YEARNING TO
BREATHE FREE

YEARNING TO BREATHE FREE

Robert Smalls of South Carolina and His Families

ANDREW BILLINGSLEY

Foreword by U.S. Congressman James E. Clyburn

The University of South Carolina Press

© 2007 University of South Carolina

Cloth edition published by the University of South Carolina Press, 2007
Ebook edition published by the University of South Carolina Press, 2021
Paperback edition published in Columbia, South Carolina,
by the University of South Carolina Press, 2023

uscpress.com

Manufactured in the United States of America

32 31 30 29 28 27 26 25 24 23
10 9 8 7 6 5 4 3 2 1

The Library of Congress has cataloged the cloth edition as follows:

Billingsley, Andrew.
  Yearning to breathe free : Robert Smalls of South Carolina and his families / Andrew
Billingsley; Foreword by James E. Clyburn.
    p. cm.
  Includes bibliographical references and index.
  ISBN-13: 978-1-57003-686-6 (cloth : alk. paper)
  ISBN-10: 1-57003-686-1 (cloth : alk. paper)
  1. Smalls, Robert, 1839–1915. 2. Legislators—United States—Biography. 3. United
States—History—Civil War, 1861–1865—Biography. 4. African Americans—South
Carolina—Biography. 5. Smalls, Robert, 1839–1915—Family. 6. Small family. I. Title.
  E185.97.S6B55 2007
  973.8092—dc22
  [B]   2006038875

ISBN 978-1-64336-215-1 (ebook)
ISBN 978-1-64336-461-2 (paperback)

To the memory of Janet "Dolly" Nash and John "Boot" Nash

and to
Judith Denise Crocker Billingsley, LMSW, ACSW

and to
Courtney Harris
Cheyanne Amy Harris
Celina Grace Billingsley Harris

and to
Ashley Nicole James
Lauryn Gross
Charles Ryann Gross

and to
David Michael Moore
Lucas Michael Greer Moore
Robert Caldwell Moore

and to
all my students

CONTENTS

ILLUSTRATIONS

Photographs

following page 74

Figures

FOREWORD

James E. Clyburn

During my studies at South Carolina State University in the late 1950s and early 1960s, I spent much of my time, some would say too much, playing a very active role in the history-making civil rights activities of the time. Of course, I am very proud of the roles I played helping to organize the first sit-ins in South Carolina and being selected by the incomparable attorney Matthew J. Perry Jr. to serve as the key defendant in the 1961 trial that resulted from the initial arrests for the sit-ins around Orangeburg, South Carolina. However, except for the occasional reference to having met my wife, Emily, during my trip to jail, I seldom discuss those experiences with anyone outside family and the close friends with whom I shared them. As an indication of pride in my actions, however, I have refused to write a letter required to have my arrest records expunged, even though, I have been asked to do so by South Carolina law enforcement officials.

Although I never thought of those activities as being of any real significance to my status as a human being or my political standing, I often think about the phone call I received some time ago from an activist in Columbia who had run across my arrest records while doing some research for an incident in which he was involved. He explained how shocked he was to find out these things about me, and that, had he known them, his attitude and actions toward me over the years would have been more respectful. He also said that he knew others who felt the same way. We had a rather interesting discussion, which I think was beneficial to both of us.

Coming of age during this historic era helped shape and influence my perception of the world around. This manifests itself today in my love of history

The Honorable James E. Clyburn, U.S. Congress, 6th District, South Carolina, is a political heir of Robert Smalls and the other black men who served in the U.S. Congress from South Carolina during Reconstruction.

and my desire to set the record straight. I have developed a real passion about our history as a people and nation and have a real problem when that history is subjected to so much omission, revisionism, and downright falsehoods. Obviously, my dear friend Dr. Andrew Billingsley shares the same sense of indignation and has taken on the laudable responsibility to tell the Robert Smalls story like it is.

The South Carolina history books I grew up with contained no mention, not even in footnotes, of Robert Smalls and his extraordinary contributions to our state's history. The military has recognized this hero of the Civil War, the navy named an Illinois training camp in his honor, and the army recently christened a transport cargo ship the *Major General Robert Smalls*. However, South Carolina has done little to honor or remember this significant figure. Outside his native Beaufort County, I know of no towns or streets named in his honor. I know of no buildings or institutions that bear his name. Yet Robert Smalls should rank among the most honored and recognized South Carolinians, but he does not simply because of the color of his skin.

I agreed to write this foreword to make a small contribution to this insightful work by Dr. Billingsley, which is a small but significant honor to the great legacy of Robert Smalls. Dr. Billingsley gracefully captures the essence of the slave, war hero, and statesman. He delves deeply into the family connections of this heroic figure. And I felt it my duty, as the first African American to represent South Carolina in the Congress since Reconstruction, to associate myself with this insight into the historic roles played by Robert Smalls.

He was a man driven, as were many of his contemporaries, by an overwhelming desire to break the chains of bondage and breathe free. But just as we used our minds and not our muscles during the so-called student movement, Robert Smalls was patient and planned for his liberation day. For those who share my experiences and did not learn his story in history books, Robert Smalls became a Civil War hero and a free man when he led other slaves to commandeer the Confederate steam ship *Planter* in Charleston in 1862 and turn it and its contents over to the Union.

Robert Smalls's dedication and ingenuity garnered him a $1,500 reward from the federal government for his actions and enabled him to purchase the house in Beaufort where he had served as a slave. Emancipation brought Robert Smalls wealth and prominence in Beaufort, South Carolina, an area that was populated largely by other emancipated slaves. He was profoundly concerned about the plight of his community, and in 1868 he served as a delegate to the State Constitutional Convention. There he offered a proposal to establish a free public education system for children of all classes. He was active in the Republican Party and served in the South Carolina House of Representatives and

Senate before being elected to the United States Congress. During his tumul-
tuous decade in the Congress, Robert Smalls remained true to his convictions.
He fought to integrate the U.S. Army and supported women's suffrage. These
concepts were all visionary at the time and indicative of the driving principles
behind this great man.

Born into a life fraught with challenges, Robert Smalls faced each with un-
yielding dignity and courage. His place in history should not be relegated to a
footnote in the history books or a plaque at his historic home. The name Robert
Smalls should fall with pride off every South Carolinian's tongue. Just as Francis
Marion, The Swamp Fox, has become our state's emblem of the Revolutionary
War, Robert Smalls should be heralded for his visionary role in the establishment of free public-school education for all children. This man of patience, per-
severance, and principles was a pioneer of his time. He is a role model of what
we seek in our leaders today, a dogged determination to fight injustice and a
deep devotion to his fellow man.

There exists a palpable connection between America's vision of democracy,
its sense of morality, and its public education system. The creation of the our
public schools indicates how crucial we believe democracy and morality to be.
French philosopher Alexis de Tocqueville once said, "The best laws cannot make
a constitution work in spite of morals; morals can turn the worst laws to advantage." Perhaps no where else in the changing winds of American history can one
view those particular juxtapositions quite as clearly as when it applies to the
education of African Americans. This was not lost on Robert Smalls.

From the time that African men, women, and children were taken from their
homes across the sea and planted on America's shores, our nation has been thrust
into a moral quandary about its very being. One must admit to the ironic, if
visible, conundrum that faced the architects of this new democracy. On one
hand, America was a country built on the yearnings for freedom and equality.

On the other hand, this burgeoning country—created by a quest for freedom
—callously deprived thousands of African men, women, and children of that
very same right. Even Thomas Jefferson, author of the Declaration of Independence and third president of the United States, participated in the moral
duplicity of slavery. America's participation in that inhuman institution and the
romanticizing of that era by so many of today's citizens continue to undermine
our views of democracy as well as our perception of ethical behavior and moral
responsibility.

How could a country trumpet, with any conviction, its belief in justice
when scores of its citizens were held in slavery against their will? What democracy created a political environment where certain of its citizens were counted
as three-fifths of a person?

Almost from the beginning of this nation's creation, it has been understood that education is the great equalizer of persons. Thomas Jefferson was one of the first American statesmen to propose an educational structure that would be operated under the control of the government. Even more radical than the idea of a nationally sponsored educational system would be that its doors would be open to many classes of American citizenry.

For the most part, before the Civil War the doors to education were closed tightly to African Americans, denying them an essential ingredient for successful pursuits of life, liberty, and happiness. The reasons behind this deprivation are well established. Many whites believed that slaves could not be educated without instilling in them a thirst for freedom and equality. Although a few slave owners believed that an educated class of slaves would augment the economy and the labor pool, the majority of whites believed that the less education a slave possessed, the stronger grew the slave owner's power.

It is within this historical backdrop that Robert Smalls emerged a national figure. Born in the wealthy McKee household, where his mother was a house slave, Robert Smalls grew up in relative privilege. Understanding the precarious nature of slavery; however, his mother, Lydia, repeatedly showed Smalls the true nature of slavery. She took her son to the Beaufort jail and made him watch as slaves were lashed. In addition, she brought him to slave auctions and recounted tales of the inhuman treatment heaped on blacks.

I believe that this particular education Robert Smalls received at the hands of his mother and the realities of his birth provided him with a unique perception of the myriad manifestations of slavery. He quickly grasped that, although he indeed lived a comfortable life, it was still a half-life, never wholly his. Much can be said about the heroic and courageous action of Robert Smalls. He was a true patriot and, like so many of us since, began his legendary career by challenging the system at great risk, which liberating the *Planter* certainly was. Spending the bulk of his life as a statesman, Smalls, after serving in both houses of the South Carolina legislature, spent five terms in the United States Congress.

While these accomplishments are inspiring and certainly noteworthy, I believe that Smalls's greatest contribution to South Carolina and the nation was in the field of education. As a member of the Beaufort County School Board in 1867, he and several other prominent African Americans acquired property that was used to establish a school for black children.

In his resolution at the 1868 Constitutional Convention, Robert Smalls proposed, "a system of common schools . . . , to be open without charge to all classes of persons." Smalls also petitioned that the Convention's Committee on Education compel mandatory school attendance for all students aged seven to fourteen for at least six months of the year. When the convention passed his resolution, it was a seminal moment in South Carolina's educational history. The passage of the act made it possible for blacks as well as whites to have access to free public schools. I often cite "free public school education for all" as South Carolina's most meaningful contribution to our nation's development.

PREFACE

Around 3:00 A.M. on May 13, 1862, Robert Smalls, a twenty-three-year-old African American then held in slavery, commandeered the Confederate ship *Planter.* This action brought him freedom and national acclaim. It was the beginning of a career that encompassed service during the Civil War, service in both houses of the South Carolina legislature, and five terms in the U.S. Congress.

Born into slavery in Beaufort, South Carolina, in 1839, Smalls died there a free man in 1915. To honor him during World War II, the U.S. Navy named an Illinois training facility Camp Robert Smalls. There Smalls's grandson Edward Estes Davidson was a trainee and his son William Robert Smalls was a graduation speaker. On April 21, 2004, nearly ninety years after Smalls's death, his descendants were called together by the U.S. Army to witness the christening of the newest army transport cargo ship, the *Major General Robert Smalls.* His oldest living great-granddaughter, Helen Greenlee, broke the ceremonial bottle of champagne on the ship's bow. Other descendants, including his last remaining grandson, his namesake Robert Smalls, who bears a striking physical resemblance to his famous grandfather, stood together there in a spirit of remarkable unity and pride.

This book describes Robert Smalls's story and legacy and their meaning for us today. Written from a sociological perspective, the book seeks to highlight the roles of family, religion, and meaningful work in the struggle for freedom during slavery and up to the present time.

ACKNOWLEDGMENTS

My introduction to the Robert Smalls story occurred at Howard University in the early 1970s. At that time, under President James Edward Cheek, there was a flowering of scholarship similar to what occurred a generation earlier, when scholars such as Ralph Bunche in political science, Abraham Harris in economics, E. Franklin Frazier in sociology, Inabel Lindsay in social work, Alain Locke in philosophy, Ernest Just in biology, John Hope Franklin in history, Sterling Brown in English literature, and a dozen others brought distinction to themselves, the university, and their disciplines. In the early 1970s, following the breakthroughs in the civil rights movement, many young black scholars came to Howard, the nation's only comprehensive black university, where they were encouraged to stand on the shoulders of their predecessors in creating new contributions to scholarship. In this group were two young scholars who had already discovered Robert Smalls and vowed to revive scholarship surrounding his legacy. One was Professor Okon Edet Uya, author of *From Slavery to Political Service: Robert Smalls, 1839–1915* (1971). The other—Russell Adams, a professor of African American studies—devoted a chapter to Robert Smalls in his *Great Negroes, Past and Present* (1969). My discussions with these two scholars about the Robert Smalls legacy led to a fascination with the subject.

As President of Morgan State University between 1975 and 1985, I came to know the historian Dr. Benjamin Quarles, whose work is cited in his book *The Negro in the Civil War* (1953). In the 1980s I conversed with the novelist Louise Meriwether at the Yaddo artists' and writers' colony in upstate New York. Meriwether was working on her novel on Robert Smalls, *Fragments of the Ark* (1994) after having already done a children's book on the Smalls story titled *The Freedom Ship of Robert Smalls* (1971). I came to appreciate not only Smalls's heroism, but also the place of his story in the study of African American families and how they survived slavery. This insight led me to publish an essay, "Robert Smalls and his Family," in *Climbing Jacob's Ladder: The Enduring Legacy of African American Families* (1992).

In 1992, when I gave a lecture on my book at the Charlotte Mecklenburg Public Library, one of the librarians, Dr. Myriette Guinyard Exechukwu, introduced herself as a descendent of Robert and Hannah Jones Smalls. She invited me to attend the next biannual Robert Smalls/Hannah Jones Smalls Family Reunion. At that 1992 reunion I met many descendants, including the oldest, Furman F. Williams, who had actually known Robert Smalls, and Smalls's great-granddaughter Janet Davidson "Dolly" Nash. This reunion and these two descendants were profiled in my essay "Family Reunion: The Family Legacy of Robert Smalls-Civil War Hero," in a 1993 issue of *Maryland Humanities*. The next reunion, held in Beaufort, South Carolina, in July 1994, organized by Dolly Nash and her husband, John, was the impetus for my photographic essay, "Robert Smalls in Beaufort Today" in a 1998 issue of *Carologue*.

Then in 1997, the curator of the Dorothy Sterling Papers in the Amistad Research Center at Tulane University in New Orleans introduced me to the Smalls materials collected by Sterling while preparing for her children's book, *Captain of the* Planter: *The Story of Robert Smalls* (1958). Finally, in 1997, editors at the University of South Carolina Press introduced me to Edward A. Miller's book, *Gullah Statesman: Robert Smalls, From Slavery to Congress, 1839– 1915* (1995). Miller's book contains an extensive bibliography of original sources.

Dolly Nash

Many times my wife and I visited Dolly and John Nash at their homes in Beaufort, South Carolina, and Cape May, New Jersey. John was a master craftsman. Both were graduates of Hampton University, and they were married for more than fifty years. Over the years they were inveterate collectors and preservers of the Smalls legacy. In Cape May they built, owned, and operated for seventeen years the Planter Motel, named in honor of the ship Robert Smalls captured. The walls of their home were decorated with photographs and drawings of the Smalls legacy. One original oil painting was done by Smalls's daughter Sarah around the turn of the century. We sat on furniture that Smalls had in his Prince Street home in Beaufort. The family collected scrapbooks of photographs, news clippings, programs, and other items of Smalls family history. Many of these objects were handed down to Dolly from her grandmother, Robert Smalls's daughter Elizabeth Lydia Smalls Bampfield.

Janet "Dolly" Nash died in March 2004, and John Nash followed her in October 2005. They were both cremated and lie side-by-side in the cemetery in Cape May, New Jersey. Helen Boulware Moore, another of Smalls's great-granddaughters, has taken Dolly's place in preserving the legacy of Robert Smalls.

Others

The participants at various family reunions have also helped me. They include attendees at the 1992 Jones-Small Reunion in Norfolk, organized by Verdonda Wright and her family; the 1994 reunion in Beaufort, organized by Dolly Nash and Helen Fields; the 2000 reunion in New York City, organized by Michelle Chaffin and family; the 2002 reunion in Norfolk; and the 2006 family gathering at the Avery Center in Charleston, hosted by Helen Boulware Moore and family. William Robert Smalls's granddaughter Linda Grigsby has provided insights into his branch of the family while Judge Gwen Bampfield tried to help me understand the various branches of Bampfield descendants.

Kitt Alexander shared her storehouse of public documents with me and invited me to numerous events she sponsored with Dolly Nash. The staffs of the Caroliniana and Thomas Cooper Libraries at the University of South Carolina, the South Carolina State Library, the Civil War Relic Room and Museum, the South Carolina Department of Archives and History, the South Carolina State Museum, and the Beaufort County Public Library have all been courteous and prompt in responding to me and my graduate students. I am grateful to Geneva Cobb Moore for her thorough critique of an earlier draft of this book while we were Fulbright Fellows at the University of Ghana—and to Carol Hall and Marie Brown for inspiration and encouragement.

At the Institute for Families in Society, University of South Carolina, directors Gary Melton, Arlene Andrews, Melinda Forthofer, Patricia Motes, and others have been most felicitous daily colleagues who helped my research along. So too did Cleveland Sellers and faculty colleagues in the Department of African American Studies as well as Pat Nolan and my colleagues in the Department of Sociology. Graduate student assistants have included Cathy Ward, Deborah Kinnard, Ubong Udoyen, and Raheem Paxton. The book surely would not have been completed without the competent and faithful administrative assistance of Sheila Heatley for nearly ten years. In the last two years of the research and writing, Renée Gibson stepped in to prepare the manuscript for submission to the press and was particularly helpful in restoring and preparing the photographs. Words alone cannot express my gratitude for her expert rendering of the entire manuscript through serial productions to make it ready for publication. She had the unenviable role of satisfying both the author and the acquisitions editor at USC Press, which she did extremely well. For commodious settings for writing retreats I continue to be grateful to the Virginia Center for Creative Arts in Sweet Briar, Virginia, and the Penn Center in Beaufort County, South Carolina.

    Not enough can be said about the expert editing by Patricia Coate and
Karen Rood that made the book more readable. My editor at USC Press, Alexander Moore, saw early on the value of this manuscript and has helped to guide
it through the labyrinth of the publishing process. He was an arduous collaborator in preparing this manuscript and invaluable to the process. Thanks to my
daughter, Angela Billingsley, for all her support and especially for conducting
research for me at the Library of Congress in Washington, D.C. Terry Stephens
and Bonita Billingsley Harris have also helped me beyond measure. My wife,
Judith Denise Crocker Billingsley, who has been an unbroken source of support
and assistance.

    My eternal gratitude goes to Congressman James E. Clyburn, who early on
agreed to write the foreword and then waited patiently for ten years while I finished the book. When the book was completed, I asked Jonathan Green to create an appropriate illustration for the dust jacket. His response was generous and
brilliant. Both these men are not only my friends but also steadfast friends of
the University of South Carolina.

ROBERT SMALLS'S FAMILY TREE

Mother, **Lydia Polite** 1796–1878; father, unknown
Robert Smalls 4/5/1839–2/23/1915 married **Hannah Jones** 1826–
    7/28/1883, Charleston, 1858
    When they married, Hannah had 2 daughters, Clara and Charlotte.
       Father/s unknown

Robert Smalls Jr. 1861–1863

Sarah Voorhees Smalls married Dr. Jay Williams, no children

Elizabeth Lydia Smalls married Samuel Jones Bampfield, 11 children

  Julia Bampfield married William Henry S., 8 children

    Thelma S. married Palmer L. B., 2 children
      Julia B. married Theo P., no children
      Palmer B. Jr. married/divorced Bernice T., 1 child, remarried
        Marion C., 2 children
        Gail B. married William R., 1 child
          Trent William R.
        Cheryl B. married David S., 3 children
          Charisse S.; Danecia S.; Dominique S.
        Palmer B. III married Beverly, 4 children
          Palmer B. IV; LaQuentin B.; Palisha B.; LaSchelle B.
    Edna S. married Audrey R., no children

    William S., unmarried

    Camilla S. married Joseph D., no children

    Julian S. married Catherine H., two children
      Linda Bampfield S., no children
      Julian Leigh S. married Lynette T., 1 child

    Juanita S. S., 1 child
      Raiven D. S.

Alberta (Roxie) S. married David M. C., 2 children
    <u>David E. C.</u>, no children
    <u>Julia Ann C.</u> married Paul J., 2 children
      Paul J; Rodney J.

Helen S. married Charles Edwin G., 3 children
    <u>Mark G.</u>, no children
    <u>Carla E. G.</u>, no children
    <u>Samuel Richard G.</u> married Andrea, 2 children
      Max G.; Samantha G.

Bampfield S. married Dorothy P., no children

Sarah Bampfield married Edward M., 2 children

Edwina M., no children

Bampfield M. married Janie L., 6 children
    <u>Edward M.</u> married Alvena D., 1 child (adopted another–
    Joanne M.)
      Edward M., Jr., no children
    <u>Freddie M.</u> married Ida J., 3 children
      Stephanie E. M. married/divorced Van J., 2 children
        Alexis Vanessa J.; Stephen Paul M.
      Jeffrey M. married/divorced Melanie M., 2 children
        Ashley Kiara M.; Brandon Arbry M.
      Jarrid Darrien M., 1 child
        Jarrid Darrien M.
    <u>Charles M.</u> married/divorced Lucille, 3 children; remarried
    Derocha
      Charles M., Mark M.; London M.
    <u>Carolyn M.</u> married Tom L., 4 children
      Sean; Sonya; Shanita;
      Sabrina, 1 child
        Brandon
    <u>Helen M.</u> married David F., 5 children
      Anthony F. married Kim T./divorced, one child
        DeJuan A. F.
      Keith F. married Judy, 2 children
        Alisha F.; Della F.

David F., 2 children
    Aujenne Chanelle J.; Xavier R. F.
Johnny F., no children
Rachel F., 1 child
    Kahleb T. F
<u>Yvonne M. R.</u> married Ollie J. III, 1 child, remarried,
Reginald B. (divorced), 3 children, remarried R.
    Ollie J. IV married Tracy Ann W., 2 children
        Nya Faith J.; Janae Hope J.
    Kevin B.; Derrick B.; Alonzo B.

Maria (pronounced Mariah—called Yaddie) Bampfield married
Charles S., 1 child
    Laura S. married Walter B., no children

Hannah Bampfield (died in infancy)

Robert Bampfield married Betty S., no children, remarried Ella D.

Elizabeth Bampfield (Lise) married Woolsey W. H.,
no children

Albert Barnes Bampfield married Lillian S., no children

Janet Bampfield (Jennie) married Edward Estes D., Jr., 2 children
    Janet (Dolly) D. married John Thomas N., no children
    Edward Estes D. Jr., married Idella D., no children

Helen Brooks Bampfield married Howard W. G., 1 adopted child
    Lois Ariana G. married Joseph E. G., Sr., 2 children
        <u>Joseph E. G., Jr.</u>
        <u>Helen Edwina G.,</u> 1 child
            Jordan E. A.

Ariana Bampfield (Arie) married Caldwell Elwood B., 1 child
    Helen Judith B. married Robert E. M., 3 children
        <u>Michael Boulware M.</u> married/divorced Kimberly G., 2 children
            David Michael Bampfield M.; Lucas Michael G. M.
        married Carla S., two children
            Israel James Pendleton M.; Robert Caldwell M.
        <u>David Caldwell M.</u>; <u>Robin Elizabeth M.,</u> no children

Samueletta Bampfield (died in infancy)

Descendants of **Robert and Annie Elizabeth Wigg Smalls**

William Robert Wigg Smalls married Helen (Marty) Martineau G.,
  2 children
  Robert Smalls married Lillian P., 1 child
    <u>Helen Smalls</u> married Roy D., 2 children,
      Shenitta E., 2 children
        Quivon E.; LaKobie E.
      DeJuan P. married Victoria L., 2 children
        Alexis P.; Christopher P.
  Anne Elizabeth Smalls married Wendell P. G., 2 children
    <u>Linda M. G.,</u> 2 children
      Shyra C.; Leah C.
    <u>Michael W. G.</u> married/divorced Lynn S., 1 child; Remarried
      Ellen C.
      Kathryn Elizabeth Smalls G.

Prologue

On May 13, 1862, one year into the U.S. Civil War, a twenty-three-year-old slave named Robert Smalls and a small band of trusted associates made a bold and brilliant dash for freedom that echoed around the world. Without firing a shot Smalls and his associates captured a Confederate warship, the *Planter.* With their families aboard they steered the ship out of Charleston harbor, safely past five armed Confederate checkpoints, including Fort Sumter, and delivered the *Planter* to the Union Navy. Smalls was now a free man. The Union had a valuable possession in the ship, its cargo and armaments, and especially Robert Smalls himself. The psychological uplift it brought to the Union and to black Americans, enslaved and free, was a priceless consequence.

In his debriefing of Smalls, Admiral Samuel F. Du Pont found him to be "superior to any of the contraband who has yet come into our lines, intelligent as many of them have been." On the floor of the U.S. Congress, Smalls was declared "the first hero of the Civil War." Congress passed legislation granting Smalls a $1,500 payment and lesser sums for his associates. After the Confederacy placed a $4,000 bounty on his head, Smalls told a black audience in New York that the only way he planned to return to Charleston was at the head of a Union invading squadron. Descendants have emphasized the fact that Smalls did not say as "a member" of the Union invaders but as their "head."

The confiscation of the *Planter* was the first of many episodes in Smalls's incessant "yearning to breathe free." Later, during an audience with President Abraham Lincoln and Secretary of War Edwin M. Stanton, Smalls regaled the president with an account of his capturing the *Planter.* But when the president asked him why he did it, Smalls said simply, "Freedom." The president, deeply enmeshed in his own struggle for "a new breath of freedom," fully understood Smalls's mission.

Smalls served the Union throughout the war, engaging in more than seventeen battles, voyages, and combat missions. After the war he returned to Beaufort, where he was elected to the Constitutional Conventions of 1868 and 1895.

Between those times he served in both houses of the state legislature and five terms in the U.S. Congress as a representative from South Carolina, while rising to the rank of major general in the state militia. He died in 1915, at the age of seventy-six, in the Prince Street house in Beaufort where he had been born and raised in slavery. His funeral was the largest held in Beaufort until that time. His house on Prince Street remained in Smalls's family for nearly one hundred years. In 1976 the Robert Smalls House was placed on the National Register of Historic Places. A small house he owned at the rear of this property was still in the family as late as 2004, when his great-granddaughter died.

The citizens of Beaufort County have paid honor to Smalls and his legacy in several ways. For a time there existed simultaneously the Robert Smalls Elementary School, the Robert Smalls Jr. High School, and the Robert Smalls High School, which for a long time (1925–1985), brought academic, cultural, and athletic distinction to the county. The current Robert Smalls Middle School continues this tradition. A section of Highway 170 leading into Beaufort has been designated Robert Smalls Parkway. In 1976 South Carolina Republican governor James B. Edwards issued a proclamation naming February 22, 1976, Robert Smalls Day throughout the state, in honor of a man who "born in slavery, exemplifies a man who through devotion to his state and people, and, by a constant faith in himself, rose above his environment to play an instrumental role in our nation's history." The governor was prompted, no doubt, by Smalls's descendants and the citizens of Beaufort County, who had gathered the previous day to install a bronze bust of Smalls in the front yard of the Tabernacle Baptist Church. Governor Edwards continued, "Whereas during the Civil War and Reconstruction the wisdom of Robert Smalls as both general and statesman was a major factor that enabled our state to mend its wounds and rebuild after such a tragic war. . . . " More than two decades later Beaufort historian Lawrence Rowland reported that in his historical research he found strong support for Governor Edwards's tribute to Smalls for helping to hold the community together during the years after the war.

On May 13, 2002, in honor of the 140th anniversary of the capture of the *Planter,* the South Carolina adjutant general awarded the Palmetto Cross to Robert Smalls "for exceptionally outstanding service while serving in the South Carolina Militia between 1870 and 1877." That same year the Republican Party of Beaufort County discovered, no doubt through Professor Rowland's work, that Smalls was a principal founder of the Republican Party in 1867. At the annual banquet, Bob Holzmacher, chair of party, gave a citation to Smalls's great-granddaughter Janet Davidson "Dolly" Nash "in appreciation for the courage, wisdom, and foresight of Robert Smalls, for patriotism and the desire for all men to live in a democracy and for being the founding leader of our Beaufort County Republican Party."

Smalls has received national recognition as well. During World War II the U.S. Navy named a training facility at Great Lakes, Illinois, Camp Robert Smalls. Smalls's great-grandson Edward Davidson was a trainee there and Smalls's son William Robert Smalls was once commencement speaker.

Since 1984 the descendants of Robert Smalls and his wives, Hannah and Annie Smalls, have gathered every two years for memorial family reunions, to which the author is regularly invited. Beginning in 1997, the University of South Carolina, under leadership of its African American Studies Program and other entities, began sponsoring annual Robert Smalls lectures.

Of all the accolades paid to Smalls by persons and institutions high and low, none can quite equal the tribute paid to him by two ordinary citizens of Beaufort during his own lifetime. Around the time of Smalls's first election to Congress, two men saw Smalls walking down the street in Beaufort. One man said to the other, "You know, that Robert Smalls is just about the greatest man that ever lived, don't you agree?" "Well," said the second man, "Smalls is great all right, but not the greatest man that ever lived." The first man responded in indignant disbelief: "Well, who could be greater than Smalls?" "Jesus Christ," said the second man. "OK," said the first man with some humble reluctance. "You're right about that. But just remember, Smalls is still a young man yet."[1]

Theoretical Perspective

The theoretical orientation of the book is based in an element of human ecology theory, which views a child's life as being shaped by a series of mutual interactions with his family and with persons and institutions of the communities within which he resides. These communities are in turn influenced by forces emanating from the larger society.[2] In this perspective Smalls was not just an individual with outstanding talents and abilities but a social being—framed, assisted, and hindered by the social forces, positive and negative, emanating from his families, his communities, and the larger American society, which underwent extreme trauma during Smalls's time and in which he was an extraordinarily active participant. In keeping with this view, however gifted Smalls was as an individual, without the nurture and guidance received from his family of origin—where, like Moses in the house of Pharaoh, he experienced bondage and privileges—he would not have been prepared at age twelve to make his way in life as he did. Without the social forces emanating from the community of Charleston and shaping his adult socialization, he would not have been prepared for his major life ventures. Also, throughout his life he was buoyed and buffeted by forces in the larger American society including slavery, the Civil War, political reform and repression. In the end his society collapsed around him, and he and his mission of universal freedom could not stand. But Smalls's spirit of adventure and his dogged yearning to breathe free outlasted this colossal calumny. While guided by this ecological perspective, we make every effort to prevent such theoretical speculation from getting in the way of our rendering of the story of Robert Smalls and his families—a story that is powerful in its own right.

This study has made use of the social-science research methods called "triangulation." These methods included analysis of documents, manuscripts, letters, and photographs at the Library of Congress, the National Archives, the U.S. Navy Museum, the Caroliniana and Thomas Cooper Libraries at the University of South Carolina, the South Carolina Department of Archives and History, and the South Carolina State Library—as well as analysis of privately held papers, letters, photographs, and memorabilia. Participant and nonparticipant observations were made at family reunions and with individual descendants and other informants. Analysis of U.S. Census data played a major role in this research. Finally field observations were carned out at cemetaries, churches, harbors, and other relevant sites in Beaufort, Charleston, and Columbia, South Carolina.

PART I

Social Background

I

Slavery, Religion, and Family in the Robert Smalls Legacy

An appreciation of Robert Smalls's life achievements requires an understanding of the role of spirituality, religious faith, and religious practice in the African American experience. Scholars of this experience have been nearly unanimous in finding that spirituality, religion, and church affiliation have been among the most important components in the survival and achievements of African American people.[1] These factors are by far the preeminent sources of African American culture, even to the present time. So it was with Robert Smalls's forebears and descendants. Indeed, when African captives landed in South Carolina during the early part of the eighteenth century, they brought with them what W. E. B. Du Bois called their "spiritual striving."[2] However, during the first hundred years of American slavery, the planters in the South and their Protestant Christian churches engaged in a conspiracy to suppress and distort the spiritual striving of their captives. Europeans who had come to the New World in search of their own religious liberty and economic independence saw no contradiction in denying both to their African bondsmen.

According to C. Eric Lincoln, "there was no consistent effort to bring Christianity to the slaves in America until the (Anglican) Society for the Propagation of the Gospel in Foreign Parts established a spiritual presence of sorts on the plantations of the South in 1701—almost a hundred years after the first Africans arrived at Jamestown in 1619."[3] Albert Raboteau found that planters were afraid that introducing the Africans to Christianity would encourage their aspirations to be free and lead them to run away and to revolt in the manner of David Walker.[4] Indeed, historians have pointed to examples of how religious faith spurred the desire to escape from slavery. In South Carolina the Stono Rebellion of 1739 and Denmark Vesey's insurrection in 1822 had their basis in the spiritual striving of the captives. The planters held on to slavery and expanded it because, according to Walter Edgar, "slavery was a tremendously profitable business and their greed outweighed their fears."[5]

In time the planters made two remarkable discoveries. First, they learned that denying their own Christianity to the Africans did not keep them from worshiping. Slave owners discovered the existence of "the invisible church" that Africans had developed so they could worship outside their masters' presence. The planters also learned that keeping Africans from participating in Christian worship was not sufficient to make them contented with slavery or to keep them from running away, which they did in impressive numbers.[6] With the coming of the Great Awakening in the early eighteenth century, planters were persuaded that conversion to Christianity might, in fact, make the Africans more accepting of their lot. The new evangelists were required to teach slaves that conversion to Christianity would not automatically lead to their emancipation. Black and white preachers instructed the Africans to be content with their slave status, often quoting Bible passages that instructed Christian slaves to obey their masters. These evangelists succeeded in converting large numbers of blacks, who were welcomed into Christian fellowship with some evangelical planters and white churches.

In Beaufort, South Carolina, three churches played important roles in the conversion of blacks to Christianity and in establishing a Christian framework for Robert Smalls's forebears, himself, and his family. St. Helena's Episcopal Church, Beaufort Baptist Church, and Tabernacle Baptist Church are located within three city blocks of each other. They changed substantially over the generations and had distinctive roles in the legacy of Robert Smalls.

St. Helena's Episcopal Church was the spiritual and social home of the McKee family—the owners of Smalls, his mother, his grandmother, and his older brother during slavery. Beaufort Baptist was the spiritual and social home of Lydia Polite Smalls and her son Robert during the first eleven formative years of his life. Tabernacle Baptist grew out of Beaufort Baptist and was the post–Civil War spiritual home of Smalls's mother, Lydia, his wife Hannah, and their children.

St. Helena's Episcopal Church

St. Helena's Episcopal Church, located on Church Street between North and King streets in Beaufort, South Carolina, represents a significant and generally unrecognized element in the legacy of Robert Smalls. In 1999 the junior high school honors class of Beaufort teacher Margaret Rushton toured sites in Beaufort relevant to the Smalls story.[7] As the group passed St. Helena's Episcopal churchyard, which was not on the tour, thirteen-year-old student Brandon Jarrell remarked to the author, "Henry McKee is buried over there."

Discovery of the McKee burial ground led to the supposition that the McKees had been members of the St. Helena's Episcopal Church. Associate rector Reverend Jeffrey S. Miller confirmed that supposition and taught us much about its leading members. The rector gave us a copy of *The History of the Parish Church of St. Helena, Beaufort, South Carolina. Church of England 1712–1789. Protestant Episcopal 1789–1990* (1990).[8] He also referred us to the historian Lawrence S. Rowland, who had written the introduction, and to Gerhard Spieler, Beaufort historian and local columnist. Professor Bobby Donaldson and I returned to the Beaufort County Library, where the librarian showed us *Old Churchyard Cemetery of St. Helena's Episcopal Church, Beaufort, S.C.* (1987), which confirmed our personal observations. While St. Helena's Episcopal Church, the McKees' spiritual and social home, upheld the system of slavery that kept Smalls and his family in bondage, it also strongly supported Christianizing the captives and treating them kindly as befits the children of God. This bifurcation of influence was not and could not be resolved by this or other white Christian churches until after the Civil War. The churches were as beholden to the planters as the planters were to the churches.

As early as 1726 Lewis Jones, the founding rector of St. Helena's Church, expressed strong support for extending Christianity to the enslaved Africans.[9] He publicly criticized efforts in the higher echelons of the community to stop the spread of Christianity among the Africans. The first Great Awakening was led by John Wesley and George Whitefield, who had come from England. When John Wesley arrived in Beaufort on December 7, 1737, from Savannah, he was warmly received by those who already knew of and admired his evangelical gifts. The Reverend Jones was among the welcoming party. Wesley, who had left his brother James Wesley to evangelize in Savannah, did not tarry long in Beaufort. He soon returned to England, where he became the founder of Methodism, which afforded him greater latitude for his brand of theology, evangelizing, preaching, and worship.

George Whitefield came to America from England in 1737 and began his work of conversion at St. Helena's in 1740. In 1743 several of the leading members of St. Helena's Episcopal Church broke from the church, signed on with Whitefield as evangelists, and formed the Stony Creek Presbyterian Church. The vigorous fusion of English/American and African worship styles in this Protestant congregation set the tone for black worship even to the present day.

Many of St. Helena's leading parishioners supported the American cause during the Revolution. Among these was the twenty-eight-year-old planter John McKee. He survived the war without injury and returned to Beaufort to take over his father's cotton plantations. In 1784, at the age of thirty-five, John McKee married Margaret Johnson of Beaufort. They eventually had five children, who were baptized into the fellowship of St. Helena's Church. Four generations of the John McKee family are shown in figure 1.1.

John McKee's status as a war veteran helped to make his wife, Margaret, a prominent socialite and beneficiary of her husband's pension when he died in 1834. In 1815 Margaret was among the women who petitioned the legislature to establish the Ladies Benevolent Society "for the relief of distressed and destitute children." In 1839 she and Ann Barnwell were described as "the last women in Beaufort eligible to receive pensions for a husband's service in the Revolutionary war."[10]

Among John McKee's holdings was Ashdale Plantation on Lady's Island, a sea island cotton property, just across the Beaufort River. The plantations owned by the McKees and on which Robert Smalls's mother was born and raised, were prime examples of the slave community. They were communities in the full sense of that term, producing and managing all the essential resources needed for the subsistence of large groups of people. Three factors helped the formation, perpetuation, and daily operations of these communities. The most important was the introduction of sea island cotton in the 1790s. A second was the new importation of African captives between 1804 and 1808 as a consequence of the cotton revolution. The third was the religious revival and plantation missions that began in the early 1830s. Thus, "the permanent retention of African cultural and linguistic traditions among sea island blacks," so actively studied today, was not only because of their geographic isolation but also because of their more recent arrival.[11]

Lydia was born in about 1796 on John McKee's Ashdale Plantation. From an early age she worked as a field hand on the plantation. During this time she was allowed to share a cabin with her mother and slept on the floor. She stayed with her mother until she was about ten years old. During this period of intimate contact, her mother told her many stories and taught her numerous skills. Lydia's mother talked about her own mother, who had been brought from the Guinea Coast of West Africa. She taught Lydia how to cook and sew and how to keep the house and yard clean. She also taught her how to dance, which was especially encouraged in this all-African community. Lydia's mother also took her to church on the plantation, which during the 1790s was a thriving Christian outpost for a Beaufort church involved in the Second Great Awakening.

A black preacher with no schooling was allowed to officiate, to marry people, and to say prayers at burials. Sometimes black men were allowed to serve as deacons. While these religious mission stations were most likely to be sponsored by Baptist churches, some were Episcopal and Presbyterian. Lydia grew up under her mother's teaching as a very bright and personable child. She said later that she almost never saw a white person, except when McKee came for regular visits to bring special rations and to oversee his crops. His wife, Margaret McKee, came with him at Christmas time and brought enough oranges for all the children.

On one of Margaret McKee's visits, Lydia walked right up to her, said hello, and thanked her for the orange. Impressed with Lydia's boldness and apparent intelligence, Mrs. McKee asked her how old she was. Lydia said she did not know, but that her mother had told her she was born during the time George Washington was president. Following Dorothy Sterling, Smalls's first biographer, other writers have approximated Lydia's birth date as 1790, during the first year of Washington's first term. However, the U.S. Census of 1870 lists Lydia's age as seventy-four, which would make her birth year approximately 1796, during Washington's second term. This later date seems more consistent with other events in her life.

Lydia's father is unknown. He was probably one of the workers on the plantation. In general within slavery the father of a child was not recognized. He had no rights to or responsibilities for an offspring; the child belonged to the mother and to the white man who owned the mother. Lydia was given the last name *Polite*, which in all probability was her mother's maiden name. We know that Polite was a rather common surname among the black population at that time and continues today in Beaufort County. We interviewed one such person in 1999, a retired teacher who was careful to point out that she was related to Lydia Polite and thus to her son Robert Smalls.

It is important that Lydia was raised by her birth mother until she was ten years of age, which was extremely uncommon at that time for persons held in slavery. This unusual situation permitted maternal bonding and care, which, then as now, is indispensable to the healthy growth and development of a child.

When Lydia was about ten years old, the McKees took her away from the plantation to their home in Beaufort, so that she could keep house, cook, wash, and help to care for the McKee children. This action was threefold in impact. First, it showed no regard for the mother-child bond, which was the only family Lydia knew. Second, by breaking this bond the McKees simultaneously strengthened their own family by providing assistance with home and child care. Third, while her removal from her mother was a wrenching experience, Lydia was not sold away and was elevated from the status of field hand to the status of house servant. Lydia grew up in this role, serving the McKee family for some fifty-five years until the Civil War came to Beaufort in 1861 and set her free. During this time the McKee family was kind and generous to her. They allowed her to visit alone with her mother on weekends. She continued to go to church with her mother and to visit her friends on the plantation until her mother died. Lydia helped to raise the John McKee family's six children. Their first-born, Elizabeth, born in 1799, was seven years old when ten-year-old Lydia arrived, and their last child, Edward, was born in 1825, when Lydia was thirty-six. (See figures 1.1 and 1.2.)

At approximately twenty-three years of age, Lydia had a son whom she named Larry Polite, giving him her maiden name. He grew up on the planta-tion, became a field hand, and was never married. Robert Smalls's son William Robert "Willie" Smalls wrote, "I have often heard my father say that he had one brother, Larry Polite, who was twenty-one years older than he." At another time Willie Smalls told the following story, which his father told him: "A white ten-ant, named Mrs. Gray came to the house to pay her rent and referred to Smalls as *uncle*." Smalls response was, "Madame, for me to be your uncle, you must be the child of my brother or sister. I never had a sister and my only brother was named Larry Polite and he never married."[12]

The Second Great Awakening

In time St. Helena's became caught up in the Second Great Awakening of the 1830s. Planters were again persuaded that religion could be an ally to their pri-mary mission of maintaining contented workers to tend their crops. Partly be-cause many of these plantation owners were active members and leaders of St. Helena's Church, the church became an active participant in the movement to Christianize the Africans, and many members became evangelists.

Thus, the church played a major role in the Plantation Mission Movement, which was a part of the Second Great Awakening. Christian missions were estab-lished on large plantations to facilitate the Christianizing of the black popula-tion. According to historian Walter Edgar, during the 1830s Episcopalians built chapels on fifty plantations for enslaved persons to worship, despite the law banning unsupervised all-black gatherings. Moreover, in Beaufort "hundreds of blacks crowded into St. Helena's as well as Beaufort Baptist Church" for spirited revivals.[13] Historians agree that the most important aspect of life in the slave community was religion. One found that "the principle behind the Plantation Mission Movement was that Christian instruction for the slaves would trans-form the plantations into harmonious and moral communities." In consequence this would "make the slaves better servants and their masters better people."[14]

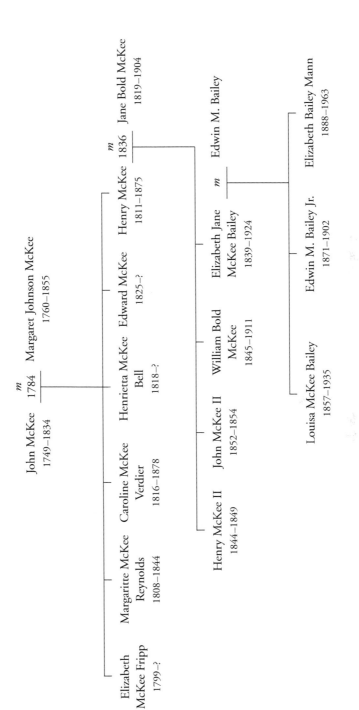

Figure 1.1   The John McKee Household

Blacks took advantage of this movement to build their self esteem and establish patterns of interaction among themselves. They eventually used it to establish their own praise houses, more permanent houses of worship, and networks of worshippers. In considering the primary purpose of this movement, it might well be said that spreading Christianity to the Africans had some effect on making them faithful and productive workers, but the strategy was a failure in making them content to be enslaved. Bringing religion to the Africans was like throwing rabbits into the briar patch. They took Christianity, made it their own, and in the process made of it a source of solace and self-esteem. They became "God's Children." As Robert Smalls's mother taught him, Christianity made blacks "as good as anybody else," and thus they were "supposed to be free." They took their religion and their relations with God personally and were not content to leave their religion in church, as some had hoped. Specifically, they drew from their newfound religion the tenets of the Christian faith that teach equality and empowerment.

During the Civil War, St. Helena's Church suffered with the landing of the Union forces in Beaufort in November 1861 under the command of Admiral Samuel F. Du Pont. On Saturday November 2, 1861, it was announced publicly that the Union fleet had landed on the island. On Sunday, November 3, the Reverend Dr. Joseph Walker, rector of the St. Helena's, spoke from the pulpit, urging his parishioners to pack their belongings and hold family prayers. On Monday, November 4, the white members fled to the Confederate-held mainland, leaving the church in the care of the black grounds keepers. When Union troops landed on November 7, there were few whites left in Beaufort District. During the war the church was used as a hospital by the occupying Union forces. They brought gravestones inside to use as operating tables. Harriet Tubman served there as nurse to the Union soldiers during 1862 and 1863.

After the war the church revived and became even stronger. In St. Helena's cemetery are buried some of Beaufort's wealthiest and most distinguished families. A large marble headstone marks the expansive McKee family plot. We have identified the graves of John McKee (1749–1834) and his wife, Margaret Johnson McKee (1760–1855). A prominent headstone is laid for their son and heir, Henry McKee (1811–1875), and his wife, Jane M. Bold McKee (1819–1904). Henry and Jane's children are buried there, including their first born daughter, Elizabeth Jane McKee Bailey (1839–1924), their son William Bold McKee (1845–1911), and two sons who died in childhood: Henry Howard McKee II, (1844–1849) who had been named for his father, and John McKee II (1852–1854), who had been named for his grandfather. Jane M. Bold McKee's parents are also buried in this family plot: her father, William Bold (1782–1852), and her mother, Elizabeth Jane Bold (1794–1840).

Figure 1.2 The McKee Family Plot

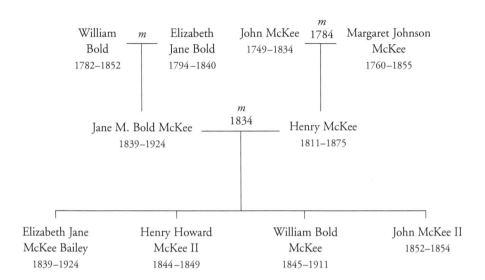

Other children of John and Margaret McKee are not buried in this family plot. Among them are Elizabeth (born in 1799), who married Hamilton Fripp; Henrietta (born in 1818), who married John Bell; and Edward (born in 1825), who married Catherine Williams. Caroline (1816–1878), who married John Verdier, is buried in another section of the St. Helena's Cemetery with her husband's family. Margaritte (1808–1844), who married Richard Reynolds, is buried here in the section with her husband's family.

Lydia Polite faithfully served this family for more than fifty years. Descendants report that she was a favored house servant and cite no incidents in which Lydia was mistreated by any member of the McKee household. Among the many gifts from Margaret McKee to Lydia were hand-me-down clothes that made Lydia one of the best-dressed women in the slave community, especially at parties and on Sundays at church. The religious values of the McKee family, honed in St. Helena's Episcopal Church, probably sustained their humanitarian treatment of Lydia, even in the midst of the abominable system of chattel slavery. The McKee's even allowed Lydia to travel to the plantation, where she visited her mother, and attended church services. When her mother died, she stopped going to the plantation and joined the black majority in the gallery of the Beaufort Baptist Church.

Beaufort Baptist Church

The Beaufort Baptist Church, located at 600 Charles Street, is even more deeply involved in Robert Smalls's legacy. It was founded in 1804 under leadership of the Reverend Henry Holcombe of the Euhaw Baptist Congregation with eighteen white members and a greater number of blacks, all previously associated with the Euhaw Congregation.[15] The first pastor elected by the Beaufort Baptist Church was the Reverend James B. Cook Jr. During the antebellum period black members outnumbered white ones consistently. Robert Smalls's mother, Lydia Polite, joined this church after her mother died. Segregated from white members, blacks were required to sit in the church balcony. The records of this church show that by the 1840s much of church business involved participation and treatment of its black members. Prior to the outbreak of the Civil War, there were remarkably 3,577 black members and 166 whites. In 1807 a split occurred in the congregation. One faction left the church and built another around the corner on Craven Street. They named it Tabernacle Church. In 1811 the two factions reunited. The Tabernacle congregation returned to worship at the Charles Street site, and the Craven Street building continued to be used as a lecture hall and for special services. When white members left Beaufort in 1861, they left the Tabernacle site in the care of black church members. After the war, the white members of Beaufort Baptist sold the Tabernacle to the black members. It has continued to be a site of black worship until today.

Lydia Polite was an active member of Beaufort Baptist Church for several years during slavery, and her son Robert was a participant until he turned twelve. The Beaufort Baptist Church was an important feature of the social environment that influenced Smalls's upbringing.

Reverend Richard Fuller, 1832–1847

One of the most impressive aspects of Beaufort Baptist Church, as it bears on the treatment of black members, was the tenure of the Reverend Richard Fuller as pastor from 1833 to 1847. An examination of Fuller and his influential role provides valuable insight into the social structure, culture, and values of antebellum Beaufort.

Fuller was converted and joined Beaufort Baptist Church in 1831, almost at the same time a revival reached Beaufort and gave rise to the Plantation Mission Movement. Fuller was born in Beaufort in 1804, the year Beaufort Baptist Church was constituted and the year his father, Thomas Fuller, a life-long Episcopalian, converted to the Baptist faith and joined this new Baptist church. One of Richard's sisters also joined this church; however, Richard and his mother remained loyal to the Episcopalian side of his family. Both his parents were wealthy, well educated, and deeply religious. His father was a cotton planter.

Fuller attended Beaufort College and then Harvard College in Massachusetts. After graduating from Harvard, Fuller returned to Beaufort, where he read law, passed the South Carolina bar and began a law practice. In 1831, at the age of twenty-seven, he married a prominent socialite named Charlotte Bull Stuart, and on October 26, 1831, he converted to the Baptist faith. In 1832 he took a step that many young professionals were taking at that time. Imbued with the spirit of the new revival, Fuller abandoned his law practice, entered the ministry, and was ordained a Baptist preacher. Later that year, he was elected pastor of the Beaufort Baptist Church, where both his father and older sister were long-time members.

By all accounts Fuller's tenure was a phenomenal success. He was especially drawn to this church because of its black majority. The only church more to his liking would have been an entirely black congregation. He felt a special calling to bring messages and deeds of enlightenment to the downtrodden, though whites of all social classes flocked to hear him preach and lecture as well.

Fuller embraced the mushrooming Plantation Mission Movement with fervor. He established five missions, which he called "preaching stations," on nearby plantations. He went to them several times a week to preach primarily to the enslaved Africans. His sermons were very well received by workers and plantation owners. Large numbers came to join his church in Beaufort. Every Sunday he preached in the Beaufort church, where the balconies were overflowing with his black-majority membership. On Wednesday nights he gave lectures on various topics, including slavery, in the education building still called the Tabernacle, where again most of his audience was black. He organized Sunday schools for the children on the plantations and recruited the wives and daughters of the planters as Sunday-school teachers.

Noting the disrepair of the church building in 1837, Fuller raised funds and led the congregation to build a new church, where he welcomed a record crowd on April 14, 1844. Because Fuller felt it unnecessary, the new building was built without a baptismal pool. While he was pastor, baptisms took place in the Beaufort River at the foot of Charles Street at high tide. On these occasions a procession marched the half mile from the church to the river accompanied by all the members dressed in white, with spirited singing by nearly two thousand black voices and a few whites. Hundreds of spectators lined the route down Charles Street all the way to the river. Along the route voices rang out, singing hymns and anthems and marching to the beat of the music. Looking back we can imagine such hymns as "Take me to the water, take me to the water, take me to the water to be baptized" and "None but the righteous, none but the righteous, none but the righteous shall see God." It is not hard to imagine Lydia Polite Smalls, a member of that church, marching along with the congregation, dressed in white clothing made from materials given her by Margaret McKee. On reaching the river, the black head marshal entered the waters first to find solid ground deep enough for complete immersion. These baptisms happened several times a year and became a major attraction in the town. People came from miles around to watch.

The Reverend Fuller also inaugurated quarterly sessions, which took place approximately four times per year. All the black members came to the church dressed in their Sunday best. Outside the church they formed a single-file line that sometimes stretched all the way down Charles Street to the river. The black deacons took their place at the head of the procession, facing the sanctuary. White members took their seats in their usual pews in the sanctuary. Then, on signal from the pastor, the black deacons led the joyful, hymn-singing, toe-tapping, smartly dressed black procession through the front doors—held open by the white ushers—down the aisle to the pulpit. They proceeded across in front of the pulpit and back down the center aisle, passing through the singing and hand-clapping white congregation. When they reached the rear of the church, they ascended the stairs on both sides to take their assigned places in the galleries, often overflowing onto the stairwells and the rear of the first floor. All during the procession the seated white congregants reached out to extend the right hand of fellowship to their marching black brothers and sisters in Christ. Fuller described this scene as a wonderful expression of union between God's black and white children. After the procession, the pastor delivered an address on the theme of black/white relations with laudatory comments on the culture, humanity, and spirituality of the black members. After another hymn, there came the part of the ceremony that young people—including no doubt Robert Smalls, aged six to eight at this time—had been waiting for. The whole congregation moved into the churchyard for the quarterly feast, where black and white, enslaved and free, young and old, male and female, members and guests picnicked together, much as the multitudes fed by Christ, whose true representative Fuller felt himself to be.

From the time he graduated from Harvard at age twenty until he left Beaufort for Baltimore at age thirty-three, Richard Fuller was the most eloquent spokesman for the interests of the planters, for the Protestant gospel, and for the souls of black folk—for all of which he was applauded on all sides. One of his most learned works was a justification of slavery. Titled "Ebony and Ivory," his sermon sought to show that both blacks (ebony) and whites (ivory) had their distinct places in God's kingdom. He taught his black members that, even though they were enslaved, God loved them and so did he and urged them to love themselves. Meanwhile, they should serve their masters obediently and well. While there may be some room for doubt about how much the blacks loved God or themselves, there was no doubt that they loved the Reverend Richard Fuller.

During the time of his ministry, Lydia Polite was an active member of this church. In all probability she brought her son Robert Smalls, born in 1839, into this fellowship and under the influence of this remarkable leader, which would last for the first eight years of Smalls's young life.

After strong recruitment by the Seventh Baptist Church, Fuller left Beaufort and went to Baltimore in 1847. There, he changed his views about slavery and urged the national government to purchase all enslaved persons from their owners and ship them out of the country. After a long, prominent career in the ministry and national exposure on the issue of religion and slavery, Fuller died in 1876 at age seventy-two in Baltimore.[16]

Tabernacle Baptist Church

The founding of the independent black church in Beaufort was the result of the landing of the Union troops in November 1861 and the flight of the whites to the mainland. The war years were growth years for the black churches of Beaufort. When the white members of the Beaufort Baptist Church departed during the first week of November 1861, they left their church properties in care of their black members. The Beaufort Baptist edifice on Charles Street was taken over and used as a hospital by the Union troops. The Tabernacle on Craven Street became a house of worship for a group of blacks under the leadership of a white minister from the North. A second group of black members worshiped at a New Street site also owned by Beaufort Baptist. These members called as their minister a black preacher from Savannah, the Reverend Arthur Waddell. Both of these became independent black churches after the war.

Of the more than 3,557 black members who belonged to Beaufort Baptist Church prior to the war, only four remained attached to the church after the war. These were Daniel Cuthbert, Daphne Codding, Caroline Cuthbert, and Celia Powel. The returning white members became a majority in their own church for the first time.

The Tabernacle Baptist Church in Beaufort, as a body of Christian believers, began long before its official founding in 1863. Its beginning as a black congregation at that Craven Street site might well be said to have begun in 1807 when a splinter group from the Beaufort Baptist Church first secured this site and named it Tabernacle. In November 1861, when federal troops landed and the white population abandoned Beaufort and the Sea Islands for the mainland, the black members took control of the Tabernacle site and have used it for worship continuously since that time. This church has chosen to date its founding in 1863, when the Reverend Solomon Peck, a white minister from Boston, served as pastor.[17] Lydia Polite, Smalls's mother, was an active member of this church, which in time became the leading repository of the Robert Smalls legend.

In addition to its use as a worship center during the war, the Tabernacle Church was used by the Union forces to launch raids by Colonel John Montgomery's Second South Carolina Volunteers into Confederate-held areas and for both somber and celebratory services when the troops returned to the church after raids. These raids were undertaken by black troops under the command of Colonel Montgomery, and they were led by Harriet Tubman, making her the first woman in modern times to lead men into military engagements. An article in the June 6, 1863, issue of the *New South* newspaper described an expedition up the Combahee River:

> On Monday evening last, five companies of the 2nd S.C. Vols., and a section of Battery C. 3rd R.I. Artillery, Capt. Brayton, under the command of Col. Montgomery, started on an expedition, which had for its main object the recruiting of soldiers for the 2nd S.C. Regiment.
>
> After gathering all the troops, and taking on board 737 negroes, men, women, and children and a few fine horses, the expedition returned to Beaufort, where a tremendous reception awaited them. All the darkies in town were in the streets, gazing with unaffected surprise and admiration at the strange spectacle of several hundred genuine contrabands, in their field suits of dirty gray, but with every lineament bearing with that intelligence which is inseparable with plantation negroes enjoying their freedom.
>
> The contrabands were placed in *one of the Beaufort Churches,* temporarily, but will be distributed on general principles, in a few days. All the able bodied negroes rescued from slavery, are to be placed in the 2nd S.C. Vols. They will be strong enough in numbers for two companies.

The Beaufort church mentioned was probably the Tabernacle because the two white churches, St. Helena's Episcopal Church and Beaufort Baptist Church, were being used as hospitals. The July 10, 1863, *Boston Commonwealth* supplied more confirmation.

> Col. Montgomery and his gallant band of 300 black soldiers, under the guidance of a black woman, dashed into the enemy's country, struck a bold and effective blow, destroying millions of dollars worth of commissary stores, cotton and lordly dwellings, and striking terror to the heart of rebeldom, brought off near 800 slaves and thousands of dollars worth of property without losing a man or receiving a scratch! It was a glorious consummation.

After they were all fairly disposed of in *the Beaufort Church,* they were addressed in strains of thrilling eloquence by their gallant deliverer, to which they responded in a song: "There is a white robe for thee." A song so appropriate and so heartfelt and cordial as to bring unbidden tears.

Then Colonel Montgomery was followed by a speech from the black woman who led the raid, and under whose inspiration it was originated and conducted. For sound sense and real native eloquence, her address would do honor to any man, and it created a great sensation.

A few short blocks away from St. Helena's Cemetery, where the McKee family is buried, lies the Tabernacle Baptist Church cemetery, where Robert Smalls's family is buried. These two families are nearly as close in death as they were in life. Buried in the Tabernacle graveyard are Robert Smalls (1838–1915); on his left lies his first wife, Hannah Jones Smalls (1825–1883), and on his right is his second wife, Annie E. Wigg Smalls (1855–1895), with his second daughter, Sarah Voorhees Smalls Williams (1863–1920) at her mother's side. The only statue of Robert Smalls faces the street a few feet away from the cemetery. It is a bronze pewter bust created by Marion Etheridge Talmidge and erected in a special ceremony at the church in 1976.

Slavery and the Churches

In Beaufort these three churches—St. Helena's, Beaufort Baptist and Tabernacle Baptist—played leading, sometimes complementary and sometimes conflicting, roles in bringing African captives into Christian fellowship. They provided the spiritual anchors for the McKee families as well as for Lydia Polite and her son Robert Smalls. Those three churches—plus the Brick Baptist Church of the Penn Center, which is still standing—are beautifully depicted by photographer N. Jane Iseley in her book *Beaufort,* published by the Historic Beaufort Foundation in 2003.

In the 1990s, as a symbol of spiritual and social renewal across racial lines, these churches, together with other black and white congregations of Beaufort, formed a group called Operation Good Neighbor. This association brings members into each other's congregations and communities to spread spiritual and community development. "It is not an effort to forget the past or the troubling conditions which divide us today," says the Reverend Kenneth Hodges, "but a sustained effort to outlive the past and prepare for the future." There is no doubt that if Robert Smalls and Thomas Fuller were alive today, they would be at the forefront of a movement such as Operation Good Neighbor.

2

In the House of Pharaoh

Growing Up in Bondage and Privilege, 1839–1851

Robert Smalls was born April 5, 1839, in a two-room shack in the backyard of the Henry McKee home on Prince Street in Beaufort, South Carolina. Because he was born and raised in slavery, he was a child of bondage. However, because he and his mother were favored house servants in the McKee household, he experienced many privileges not routinely available to enslaved persons. Thus, like Moses in the house of Pharaoh, Smalls was a "child of bondage and privilege."

The bondage of slavery was palpable. Indeed, Smalls came into the world under a cloud of danger. First his mother, on whom he depended for life and sustenance, was already forty-three years old, a dangerous age for giving birth. Lydia had lived a sheltered and protected life, however, and was apparently in good health. Her only other child had been born some twenty years earlier.[1] A second danger was a heightened sense of fear that ran through the slave quarters. The midwife who came to attend Lydia reported that a black man had been hanged in the Beaufort Armory by members of the Beaufort Volunteer Artillery, which used the armory as headquarters. They had then paraded through the town frightening other blacks. At a family reunion in Beaufort in 1994, Janet "Dolly" Nash, great-granddaughter of Robert and Hannah Jones Smalls, took the group on a tour of locations in the city related to the Smalls legacy. One stop was at the Beaufort Armory, which now serves as the Beaufort Museum. Nash told the group about the hanging, having heard the story many times from her mother and grandmother. Her mother, Janet Bampfield

Davidson (1895–1975), left among her possessions a handwritten account of family history. She wrote of Smalls's birth: "In the 'low country' of S.C. in the beautiful coastal town of Beaufort, while everyone was down on Craven St. to see the hanging, Lydia Smalls was at home lying on her pallet in the deserted slave quarters admiring her new born baby Robert, who was born that very day, April 5, 1839."[2] The destruction of court records and the absence of newspaper accounts might be sufficient for scholars to conclude that the incident never occurred, but not so for the descendants. The descendants are persuaded that the incident happened and was lost to history by the impact of slavery, warfare, and other factors in African American history.

There were many other reminders of the bondage. For example, a Beaufort ordinance required all enslaved persons to be in their quarters after sundown unless in the company of their owners. A bronze bell mounted atop the town jail was rung every night to signal the beginning of the black curfew. Smalls grew up hating the sound of that bell and often got into trouble for violating curfew. He said later that he especially resented the fact that, when he was playing with white boys, he had to stop and go inside while they did not. As a result he sometimes refused to go inside when the curfew bell rang. On such occasions he was arrested and put in the town jail, and his owner, Henry McKee, was notified. After getting Smalls released from jail, McKee often warned Smalls not to repeat his offense, but Smalls continued to violate curfew, knowing that McKee would spring him from jail each time.

In the essay she left behind, Janet Bampfield Davidson described the conditions under which Smalls grew up:

> For a few years, Robert grew up like any Beaufort boy—climbing trees, hunting lizards, and catching crabs on the low tide. He learned to swim like a fish. Life was not all play. There were errands to be run for his Masters, boots to be cleaned, bring water from the pump, carry logs for the fire, cleaning chandeliers, etc.

Davidson also described Lydia's efforts to teach her son about the reality and harshness of slavery:

> One morning when Robert and his mother had finished morning chores, Lydia took him for a walk. They passed the arsenal, where the slaves, frightened and trembling, were being sold on the block. The auctioneer was pointing to a boy no bigger than Robert. "Could be you," Lydia whispered. Lydia led Robert past the market to the jail. There she held him on her shoulder so he could look over the wall, where his eyes fell on a whipping

tree. A woman's wrist was tied to its lowest branch. A lash whistled through the air and landed on her bare back, shoulders, and arms once, twice, more times than Robert could count. Robert closed his eyes but could still hear the woman's screams. The jailor untied the woman's wrists and she fell to the ground. Robert caught a glimpse of her face. It was Susan—one of his friends. Robert sobbed all the way home. Robert chafed under these conditions.

Time passed and Robert went with his Master to carry rations to the plantation on the Island. He asked permission to stay overnight. There he met some slaves who had recently been brought to the Island. They could read and they had a copy of Frederick Douglass' latest talk, which is as follows: "The law gives the Master absolute power over the slave. He may work him, flog him, hire him out, sell him, kill him. In the law, the slave has no wife, no children, no country, no home. He can own nothing, possess nothing, acquire nothing, but what must belong to another."[3]

Smalls was deeply touched by this experience and on his return told his mother that when he grew up he wanted to meet Douglass. He also said that he was inspired to "be a man" like Douglass and be free. Moreover, In his 1863 testimony before the American Freedmen's Inquiry Commission during the war, the twenty-four-year-old Smalls commented, "The people here on the plantations had no chance. They have been kept in ignorance and punished if they attempted to learn." The commissioners then inquired further of Smalls, "What are the punishments for the colored men?" Smalls replied, "I have had no trouble with my owner but I have seen a good many while traveling around on the plantations. I have seen stocks in which people are confined from twenty-four to forty-eight hours."[4]

Stocks were instruments of physical punishment and public humiliation. Smalls also described other forms of torment:

> In whipping, a man is tied up to a tree and gets a hundred lashes from a raw hide [whip]. Sometimes a man is taken to a blacksmith's shop and an iron of [many] pounds weight is fastened to his feet so that when it is taken off, he cannot walk for days. He has been used to the heavy weight and when it is gone and he attempts to lift his foot, his leg flies up and he cannot get along. To prevent this iron from bruising his leg, moss is placed between it and the flesh. In this very place I have seen a man owned by John Verdier wearing an iron collar with two prongs sticking out at the sides like cow's horns.
>
> I have heard of a good many other punishments. For instance, one man had sets of stocks made, one placed before the other; and when a slave did

anything, he was not punished immediately but kept until there were enough [other persons] to be punished to fill the stocks. Then the man to be punished most would be placed in the lower stocks and the others above him. Then they would be required to take a large dose of medicine [castor oil] and filth down upon each other. I have heard of whipping a woman in the family way by making a hole in the ground for her stomach. My aunt [perhaps "fictive" kin] was whipped so many a time until she has not the same skin she was born with.[5]

Then the commissioners asked Smalls, "What were the crimes for which these punishments were inflicted?" Smalls answered: "For the simplest thing if it was not done to suit the owner's notion. They were whipped till the blood came and then washed down with salt and water. I have often gone with Dr. Reed, who lived here at Beaufort, in a buggy to his plantation, and as we were riding through the field if he saw anything that did not suit him, he would call up the man in the presence of the women and strip him, whip him till the blood streaked and then send to the house for salt and water to pour over him. The only person down here who treated his people well was Governor Aiken. He gave them everything they wanted."[6]

Smalls observed, in the style of Frederick Douglass: "Our lives were one long eternal night, not even an occasional silver lining to bid us hope for a happier day."[7]

Henry McKee

The Henry McKee household served as Smalls's "family of origin." Henry McKee was born to John and Margaret McKee in 1811, when Lydia was fifteen and she helped to raise him. In 1836, two years after his father died, twenty-five-year-old Henry McKee married seventeen-year-old Jane Bold. They moved into the house at 501 Prince Street, which his father had built for him and willed to him. They had four children. Elizabeth Jane, named for her mother, was born the same year as Robert Smalls (1839), and William arrived six years later (1845). Both these McKee children were allowed by their parents to be playmates of Robert Smalls. Two other children, John II (1852–1854), named for his grandfather, and Henry II (1844–1849), named for his father, died in childhood.

Despite their caste, status, and gender differences, Robert, Elizabeth, and William grew up in a conflicting pattern of intimacy unusual but not unknown in the antebellum South. This was undoubtedly because of the McKees' generous attitudes toward their enslaved house servant Lydia and her son Robert. These relationships survived the war and flourished again during those years

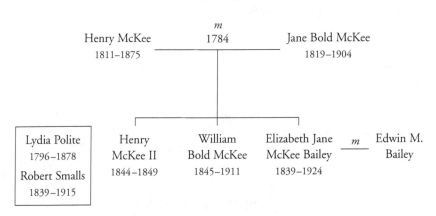

Figure 2.1   The Henry McKee Household
1836–1851

Note: Robert Smalls and his mother, Lydia Polite, were enslaved servants in the Henry McKee household from the time of his birth until he was twelve years old.

after the war when Smalls was in a position to return the kindnesses he and his mother had been shown by the McKees during slavery.

The Henry McKee family was prosperous and expanding while Smalls was growing up.[8] In 1840 the twenty-nine-year-old Henry McKee owned the Prince Street house, and lived there with his wife and their one-year-old daughter, Elizabeth Jane McKee. Forty-four-year-old Lydia Polite, her one-year-old son, Robert Smalls, and George, the family driver slept in small cabins in the backyard. In addition Henry McKee owned sixty other enslaved persons, also inherited from his father. Of these field hands, eighteen were males; and forty-two were females; eighteen were children under ten years of age, while only one male and one female were over fifty-five years old. This was a valuable work force.

A decade later, in 1850, the family had experienced considerable growth. Still living in the Prince Street house, the McKee family now included thirty-nine-year-old Henry, thirty-one-year-old Jane, eleven-year-old Elizabeth, and five-year-old William. During the 1840s Henry McKee II had died in childhood. Lydia, now fifty-four, and eleven-year-old Robert were still members of this household, as was George.

The next decade brought many changes to the McKee household. In 1851 Robert Smalls was taken to Charleston to live with Jane McKee's married sister, Mrs. Eliza Ancrum. That same year, after fifteen years in the Prince Street house,

McKee sold it to the William DeTreville family and built another house near the corner of Carteret and Bay streets. The family lived in this new house for ten years, until the Union troops landed in Beaufort in November 1861. According to Beaufort librarian Mabel Runnette's August 29, 1955, letter to Dorothy Sterling, the house burned down in 1907, but the library has a photograph of it taken in the 1860s.[9]

Social scientists hold that early sustained and loving care provided by a mother or mother figure is essential for a child's healthy and successful mastery of the pathway to adolescence and adulthood. It is also known that a child needs more than a supportive environment and mother figure to maximize her or his potential. A child also needs a father figure to provide protection, training, and a model of manhood. Smalls never had a father to fulfill these roles. Among the cruelest of the many cruel aspects of slavery was robbing children of the care and protection of their fathers, robbing black women of the care and protection of husbands, and robbing both parents of the chance to raise their children. Under slavery it was impossible for a black man to be the head of his family. If there was a head, it was the white man who owned mother and child. This severance of the father from the family is among the most crippling and long-lasting legacies of American slavery. Even today we live with this historic emasculation of the black man, which systematically drains strength from many black families.

Smalls never had a father to love, protect, provide for, and teach him. Still, he was more privileged than most enslaved blacks because he had available to him a father figure or substitute father for the first eleven years of his life. It was a grossly inadequate substitute, but it served both Smalls and his mother as well as the system and the circumstances would permit. This substitute father figure was Henry McKee.

When Smalls testified before the American Freedman's Inquiry Commission, the commissioners never asked him about his father. Characteristically, they took for granted that children born in slavery had no fathers, but this supposition ignored the fact that Smalls had a father figure. Had the commission understood the extent and impact of McKee's role, they would not have been as baffled by the presence and accomplishments of the twenty-four-year-old man before them. When they asked Smalls about the cruelties of slavery, he was careful to volunteer the observation that "I have had no trouble with my owner" before proceeding to describe others who had suffered severe abuse at the hands of their owners.

Henry McKee was kind to Lydia—as was his father, John McKee, before him for the some thirty years in which Lydia helped to raise Henry and his siblings. In allowing Robert to stay around the house until the age of twelve and to be raised by his own mother, even as Lydia was also helping raise the McKee children, Henry McKee made a gift of incalculable proportions to both mother and son. Also, from early in Smalls's life, McKee adopted the child as a sort of pet. He took Robert with him on horseback as he went out to inspect his plantation. He taught Robert how to ride a horse and how to take care of the animals. He also taught him to hunt with a gun and instructed him how to handle himself in the water by teaching him swimming and boating.

The protection and the skills that McKee provided Smalls—combined with the love, nurturing, and teaching of his mother—gave Smalls a head start in life that equipped him to function as a competent and confident young man by the time he turned twelve. Indeed, Smalls seemed to skip adolescence altogether, passing from childhood into adulthood. His descendants have made a persuasive case that this early childhood upbringing, or socialization, was the key to Smalls's survival and to his remarkable achievements in life, which in turn brought enormous satisfaction and pride to his mother, to his people, and even to his former owners. As to why McKee helped Smalls so much, no one knows for sure. Some say that Henry McKee—like his father, John McKee—was by nature a kind and considerate person influenced by his religious upbringing in St. Helena's Episcopal Church. Others say it was because Henry McKee was grateful to Lydia for helping to raise him and his own children. Then there were those who say that Lydia was just the kind of person who demanded such treatment. Some believe that Smalls was Henry McKee's blood brother, the biological son of John McKee. Still others say that Henry was Lydia's lover and Smalls's biological father.

Privileges

Despite the bondage of slavery, Smalls enjoyed certain distinct privileges when he was growing up. He was a "house slave" rather than a "field slave." In slavery, house servants had the privilege of doing mostly domestic, indoor work, which was not nearly as grueling as sunup to sundown field work. In addition, house servants lived close to and learned from their owners. They learned to speak proper English, developed proper eating habits and manners, dressed in owners' hand-me-down clothing. In the process of interacting with their white and sometimes educated owners, house servants became socialized with a dose of white culture. Little wonder that a historic animosity often existed between house servants and field hands. Smalls and his mother before him benefited enormously from growing up in the McKee household. Lydia was therefore able to transmit some European culture to her son indirectly.

A further privilege flowed from the length of this socialization process. At Smalls's birth Henry McKee had promised Lydia that her son could stay around the house with her, doing errands until he reached his twelfth birthday. Only then would Robert be sent to the plantation as a field hand. Not only did Smalls have the privilege of being raised by his own mother for the first eleven years of his life, but they even slept together in the same cabin, as Lydia had done with her mother for the first ten years of her life. This situation was unusual even for children of house servants. It was also different from the treatment Lydia had received from Henry McKee's father some twenty years earlier, when her first son, Larry Polite, was born. He was not allowed to stay with her but was sent out to the plantation to be cared for along with the children of the plantation field hands. When her son Larry Polite became five or six years old, he was assigned to work as a quarter hand (a field hand who, because of age or condition, was assigned one quarter of the daily work expected of a "full hand" and did progressively more hard labor. Robert Smalls was allowed to bypass that treatment until he turned twelve.

Lydia loved her son dearly and bestowed daily affection on him. More important, she cared for his physical, emotional, and learning needs. She also taught him about her mother and her grandmother and how they had come from Africa. She told him that he too was African and as good as anybody else. When Robert got old enough, she took him to the Beaufort Baptist Church, where they joined other black members in the balcony and where he heard the Reverend Richard Fuller preach and lecture. She also took him to two major ceremonial occasions: the regular baptisms and the quarterly meetings. All the while she taught her son the value of hard work and obedience to the McKees, other white people, and black adults as well.

The Search for Smalls's Father

The identity of Robert Smalls's biological father is unknown. Whenever Smalls was asked about it, he said he did not know. There is no indication that Lydia was ever asked or ever said. Nevertheless, four men have been nominated by writers and descendants as possibly being his father. These are John McKee, Lydia's owner; Moses Goldsmith, a wealthy slave merchant in Charleston; Robert Smalls, an enslaved man on the McKee plantation; and Henry McKee, Lydia and Robert's owner.

John McKee

Some writers and descendants have nominated John McKee, mistakenly believing that he died in 1848, when Robert Smalls was nine years old. But, according to his gravestone, John McKee died on September 9, 1834, some five years before Smalls was born.[10]

Moses Goldsmith

While some scholars and descendants have asserted that Moses Goldsmith (1815–1884) of Charleston may have been Smalls's father, there is no evidence to support this theory, nor have any firsthand accounts mentioned this possibility. Some descendants, noting that Goldsmith was a Jewish slave merchant, have succumbed to stereotype speculation that Smalls's business acumen might be traceable to Goldsmith. Smalls's great-granddaughter Dolly Nash wondered "Why should a slave merchant from Charleston come over to Beaufort to have sex with Lydia since he had access to plenty of slave women of his own in Charleston?"

Some of those who propose Goldsmith's paternity have erroneously suggested that Smalls was born in Charleston. The 1870 federal census records that a black male child named Robert Smalls was born into slavery in Charleston in 1836, some three years before the subject of this book was born in Beaufort.[11] The 1900 federal census lists a sixty-seven-year-old black man named Robert Smalls, who was born in October 1832 in Charleston to a mother held in slavery, with no father indicated. This was seven years before Robert Smalls of Beaufort. A black man named Robert B. Smalls lived in Berkeley County. Born in 1856, he was seventeen years younger than Robert Smalls of Beaufort. The 1900 census also lists the subject of this book as sixty-one years old and living in his Prince Street house with his thirty-six-year-old daughter, Sarah, and his eight-year-old son, William Robert Smalls.

These findings show that the name Robert Smalls was quite common then, as now. It is quite possible that Goldsmith of Charleston fathered a child named Robert Smalls by an enslaved woman in Charleston, but that child is not the Robert Smalls who is the subject of this book. Years later, given the fame of this Robert Smalls and given the fact that Smalls grew up in Charleston and sailed from there, some historians might have confused the Charleston-born Robert Smalls with Robert Smalls of Beaufort. An examination of the available data, however, eliminates Goldsmith as Smalls's biological father.

Robert Smalls

Several sources have speculated that an enslaved black man on the McKee plantation named Robert Smalls might have been Smalls's father. Again, they cite no evidence to support this claim. One writer has written that Smalls's parents, Robert and Lydia, both belonged to the McKees.

In writing about Robert Smalls's first trip to the Ashdale Plantation as a child, Dorothy Sterling stated that "an older woman named Chloe Barnwell asked him 'Ain't you Lydia Smalls's boy?' He said yes."[12] In the 1870 census Smalls's mother was also listed as "Lydia Smalls." But why was she referred to as Lydia Smalls when her maiden name was well known as Lydia Polite? She had given her first son her maiden name, so clearly the surname *Smalls* had some special meaning for Lydia. While the *Biographical Directory of the South Carolina State Senate 1776–1985* (1985) states, "His father was probably his mother's owner, John McKee," it calls him "Son of Lydia Smalls."[13] At the time of her second son's birth, Lydia may have considered herself married to a man named Smalls, which might explain why she gave that name to him and why she called herself Lydia Smalls in the 1870 census. Robert Smalls's physical appearance also buttresses the contention that Smalls's father was a black man. None of his photographs depicts him with distinctive white features or shows him to have any resemblance to the McKees.

The McKees allowed Lydia to travel freely around the town and to make weekend visits to their Lady's Island plantation, so it is possible that she developed a relationship with one of the men there, several of whom were named Smalls.

While Smalls was often described as mulatto on the assumption that his father was white, he is called a "Negro" on his death certificate.

Still, the evidence that a Robert Smalls on the McKee plantation might have been the biological father of the subject of this book is sketchy and circumstantial. If such a person existed, he was not still alive at the time of the 1870 census, and nobody has been able to find any historical record of him.

Henry McKee

While John McKee, Lydia's owner, has been ruled out, the evidence that John McKee's son, Henry McKee, might have been Smalls's biological father is quite strong, much stronger than for any of the three other men. Henry was in more intimate contact with Lydia over a longer of period time than any of the other men. He was born in his father's house in 1811, when Lydia was fifteen years old and had been a house servant for five years. She helped his parents to raise him. When her first child, Larry Polite, was born, Henry McKee was five years old. By the time Smalls was born in 1839, Henry McKee was twenty-eight and Lydia was forty-three. Lydia and Henry spent a great deal of time together, slept on the same premises, and were very close. Henry McKee could have had sex with Lydia anytime he wished as he grew up. There are many stories about young white "masters" having sex with their female captives; it was considered part of the maturation process to "sow wild oats." It is worth noting, however, that at the time Smalls was conceived, Henry McKee owned two dozen other black women much younger than Lydia.

While we, like the other writers on this subject, have no firsthand data on the matter, we are inclined to doubt that Henry McKee was Smalls's biological father. The close relationship between Henry and Lydia was more likely that of a mother and son. The reason he was so good to her was because she had raised him and his siblings and later raised his children. Even if he wanted to have a physical relationship with his female property, he would more likely have chosen one of the younger women. Another factor of note is that Henry had an active and productive sex life with his own young wife, Jane. They produced six children together, including their first child, Elizabeth Jane, born just four months after Robert Smalls. Nor has any animosity between McKee's wife and Lydia or Robert been reported; quite the contrary seems to have been the case.

We conclude, however, that if Henry McKee was not Smalls's biological father, he was certainly Smalls's sociological father. For this proposition the evidence is quite strong. Henry helped Smalls's mother to raise him, providing the protection, the teaching, and the care that a father is expected to provide. It is true, of course, that no matter how kind he was, Henry McKee did not set his captive free. And for all the skills he taught Smalls, he never taught him to read and write, nor did he allow anyone else to teach him. For this unfatherlike behavior, however legal it was, Henry McKee must be condemned. There were slave owners who did set their progeny free and saw to it that they were educated. McKee did not set Smalls free but gave Smalls the skills that enabled him to free himself. For that McKee should be commended. He deserves the title *father figure* because he was the closest Smalls ever had to a true father. It does not matter who Smalls's biological father was. What matters is that every child, in order to grow up and reach his potential, needs a father or a father figure, and Smalls had that, an unusual resource for a boy held in bondage.

Thus, the family that helped to socialize Robert Smalls for the first eleven years of his life was a peculiar family, indeed, but family nevertheless. It was a family, not in the legal sense but in the sociological sense. It was the unit responsible for his early childhood socialization, the unit that nurtured and raised him. At the same time, however kindly disposed his owners were to him during this period, aspects of his bondage were ever present. Smalls's mother, ever aware of their status, even if he sometimes forgot, often took special measures to instill in him an understanding of the evils of slavery and the desire to be free.

As her son's twelfth birthday approached, Lydia was worried and expressed her concern to Henry McKee. Grateful to McKee for allowing her to keep

Smalls with her, she was, however, worried that Smalls would not make a good field hand because he had been spoiled and had developed some attitudes that would make it hard for him to adjust to regular slave life. Lydia proposed that instead of sending Robert to be a field hand, McKee might take him to Charleston to live with McKee's sister-in-law and hire himself out as a workman there. Smalls was now big and strong and extraordinarily gifted. In Charleston he could earn money, which would belong to McKee. And so this was done.

As Henry and the family driver, George, climbed aboard the horse-drawn carriage for the thirty-some-mile drive to Charleston, none could have known, except perhaps his mother, that they had prepared him well and were sending him into the wide world to make a difference. Nor did they know that they would all meet again someday and that, when they did, the roles of the two families, the McKees and the Smallses, would be substantially reversed, yet as close as ever. It might well have been at this juncture that Smalls decided if and when he had children he would give them names of the McKee children, who had been his family for the past eleven years. And so he did with his first child, Elizabeth Lydia Smalls, and his last, William Robert Smalls.

3

On the Waterfront

Growing to Manhood in Charleston, 1851–1862

Smalls spent the first eleven years of life in the small township of Beaufort surrounded by tidal creeks, rivers, and huge plantations. During this time his
enslavement in the McKee household brought him both bondage and privilege.
Moreover, through the agency of his mother and his owner, Smalls successfully
made the transition from birth through infancy, childhood, and early adolescence. By 1851 the experiences of these early years had provided him with the
values, attitudes, habits, and skills that served him as he grew into manhood.
Smalls spent the eleven years from 1851 to 1862 in Charleston, South Carolina, and his experiences there prepared him for the challenges of his new life as
a free man. This chapter describes the salient aspects of this period in Smalls's
life and advances the proposition that had his owner, Henry McKee, deposited
Smalls in any city other than Charleston, it is highly unlikely that we would
know his name today. Nor would he have been prepared for the event that
launched his career, his seizure of the Confederate ship *Planter.*

When Robert Smalls was taken to Charleston in 1851 by McKee and
George, the aging McKee family driver, Smalls entered a new, unknown world.
Unlike Beaufort, Charleston had many tall buildings that were close together.
As the horse-drawn carriage crossed the Ashley River into the city, he remarked
that he missed his mother and his friends in Beaufort. Both older men tried to
assure Robert that he would get used to his new life. But neither they nor he
could have possibly imagined the impact this strange new place would have in
molding him into manhood, nor how well they had prepared him for it. He

was delivered to the home of McKee's sister-in-law, Mrs. Eliza Ancrum, where he was to board in a cabin behind the house during the first five years of his stay in the city. McKee and George stayed around for two weeks in Charleston to see that Robert was settled. Always rather outgoing, Smalls soon began to make new acquaintances. McKee had taught Smalls survival skills. His mother had provided him with values that served him well in Charleston. Primary among these values was a strong self-concept. He had absorbed her teaching that he was as good as anyone else and that hard work was a virtue and imperative. She believed deeply in her son, and he was fortified by her belief.

Charleston

Charleston was a major city, a busy seaport nestled between the Ashley and Cooper rivers. It was bounded by Charleston harbor, which led past Fort Sumter into the Atlantic Ocean. Charleston historian Bernard E. Powers has shown how these natural aquatic and physical resources of Charleston provided the context and environment that helped to nurture Smalls's ambitions. When Smalls arrived in Charleston, he found an urban and cosmopolitan community. In a state that was overwhelmingly rural, Charleston by 1860 had a population of 40,522 and was the largest urban area in the state. The majority of the population was black. Over the following decade, however, owing largely to the increased immigration of working-class Europeans, the city gradually gained a white majority.[1]

What drew working-class Europeans to Charleston was what generally feeds immigration—the relative abundance of economic opportunity in the new land versus its absence in the homeland. In the case of Charleston, the booming manufacturing enterprises swelled the working-class population—a factor that also provided work for the free black population and the enslaved persons who, like Smalls, were hired out by their owners. However, the availability of white Europeans who were willing to work for low wages gave them priority over blacks for expanding the workforce.

Charleston's seaport location was a boon to its manufacturing and its immigrant population. During the antebellum period Charleston became the major manufacturing center in the state and the third largest manufacturing center in the South, following Richmond and New Orleans.[2] Finished products and a wealth of agricultural staples flowed from the Charleston economy and harbor to national and international destinations. The list of products was long. According to Walter Edgar, they included "umbrellas, cordage, hats, organs, stained glass, railway cars, furniture, crockery, silverware, carriages, wagons, bricks, saddlery, tin ware, sails, gristmills, rice mills, turpentine distilleries, and boat works."[3] The docks and boat works became of particular interest to Smalls. This manufacturing sector attracted a cosmopolitan population similar to that in northern cities, and after a while enterprising Charlestonians began to hold annual fairs to showcase the industrial goods made in the state.

Despite this vigorous manufacturing center, however, Charleston was far from the wealthiest district in white per capita income—a distinction that still belonged to the large agricultural areas with large plantations and large enslaved black labor forces. Sumter, Georgetown, Fairfield, and Beaufort were the wealthiest districts, with Charleston ranking eighteenth of the state's thirty districts.[4] Even so, Charleston citizens prospered along with those in the rest of the state. Edgar found that by 1860 "the average free South Carolinian was better off financially than most other Americans."[5]

Charleston was home to a large and diversified black population. A year before Smalls arrived, the black population of Charleston numbered nearly 23,000. Moreover, blacks had outnumbered whites in seven of the eight decades from 1790 to 1860.[6] Some were enslaved, some free; some were black, others brown; some were born in Africa, others in South Carolina. A prominent social organization in Charleston at the time of Smalls's residency was the Brown Fellowship Society, open only to free blacks of distinctly light or mulatto complexion.[7] Free blacks of Charleston had founded this mutual aid association in 1790 and purchased their own burial ground at 52–54 Pitt Street in 1794. The burial ground was sold to the Roman Catholic bishop of Charleston in 1857, and most of the gravestones were moved to Magnolia Cemetery. In the same area, but separated by a fence, was the burial ground of the Society of Free Dark Men, later called the Humane Brotherhood, founded in 1843. It was founded by a free black man named Thomas Smalls, who had been refused membership in the Brown Fellowship Society because of his color.[8]

A house at 2 Green Street was the home of Mrs. Elizabeth Johnson, a free black woman, and her descendants. Later it was the residence of the Bell family, who became active in the civil rights movement. Records of the Brown Fellowship Society were found inside this house when it was being restored by the College of Charleston in the 1970s.

As a result of the relatively independent lifestyles made possible by city life, the living conditions of slaves residing there were somewhat mitigated. Moreover, this diversity facilitated the development of what Powers has described as "attitudes and activities antithetical to slavery."[9] If there was any place in South Carolina where Smalls could implement his desire "to be a man" like Frederick Douglass, Charleston was it.

Many characteristics of the city enabled Smalls to grow. According to Powers, interactions between the Africans newly arrived in Charleston and those born in America "allowed many of Charleston's slaves to maintain a profound sense of their original heritage and culture."[10] Smalls could appreciate this because African heritage had been introduced to him by his mother, whose mother had come from Africa. There were also strong patterns of interaction between blacks and whites. One prominent local white minister commented on the relationship between the races: "They belong to us. We also belong to them. They are divided out among us and mingled up with us and we with them in a thousand ways."[11] Smalls was comfortable interacting with whites because he had done so on a small scale in Beaufort all his young life.

Another feature of Charleston was its diverse economy. Unlike Beaufort District or the Sea Islands, Charleston offered a broad range of opportunities. A majority of enslaved blacks in the city worked in domestic occupations or as unskilled laborers. However, there had evolved, as early as 1848, at least thirty-eight different occupations among blacks.[12] Many of these occupations required or taught considerable skills. They included needleworking, laundering, and housekeeping for women, and bricklaying, blacksmithing, carpentry, tailoring, baking, plastering, cooperage, shoemaking, and miscellaneous mechanical trades for men. Blacks were also regularly employed in manufacturing and shipbuilding. As a major port city, Charleston used blacks extensively for the demanding physical labor on the waterfront, where Smalls found his niche.

In the realm of education Charleston blacks were more privileged than those in many other places. As early as 1855 a system of free schools for free blacks was developed in Charleston and operated by free black men and women. The students benefited not only from what they learned but also from the relationships they formed. One of the persons associated with these schools was Francis Cardozo, who became Smalls's lifelong friend and colleague. The lives of these two men became intertwined in many ways over the years in Charleston, Beaufort, Columbia, and Washington, D.C. When Smalls arrived in 1851, Cardozo was teaching in one of these schools.

Another personality in Charleston at this time was Alonzo Ransier, who was born free in Charleston just five years before Smalls's birth. He also studied in one of Charleston's several schools for free blacks. Ransier and Smalls were contemporaries not only in their youth before the war but also during Reconstruction.[14] During this time Ransier's home was at 33 Pitt Street in Charleston. Mary Weston, Cardozo's classmate at a school for free blacks, later operated her own school for free blacks. Other prominent black antebellum educators included Dr. Benjamin A. Boseman, the first black to be appointed to the University of South Carolina board of trustees after the war, and Henry E. Hayne, postwar South Carolina secretary of state and the first black medical student to attend the University of South Carolina. One of the most prominent free blacks was T. McCants Stewart. Born in 1852 to free black parents in Charleston, Stewart attended a school for free blacks and ultimately became a national and international leader.

Smalls could not attend these schools because he was not free, but he associated with free blacks who did. Moreover, the intellectual atmosphere in Charleston at midcentury was like nothing Robert Smalls had known or imagined. He mingled with free and enslaved blacks at meetings of the seven secret societies he regularly attended, where attendees spoke mostly of welfare measures for blacks, enslaved and free, but also about their aspirations to set free the enslaved blacks. With his high native intelligence and gregarious nature, and with the support of his family and owners, Smalls thrived in this intellectual environment. The preeminent source of his practical learning, however, was the waterfront, where he met and mingled with blacks and whites, enslaved and free, from all parts of the world.

Having been trained by his mother to be a highly religious person, Smalls benefited from the many churches and church leaders of Charleston. A city of churches, Charleston underwent a dramatic increase in black church membership between 1831 and 1860. By 1845, after the Second Great Awakening, the galleries of Charleston's white Baptist and Methodist churches were crowded with black members. And while the Presbyterians and Episcopalians had fewer members, they too reached out to blacks, especially through their Sunday schools.[15] On the plantations the white planters had opened their churches to blacks to sustain a peaceful labor force and thus thwart their constant fear of rebellion. They also considered that they were doing their Christian duty to proselytize. No doubt the Charleston whites had similar motivations. Blacks flocked to the plantation churches in large numbers despite their dislike for their mistreatment and the style of worship.

When Smalls met with the American Freedmen's Inquiry Commission, he spoke about the role of the church during slavery in trying to uphold family life, youthful behavior, and morality:

QUESTION: What proportion of the colored girls join the church?

SMALLS: Most all the girls join the church . . . no matter how bad a girl may have been as soon as she joins the church she is made respectable.

QUESTION: Does this joining the church make a difference in their conduct?

SMALLS: Yes sir, the change is very great—as great as between the sunshine and a hailstorm. She stops all this business with men. The rules of the church are very strict about that.[16]

Blacks constantly agitated for their own separate worship experience. They disliked restricted participation in all aspects of the services. They were particularly bored by the European styles of preaching and hymn singing, and they were unhappy not to be allowed to "shout" or "get happy" or dance to the rhythm of their own music. During the early part of the nineteenth century black Methodists had considerable autonomy, but in 1815 white authorities decreed that blacks could not have meetings thereafter unless a white person was in charge. The whites had discovered that some of the class leaders in the black Methodist churches had been using church funds to purchase and emancipate enslaved persons. Blacks resented this change in their semi-independent status and so raised funds to send two of their lay preachers to Philadelphia to be trained and ordained by Bishop Richard Allen in the newly organized African Methodist Episcopal (AME) Church. Morris Brown, a free black preacher, was one of these two. In 1818 Brown returned to Charleston, where under his leadership the AME Church flourished, leaving the white Methodist churches almost empty.[17] It is well known that throughout history the church has been used both as means of suppressing black aspiration and as a source of their agitation for liberation. Nowhere was this dual function of religion more vividly illustrated than in Charleston.

Powers has written that "the formation of the African Church in Charleston was a rebellious act of revolutionary proportions."[18] City authorities began to harass the black congregations. For instance, in June 1818, 140 black worshippers were arrested by the city police for illegally congregating. Five ministers, among them Morris Brown, were sentenced and given the choice of leaving the state or suffering imprisonment for one month. Dedicated to his church, Brown elected imprisonment in order to remain in Charleston. Despite harassment by whites, the African Church continued to grow. However, the discovery of the Denmark Vesey slave conspiracy in 1822 precipitated the destruction of the African Church.[19]

The memory of Morris Brown's activities was still fresh in Charleston when Smalls was there. The house built by Brown around 1814 is still standing at 99 Smith Street. Brown apparently erected the plain frame house as an investment because, as a free black minister, he lived at the corner of Wentworth and Anson streets until he was forced to leave Charleston after the Vesey insurrection.

Even though Brown's church was apparently destroyed by the authorities in 1822, it went underground and continued to function. Thus, when the Reverends Daniel Payne and Richard Cain, AME missionaries, arrived in Charleston after the war, in the spring of 1865, they were able to round up over two thousand AME members who had been meeting secretly since before the war.[20]

After the war, Smalls and Cain became active collaborators and leaders in the Republican Party.

In addition to churches, there were many of other black organizations in Charleston. Smalls reported that during his eleven years in Charleston before the war broke out, he was a member of at least seven secret charitable organizations and that sometimes members discussed means of obtaining freedom for enslaved blacks.[21] He testified as much before the American Freedmen's Inquiry Commission:

> QUESTION: Were there any societies among people for discussing the question of freedom?
>
> SMALLS: No, sir. They used to talk about these things at the meetings of charitable societies to some extent but they were afraid to trust each other fully. On the plantation, I do not think there are any secret societies except the church societies and they do not introduce that subject there. They pray constantly for the day of their deliverance.[22]

Property ownership among free blacks was widespread during Smalls's sojourn in Charleston. Social stratification was a prominent feature of black life in Charleston as well.[23] One landmark is the house at 67 Alexander Street, built around 1838 by Richard Edward Dereef, one of Charleston's wealthiest free blacks. A prominent wood merchant and real-estate developer, Dereef also owned a wharf at the foot of Calhoun Street. The birthplace of Ernest E. Just, a distinguished chemist and the founder of Omega Psi Phi fraternity, is still standing at 28 Inspection Street. Just's father, Charles Just Jr., was a wharf builder, and his mother, Mary, was a schoolteacher. Just's grandfather Charles Just Sr. Had founded of the Unity and Friendship Society, a mutual insurance agency for free blacks, in 1844. Richard Holloway, a member of the Brown Fellowship Society and a free black master carpenter, built about twenty small frame houses in the city between 1822 and 1830. One of these, at 96 Smith Street, is still standing. Another was at 221 Calhoun Street, which had a school in the rear for free blacks.[24]

The small, two-story wooden house with pantile roof at 42 Amherst Street, still standing today, was built sometime after 1818 by James Brown. A prosperous free mulatto butcher, Brown purchased his wife, Nancy, and held her and their two sons, John and James, in slavery; yet he cared for them well, treating them as the family members they were. It was not unusual during slavery for free blacks to purchase their wives and children not only to profit from their labor but also to protect them as family. There are also the houses built in 1835 by Jayne Wright, a wealthy black woman, at 36 and 38 Chalmers Street, which were occupied by her family.

A three-and-one-half-story wooden mansion at 71 Broad Street was the location of the Mansion House Hotel during Smalls's time in the city. Built between 1772 and 1774 by William Barrows, the building was purchased by Jehu Jones, a free black man, in 1815. Jones operated it as a hotel until his death in 1833. Jones Hotel was considered one of the finest in the city and was patronized by wealthy, distinguished visitors. When Smalls arrived in Charleston in 1851, Jehu Jones's stepdaughter Ann Deas, owned and operated it as the Mansion House Hotel. The hotel was a major part of the social environment that helped to inspire Smalls toward his goal of freedom. The building was dismantled in 1928, and some of the interior furnishings were moved to the Winterthur Museum in Delaware.

Several free blacks owned enslaved persons when Robert Smalls entered Charleston in 1851. By 1860, 131 free blacks in Charleston owned a total of 388 enslaved persons.[25] Two-thirds of the free black heads of households owning enslaved persons were women. Many had inherited these properties from their owners who freed them in their wills. Most of these free black slave owners were also holders of real estate. Both economic reasons and the desire to protect family members motivated the practice of free blacks owning enslaved persons.

In the urban and cosmopolitan city of Charleston, free blacks could move around at will, as long as they carried their passes. They could be educated, and they could follow a variety of occupations. They could sue and be sued in courts, marry, own property in their own names (including enslaved blacks), and make court-enforceable wills. They could sit in the balconies of the many white churches of the city, and for a time they could even establish their own churches.

After extensive interaction with free blacks, many whites in the city, including prominent business and political leader Alfred Huger, came to value that class. Huger argued that the free black class acted as a buffer between whites and slaves and showed how industry and thrift could be rewarded, even in the South.[26] There was a fourth strata in the city as well, one that included Robert Smalls. This strata was composed of enslaved persons hired out to work as independent workers. They enjoyed many privileges denied field hands, yet not as many as free blacks because they were still controlled by their individual owners. But, whatever the privilege of this class, they lived in an era of slavery and could not escape its dehumanizing features.

There were vivid symbols of slavery all over Charleston during Smalls's time there, especially the workhouse at 15 Magazine Street. For a small fee paid by their owners, enslaved persons who were considered unruly by their "masters" were brought to the workhouse for punishment. It became infamous in 1822 as the place where four of Denmark Vesey's chief deputies—Peter Poyas, Ned Bennett, Rolla Bennett, and Gullah Jack—were kept in chains prior to their hanging. After they were hanged, blacks memorialized the event by changing two words of the spiritual "See How They Done My Lord" to "See How They Done Them Boys."[27] After 1840 this location became one of the prominent places for selling slaves in Charleston.

Built in 1802, the city jail at 21 Magazine Street was also in operation during Smalls's time in the city. After the Vesey insurrection, it was used to house free black seamen who stayed in Charleston until their ships left the port because white Charlestonians feared that these free black seamen might bring ideas of revolt to the local blacks.

The physical, economic, social, and cultural attributes of Charleston—as well as its large black presence and diverse population—combined to make Charleston a fertile ground for Smalls. Smalls took advantage of the inspiration and resources of Charleston, building a successful career, laying the foundation for his own "Family of Procreation," and developing a plan of escape from slavery—all of which proved to be enormously successful. Charleston also offered Smalls role models. Among the individuals in his environment who were critical to his development were John Simmons, a rigger; John Ferguson, owner of the *Planter;* and Hannah Jones, who became his wife.

Smalls's Occupational Development

Within his first two weeks in the city, just before McKee and George departed, Smalls had found his first job. As a waiter in the Planters Hotel at the corner of Church and Queen streets, he was paid five dollars per month, which went to his owner, Henry McKee. He was such a good worker and fast learner that he was soon raised to seven dollars a month. In that job he often overheard the conversations of the white planters, who spoke about the impending conflict with the North over slavery and secession.

After six months, by traveling about the city, which he was allowed to do at will, he found his second job, as a lamplighter. He could be seen at dusk each day with a huge rag slung over his shoulder and a ladder under his arm. He went from one street corner to another, wiping out the lamp globes and cleaning the soot from the jets. Then in the early evening he repeated his rounds and lit the lamps with a long taper and matches.

John Simmons

After two years on this job, Smalls longed to work on the waterfront. During one of his regular trips to Beaufort to visit his mother and friends at Christmas, he asked his owner, Henry McKee, if he could do so, and McKee agreed. At the harbor Smalls first became a stevedore, loading and unloading cargo from the ships. An eager learner and a willing worker, he was big and strong for his age, and he impressed his supervisors. After a year on the docks, when he was only fifteen years old, he was elevated to supervisor, overseeing men twice his age. Then Smalls got an even better job, as a rigger in the employment of John Simmons. During the winter Simmons taught Smalls how to make rope lines to hold the sails of boats together. As with his other jobs, Smalls excelled in his work, becoming an expert rigger.

Smalls developed a remarkable set of skills on the waterfront and a warm, enduring, mutually respectful relationship with Simmons. During the summer Simmons employed Smalls as a sailor and pilot on coastal vessels. The docks provided Smalls with a practical education of profound importance. Thomas Miller, his political protégé, wrote that "Smalls was educated practically in the school of contact with the very best cultured minds of business men on the wharves and warehouses in the city of Charleston," which was "a kind of education that fits a man for service."[28] Smalls worked for John Simmons for seven years, learning and executing a wide variety of functions. Simmons elevated him to wheelman, or boat pilot, on the inland waterways, where he traveled from Charleston through Georgia and northern Florida. In time he became one of the best wheelmen in that region. Smalls often expressed his indebtedness to Simmons and his appreciation for Simmons's teaching him and allowing him this privilege.[29]

Simmons not only taught Smalls many skills but also raised his salary to sixteen dollars per month. Smalls was trusted to deliver the funds to his owner Henry McKee. Whenever he did so, McKee returned one dollar to Smalls. By now Smalls had developed his legendary thrift and entrepreneurial skills. He began using his money to purchase vegetables and fruits on the islands he visited, and then he sold them to the men on the docks when he returned. He saved some of his profits and used some to purchase more goods to sell. At this time enslaved persons were not allowed to have bank accounts or to own real property, so Smalls stored his earnings in his little cabin in the backyard of Mrs. Ancrum's home. He enjoyed watching the funds accumulate and especially earning more. He already knew the value of money and knew that he would find good use for it.

Family Life

When he was sixteen years old, Smalls began a courtship with thirty-year-old Hannah Jones, who had two children: fourteen-year-old Charlotte Jones and twelve-year-old Clara Jones. The father of these children is unknown, but because they both were later considered by the U.S. Census to be "black" rather than "mulatto," as was Hannah, it may be presumed that the children's father was an enslaved black man in Charleston whose last name was taken by Hannah. At the time she and her children were considered the property of Samuel Kingsman, and they lived together in a cabin at the rear of Kingsman's home. Kingsman allowed Hannah to hire herself out as a local hotel maid, which meant that, like Smalls, she had considerable freedom of movement.

After six months Smalls and Hannah began to spend all their Saturday nights and Sundays together. They visited the various churches and went sightseeing along the waterfront. There is no indication either then or later that their different ages had the slightest impact on their relationship. At seventeen, Smalls was five-foot-five with broad shoulders, a slim waist, and an air of self-confidence. He liked Hannah, he said, because of her sparkling eyes, her black curls, and the way she danced. She was merry; she also had a daring manner that matched his and a quiet wisdom that reminded him of his mother's. He told the American Freedmen's Inquiry Commission: "My idea was to have a wife to prevent me from running around—to have somebody to do for me and to keep me."[30]

Smalls noted that when white men and women got married, they lived together in the same house. In Charleston he knew free black men and women who got married and lived together. Enslaved persons on the other hand, even when permitted to get married, had to continue living separately in quarters provided by their respective masters. Smalls was not willing to settle for that. So before getting married, he and Hannah made a plan to ask their respective owners for permission not only to get married but to live together as well.

Their first proposal was relatively easy. Both owners gave them permission. Robert and Hannah were considered responsible, loyal, and deserving of such companionship. Moreover, the owners considered that marriage would make them more content and more effective workers. Indeed, it did that and more.

Robert, who by now had as easy a conversational manner with Hannah's owner as he did with his own, took the initiative and asked Kingsman to allow them to live together in their own place. This would require money for rent, food, and furniture. Smalls was earning sixteen dollars per month, from which McKee still gave Smalls one dollar. Smalls now made a proposition to McKee. He said he would continue paying McKee fifteen dollars a month, but asked to be allowed to work extra and keep for himself all the money over fifteen dollars that he could make. Then Smalls and Hannah asked Kingsman to accept a monthly payment of five dollars from Hannah and to allow her to keep all her extra earnings. This way they could afford to rent a room and stay together. It is a commentary on Smalls's ambition, his persuasiveness, his reputation, and human relations skills that both McKee and Kingsman agreed to this unusual proposition and gave their permission for the wedding and for the new couple to live together.

The wedding was spectacular. It took place on December 24, 1856. Henry McKee had given the couple permission to come to Beaufort and get married at his new home on Carteret and Bay streets, the house McKee bought in 1851, the same year he took Smalls to Charleston. George, who had delivered Robert to Charleston five years earlier, drove the couple from Charleston to Beaufort for the wedding. Then assuming the role of the father, he gave away the bride. Henry and Jane McKee and the McKee children, seventeen-year-old Elizabeth Jane and eleven-year-old William, were in attendance. The food was provided by McKee. Lydia, Smalls's mother, presided over the entire affair. The couple held hands and jumped over the broom and were pronounced married by McKee. Then they celebrated and lit firecrackers until the wee hours of Christmas day in 1856. Lots of friends, black and white, were there. This was the beginning of Smalls's role as head of his own family with enormous responsibilities, for which history shows him to have been fully prepared.

After the wedding George drove the newlyweds back to Charleston. Robert and Hannah moved into a little apartment, two rooms above a livery stable on East Bay Street. They were permitted to live there in exchange for Robert's cleaning the stalls, so they did not have to use their extra money for rent. Instead they saved and invested it in Smalls's business enterprise. As they set up house over the stable, people, black and white, gave them furnishings and supplies.

Smalls reported later that these were among the happiest moments of their young lives. They were both hard workers, idealistic, and longing for complete freedom. They made no small plans. Robert's entrepreneurial talents were especially useful, and they made extra money through their enterprises on the waterfront. Sailors who had been at sea for weeks paid Hannah to launder their clothes. Robert sold them fresh eggs, strawberries, and chickens he had purchased on the islands. At the Mills Hotel, where Hannah now worked as a chambermaid, she earned seven dollars a month and paid Kingsman five. At the hotel she got free food, leftovers, and surplus clothing. They gave up their Sunday picnics, so Robert could work a part-time job as a deck hand on an excursion steamer.

Within a year, Hannah's fifteen-year-old daughter, Charlotte, had a baby whom she named Emily Brown, giving the baby her father's last name. Robert and Hannah's first child was born on February 12, 1858. They named the child Elizabeth Lydia Smalls. Lydia was for Smalls's mother, and Elizabeth was for Elizabeth Jane McKee, with whom Robert had grown up under the care of Lydia until they turned twelve. We have no record of what Henry, Jane, or Elizabeth McKee thought of this action. In all probability, they were pleased and honored. Lydia was certainly pleased.

By law, Elizabeth Smalls, like her mother, became the property of Kingsman, who was certainly pleased. Hannah had given him another property and, no doubt, others were on the way. But Robert brooded over the fact that his wife and daughter belonged to another man, who could do with them as he willed. Just as he was not willing to settle for the status quo on living arrangements for enslaved persons, he railed against the ownership norms as well. He said later that after their first child was born, he longed even more for his family's freedom and to be the head of his own family.

Smalls then got another idea, which he and Hannah discussed several times. Robert put the question to his owner, Henry McKee, from whom he needed permission for so drastic a proposal. Robert reminded McKee that he now had a good job with a solid future. He was well respected, well treated, and well paid on the docks. He was in an excellent position to make extra money and was very frugal. In addition, his wife had also been given permission by her owner to work and make extra money for herself. Robert asked McKee what he would think of Robert purchasing his wife and daughter from Kingsman.

The practice of free blacks owning enslaved persons in Charleston was well established. For example, Jehu Jones owned the workers he employed in his various business operations.[31] But the idea of an enslaved person owning another was not recognized in law or practice. Because the law was usually interpreted at the whim of powerful white men, however, Robert knew that he had a chance. After discussing the matter, McKee readily consented to Robert's newest request. McKee had nothing to lose by this proposition. Since he owned Smalls, he consequently possessed everything and everybody that Smalls owned. But knowing of the close relationship between these two men, it is clear that his consent was just another favor McKee was prepared to do for Smalls.

Then came the hard part. Robert approached Kingsman with his strange and illegal proposition. Smalls had learned by now that slavery was essentially a commercial enterprise; his proposition was commercially beneficial and profitable to Kingsman. He also had a high degree of confidence in himself, buoyed by his mother's teaching that he was good as anybody else. Kingsman knew

Robert to be a responsible and industrious young man. Because Robert and Hannah had kept up the payments negotiated in the marriage arrangement, Kingsman agreed to sell Hannah and Elizabeth to Robert for $800. Because Robert and Hannah had only $100 saved up, Kingsman agreed to let Smalls give him a $100 down payment and the rest later. It was a gentleman's agreement, settled with just a handshake. But both men, and others too, knew that this was serious business. Smalls, legally enslaved himself, was the contractual owner and master of his wife and daughter. Not many enslaved persons could make that statement or make that kind of deal. It was a multifaceted contract. Kingsman had contracted to sell his two slaves to Robert. McKee had contracted to permit Smalls to own them. Robert and Hannah had contracted to pay a specified price over an unspecified period of time. It is a testament to all persons involved in this complex, partly commercial and partly family, relationship— and to Charleston—that all would sanction such an arrangement. In 1861 Robert Smalls Jr. was born.

During the next three years, Robert and Hannah saved all their extra earnings. The next few months were busy ones for Smalls. He pored over maps and charts, traced channels, studied currents and tides, and memorized the location of the shoals and reefs in Charleston harbor to better equip himself for the challenges of making money on the waterfront. Within a few years, Smalls had complete mastery of the harbors and waterways of the South Carolina and Georgia coasts. He became an expert boatman and a great manager of boats. It was said that few men along the South Carolina coastal waters could handle a boat as well as Robert Smalls. By the time war broke out in 1861, Robert and Hannah had saved up the $700 they owed Kingsman. However, Smalls and Hannah never had to pay Kingsman this additional money.[32]

In Hannah Jones, Robert Smalls had found a perfect match. He and Hannah planned and worked together through good times and bad, through dangers seen and unseen, until her death parted them some twenty-seven years later.

PART II

Fighting for Freedom

4

The Seizure of the Planter

A Family Affair, May 13, 1862

On May 13, 1862, Robert Smalls took control of the Confederate ship *Planter* and sailed it out of Charleston harbor. It takes nothing away from Smalls's feat to note that his was not the first escape made by enslaved blacks from that harbor. According to Charles Cowley, "In 1862 the crew of General Roswell S. Ripley's gig [barge] were the first to act upon this plan. One night when General Ripley had kept them waiting for him for some time they concluded to wait no longer and they ran away with his gig, and took her over the bar to the blockading fleet. . . . Gabriel Pinckney and another of this gig's crew named Bull found remunerative employment as pilots in the federal fleet and they more than intimated that Robert Smalls was liable to follow them and bring the *Planter* with him."[1]

The capture of the *Planter* thrust Robert Smalls into the history books. This event was also the beginning of Smalls's notable career in the Union Navy during the Civil War and his even more notable political career after the war. While it might well not have been his most important achievement, his seizure of the *Planter* was an impressive and influential gateway to an adulthood of remarkable achievements, and not a few downturns as well. Emma Lou Thornbrough has called him "daring, cool-headed, keen of mind, courageous, and firm on the principle of equality of all men."[2]

The *Planter* was carried off by a group of people we may call Smalls's "family of liberation," which consisted of nuclear, extended, and augmented family members, who were not only kindred spirits in their struggle for freedom but were also specifically related to each other by marriage, bloodline, and simple affirmation.[3]

This event was not a spur of the moment affair and was not an individual achievement; rather, in a profound sense, it was a family affair, building on Smalls's attachment to freedom and family. If this action was not and could not have been accomplished by Smalls alone, neither was it undertaken for himself alone.

The *Planter* was officially entered in the U.S. Ship Registry by John Ferguson on October 23, 1860, in Charleston. The ship—147 feet long, 30 feet wide, and 45 feet in beam—drew only 3'9" of water, making it especially suitable and fast moving for the inland waterways. The *Planter* was planked with red cedar on a live-oak frame and had two oscillating steam engines, each driving a side paddle wheel. With a carrying capacity of fourteen hundred bales of cotton or one thousand men, it was one of the speediest ships out of Charleston harbor. Because two engines could be rotated simultaneously in opposite directions, she could be turned on a dime. The *Planter* therefore was quite handy for transporting troops and material in the coastal waters of South Carolina and through the labyrinth of rivers and creeks. Ferguson assigned himself as pilot and three of his enslaved persons as crew. He contracted further with other owners to supply him with five additional enslaved crewmen. Robert Smalls was one of these crewmen. When the war broke out, Ferguson leased the *Planter* to the Confederate Navy for $100 per day. By April 1862 Robert Smalls was a strong-minded, strong-bodied young man. He was the son of a proud mother, husband of an adoring wife, father of two children, and stepfather of two others. In the occupational sphere he was a pilot and a businessman of extraordinary talent and accomplishments. After ten years on the Charleston docks, he had learned from sailors and merchant seaman from many parts of the world. Beyond that, he had established a strong commitment and leadership pattern among his peers. He was well respected and trusted by whites and blacks, men and women, enslaved and free. He was self-confident, a planner, and focused in all his endeavors. Moreover, he was a mature and expert boatman after seven years under the supervision and training of John Simmons, and he handled boats with expert skill and assurance. Early on Simmons had said to another white man on the docks, "That boy's got the makings of pilot."[4] John Ferguson, the original owner of the *Planter,* also recognized and rewarded these talents. So, too, in time, did Captain C. J. Relyea, an officer assigned to the *Planter.*

By the time war broke out Smalls had completely mastered the harbors and waterways of the South Carolina and Georgia seacoasts.[5] All these experiences had sharpened his desire for freedom. But Smalls was still enslaved, and making his situation even more intolerable, he was assigned to work on a Confederate warship fighting to defeat the Union and to maintain slavery. By the time Smalls had served on the *Planter* for almost a year, he had become quite valuable to the Confederacy. His duties consisted of carrying war supplies and men to the various Confederate fortifications around Charleston harbor, laying torpedoes strategically to warn off Union ships, and keeping the *Planter* cleaned, fueled, and loaded with supplies, as well as other work assigned to him by the officers. He said later, in his address to the 1895 Constitutional Convention, "I fought for the Confederacy and they didn't treat me right so I left."

General Hunter's Initiatives

Perhaps the series of events that bore most directly on Robert Smalls's historic action were orders issued by Major General David Hunter to enlist blacks to fight in the Union Army under his command. The capture of Port Royal harbor on November 7, 1861, and the subsequent founding of Hilton Head Naval Station brought Hunter to South Carolina, where in March 1862, he was placed in charge of the Union forces in the Department of the South headquarters at Port Royal on the Sea Islands. Hunter, an abolitionist, a former associate of John Brown in Kansas, and a personal friend and former guard of President Lincoln, was a passionate advocate for freedom. The relationship between Hunter and Smalls became close, warm, respectful, reciprocal, and lifelong.

Two forces motivated Hunter's historic initiative. The first was his deeply held belief in freedom and his antipathy toward the slave system. Second was the shortage of manpower owing in part to the desertion of white Union soldiers and to the deployment of some of his troops in support of the campaign at Richmond. Because of these factors, Hunter had concluded that the Union forces could not win the war without the military participation of blacks.

Hunter communicated as much to the secretary of war, but to no avail. Then, in a bold and daring move, Hunter issued an order on April 13, 1862—one month before Smalls's seizure of the *Planter*—declaring all persons held in slavery, in the territory under his command, to be free and the men eligible to be received into the Union Army.

In practical terms this order was a fiasco. Several thousand black men were rounded up and forced into the Union Army. But Hunter had no authority to pay these men or to order weapons and rations for them. As a result, he was forced by President Lincoln and Secretary of War Edwin M. Stanton to dismiss them.

Then, on May 9, 1862, four days before the seizure of the *Planter* and apparently without clearing his actions with Washington, General Hunter issued a second proclamation declaring all persons held in slavery in the states under his command—South Carolina, Georgia, and Florida—to be free. This was perhaps in anticipation of Lincoln's preliminary Emancipation Proclamation. Hunter's rationale was that the territories under his command were under martial law and that martial law and slavery were incompatible. This time Hunter was better prepared, so he recruited several companies of black soldiers by persuasion. Because of political pressures in Washington, however, Hunter's second order was later set aside by the secretary of war.[6] Even so, Hunter continued to insist that, if the captives could reach the Union lines in his area on their own, they would be treated as free persons. Since Hunter's plans were widely discussed by Smalls and his associates on board the *Planter* and were well known on the docks, the general's actions might well have given immediacy to Smalls's plans.

Meanwhile, inside Charleston harbor the Confederates amassed their military forces on a series of islands and proceeded to mine the harbor against further encroachments by Union forces. When they leased the *Planter* from John Ferguson, Smalls and the entire crew who had been working under the civilian command of Ferguson were assigned to the Confederate forces under General Roswell S. Ripley. The *Planter* was then given the task of laying torpedoes and supplying guns, ammunition, and other equipment to the Confederate troops around the harbor. Smalls and the other blacks were supervised by three white officers. Smalls's talents were quickly recognized, and he was named wheelman, a considerable promotion for an enslaved person. Smalls did his duties on the *Planter,* biding his time and laying plans for escape.

On a Sunday afternoon in April 1862 the crew gathered for their final strategy session in Smalls's two-room quarters above the horse stable on East Bay Street in Charleston. Smalls explained the plan in detail. He suggested that if they were apprehended by Confederate forces, they should set fire to the boilers, blowing up the ship and themselves as well. Better to take their lives into their own hands, he argued, than to turn themselves over to the Confederates. They all agreed. Then, in the most poignant moment of the meeting, descendants have reported that Smalls turned to Hannah, who had intimate knowledge of all the plans and discussions. He suggested that because they might be killed or kill themselves, perhaps she and the children should stay behind. After he reached freedom, he would surely return for them. Filled with love for her husband and for freedom and with supreme confidence in God, Hannah responded, in the manner of Ruth in the Hebrew Bible: "I will go," she said, "and where you die, I will die."[7]

By Monday, May 12, 1862, Smalls and the crew of the *Planter* had had an arduous two weeks of supply duty. The ship had been moving Confederate guns and ammunition from Coles Island to James Island. The night before, around two hundred pounds of ammunition had been loaded onto the *Planter* for transport to the other forts. At the end of the day, the white officers tied the ship to the southern dock. The officers—Captain C. J. Relyea, pilot Samuel H. Smith, and engineer E. Zerich Pitcher—took advantage of the completion of this task to spend the night ashore with their families.

After night fell, they left the black bondsmen on board to get the ship ready for the next day. This was the opportunity for which Smalls and his crew had been waiting. The other black crewmen who had joined Smalls were John Smalls (no relation), J. Samuel Chisholm, Abraham Allston, Gabriel Turno, Abraham Jackson, and Alfred Gradine. Another black crew member, David Jones, had decided not to join the expedition out of concern for what might happen to his family. Smalls excused him on his pledge of secrecy, which Jones kept.[8]

The white officers, of course, were violating military orders by staying on-shore overnight. It was not the first time they had done so, and Smalls anticipated their behavior precisely. Meanwhile, Union forces had placed a blockade at Charleston harbor to prevent the Confederates from getting out to the Atlantic Ocean and engaging in foreign trade that would help them conduct the war. Ten Union ships—armed and ready to attack any Confederate ship that approached them on their way to the ocean—enforced this blockade. The most notable of these ships was the *Onward,* commanded by Lieutenant J. F. Nichols.

Smalls Makes His Move

The time had come to execute the long-prepared plan. At about 3:00 a.m. on May 13, 1862, Smalls and his crew were ready. They put extra wood on the fire and got up a full head of steam. Smalls ordered his crew to raise the South Carolina state flag and the Confederate battle flag and to fire up the boilers. At this point Smalls, always a religious man, said a prayer: "Oh Lord, be with us on this fateful journey." Then, with John Smalls as engineer, he backed the vessel out of her berth at the southern wharf, just in front of General Ripley's head-quarters, and into the channel. They successfully passed the first checkpoint, a Confederate sentinel stationed only fifty yards away. This sentinel later testified at the trial of the three officers who had spent the night onshore that he did indeed see the *Planter* pull out from the dock at an unusually early hour on the morning of May 13; however, he thought that Captain Relyea was in command of the ship and so did not attempt to apprehend the vessel.

The sentry might be excused for thinking that Captain Relyea was in charge of the *Planter;* for, in a brilliant act of camouflage, Smalls had donned the captain's large floppy straw hat and put on his gold-trimmed jacket, hoping that the dark shadows of the predawn hours would give him the appearance of Captain Relyea.

Smalls eased the *Planter* along the shore to the north Atlantic wharf, where another Confederate ship, the *Etowah,* was moored.[9] Smalls dispatched two of his men in a small rowboat to pick up nine passengers who had hidden on the *Etowah* the night before. The two black stewards on the *Etowah* had been enlisted in this conspiracy. Hannah; the Smallses' two children, Elizabeth Lydia and Robert Smalls Jr.; Hannah's eighteen-year-old daughter, Clara Jones; and W. William Morrison, one of the black stewards on the *Etowah,* were quietly taken into the rowboat and boarded the *Planter.* Left behind in Charleston was Hannah's twenty-year-old daughter, Charlotte, who might have chosen to stay behind with a man named Brown who was the father of her five-year-old child, Emily Brown. After the war Charlotte and her child came to live with the Smalls family.

Just as swiftly John Smalls's wife, Susan Smalls; their small child; and Susan's sister were brought aboard. Two other women, Annie White and Lavina Wilson, were also in this party; they were probably girlfriends of crew members. The escape had become a family affair, and the traditional African American extended family was in full evidence. Members of this "family of liberation" were bound together by marriage, blood, and affinity. They were also bound together by faith, fear, and a determination to be free. The women and children were placed in the bottom of the ship, and each man took his preassigned post. Speed and quiet were of utmost importance. Within half an hour the *Planter* was steaming out of the harbor past Castle Pinckney, the second checkpoint and the first fort to fall to the Confederacy at the outbreak of the Civil War. Without military defenses, the fort had been captured by Confederates in a bloodless takeover on December 26, 1860.

Smalls gave the proper signal and was ordered to pass. The men breathed another sigh of relief. The third checkpoint was Fort Ripley, where the four guns taken on board the *Planter* the day before were scheduled to have been deposited. Smalls gave the correct signal and was ordered to proceed. Their fourth checkpoint was Fort Johnson, from which Confederate troops had fired the first shot of the Civil War on Fort Sumter at 4:30 A.M., April 12, 1861. Here again Smalls sounded the correct signal and was ordered to pass. Now miles from the Charleston shoreline, the crew and passengers of the *Planter* noted that the early morning light beginning to pierce the darkness as they headed toward Fort Sumter.

This Confederate installation had huge guns, which could have blown the *Planter* into pieces if the plot had been discovered. Knowing he would be shot

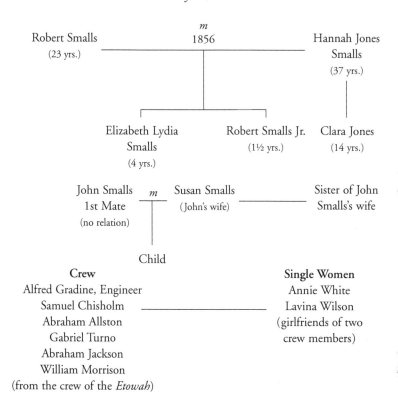

Figure 4.1   Robert Smalls's Family of Liberation
May 13, 1862

by the Confederates if he were caught, Smalls played the role of his life, imper-sonating Captain Relyea. Still wearing the captain's garments, Smalls stood in the pilothouse leaning on the windowsill with his arms folded across his chest —just as Captain Relyea often did. His figure was trim like the captain's; some said later that except for his dark complexion, Smalls bore a striking resem-blance to Captain Relyea.

The men of his crew played their parts as well. Having crewed together on this ship for nearly a year in the service of the Confederacy, they were now in no-man's-land, halfway between slavery and freedom. They knew they must work together or perish; this voyage had become a life or death struggle. They gave their best efforts and prevailed—over the Confederate forces of Charleston harbor; over their fears; over the rough waters, shoals, and mines in the harbor; and over slavery. These men had extraordinary faith in their mission, in their God, in themselves, and in their leader, Robert Smalls.

As they approached Fort Sumter, it was 4:15 A.M. and the ship was clearly in sight of the fort. Some men had advised cutting a wide birth around Sumter so as not to be seen. Smalls disagreed. He wanted the ship's passage to appear as a normal voyage, which would go closer to the fort. Smalls said another prayer: "Oh Lord, we entrust ourselves into thy hands. Like thou didst for the Israelites in Egypt, please stand guard over us and guide us to our promised land of freedom."[10]

When the *Planter* came abreast of Fort Sumter, it could be seen plainly by the sentries. Still in the pilothouse impersonating Captain Relyea, Smalls calmly and deliberately pulled the cord giving the appropriate signal: three shrill sounds and one hissing sound. After a pause that Smalls would later say seemed eternal, the countersign came back: Pass on by! It has been said that after the sentry at Fort Sumter ordered the *Planter* to pass he shouted out "Blow the damned Yankees to hell, or ring one of them in." "Aye, aye," shouted Smalls and kept on his way.

After successfully passing Fort Sumter, Smalls headed out to sea, where the Union blockaders were stationed. He demanded of his loyal crew more speed. Now the quickened pace of the *Planter* alerted the guards at Fort Sumter that something was amiss. Why should their Confederate warship be heading toward the enemy lines all alone at this hour in the morning? They called out to the *Planter* to halt and readied their guns. They signaled to the Confederate light artillery battalion on nearby Morris Island to stop the *Planter*. But they were all too late; the *Planter* was safely beyond the reach of all Confederate guns. The sentry at Fort Sumter then alerted the Confederate command at Charleston harbor that a ship was heading out to sea, but it was too late to dispatch another ship to intercept the *Planter*. The *Planter* was now in Union-controlled waters, and her crew breathed a collective sign of relief—but only for a moment.

Although they had experienced spectacular success on their journey so far, another equally perilous danger confronted Smalls and his crew. They were headed toward the Union blockade in a ship flying a Confederate flag and a South Carolina state flag. Union troops did not know of the plan to turn over the *Planter* to the Union fleet.

Smalls reported later that this was the moment he had feared the most. He had thoroughly familiarized himself with Charleston harbor and Confederate strategies, but he knew nothing about Union strategies. What, he thought, if having successfully taken control of the *Planter* and having successfully outwitted five Confederate checkpoints, they were now attacked by the Union forces to whom they were trying to deliver the vessel and themselves? Smalls prayed again.

Smalls and his crew continued steaming straight toward the Union fleet with the South Carolina flag and the Confederate flag flying high. At sunrise on May 13, 1862, Lieutenant J. F. Nichols, commanding officer of the *Onward,* the lead warship in the ten-ship federal blockade, saw this Confederate vessel speeding out from Fort Sumter and headed directly toward his ship. Nichols alerted his crew and the other nine ships to prepare to fire at the approaching vessel.

But then Smalls had his men take down the flags and run up the flagpole a white bed sheet that Hannah had brought along for the occasion. As the *Planter* got closer, Nichols and his crew saw the white flag of surrender. Obeying the rules of warfare, Nichols ordered his men to hold their fire.

When the *Planter* got into shouting distance of the *Onward,* Robert Smalls, seeing that the ship was holding its fire, bristled with confidence and pride. He pulled the *Planter* up close to the *Onward.* In his May 13 dispatch to his supervisor Nichols reported:

> The steamer ran alongside and I immediately boarded her, hauled down the flag of truce, hoisted the American ensign, and found that it was the steamer *Planter,* of Charleston, and had successfully run past the forts and escaped. She was wholly manned by negroes, representing themselves to be slaves.[11]

The women were jumping up and down on the open deck crying, shouting, hugging each other, pointing back toward Fort Sumter, and uttering sounds of disbelief. Presently Smalls stepped forward and addressed Lieutenant Nichols, "I thought this ship might be of some use to Uncle Abe," he said and added, "I have some guns the Confederates took away from Fort Sumter."[12]

Robert Smalls, seven other men, five women, and three children gathered on the deck of the *Planter.* They were now free, according to the canons of war, and the Confederate warship *Planter* now belonged to the Union forces.

Nichols ordered the ship and its passengers to be taken sixty miles down the coast to Port Royal and turned over to Admiral Samuel F. Du Pont, the commanding officer there. The *Planter* arrived off Port Royal shortly after 10:00 P.M., on May 13. It was a glorious end to a fifteen-hour day, the longest and most adventurous of Smalls's life. The ship was then anchored off Hilton Head near Beaufort. The arrival of the *Planter* interrupted Du Pont while he was writing a letter to his wife, Sophie. He added to his letter a description of the incident and his assessment of Smalls:

> She is a fine boat, can carry seven hundred bales of cotton, has a fine engine, and draws but little water and will be of the greatest use to us—so that in

herself she is a valuable acquisition, quite valuable to the squadron. I sent for the hero, Robert, and he soon came, a pleasant-looking darky, not black, neither light, extreme amount of wooly hair, neatly trimmed, fine teeth; a clean and nice linen check coat with a very fine linen shirt having perhaps been of the wardrobe of the Navy officer who commanded the boat but fitting him very well if they were.

His information is thorough and complete as to the whole defense of Charleston: Stono Inlet is abandoned, they are building a fort on the middle ground in the harbor and making it stronger and stronger, but there is not much land near.

I told Robert I would take care of him and his people, that he was a hero. When we asked him what they said in Charleston when General Ripley's barge was carried off, he said in a quiet pleasant way, "They made much to do about it and talked a great deal, ordered sharper look-outs and more pickets. I think they had more to say this morning about me, though, when they found the steamer gone."[13]

In the months and years ahead, Smalls and Du Pont became active collaborators in the cause of freedom. The next morning, May 14, Du Pont forwarded to the Navy Department an extended report.

Sir: I enclose a copy of a report from Commander E. G. Parrott, brought here last night by the late rebel steam tug *Planter,* charge of an officer and crew of the *Augusta.* She was an armed dispatch and transportation steamer attached to the engineer department at Charleston, under Brigadier-General Ripley, whose barge, a short time since, was brought out to the blockading fleet by several contrabands.

The bringing out of this steamer, under all circumstances, would have done credit to anyone. . . .

The armament of the steamer is a 32-pounder, on pivot, and a fine 24-pounder howitzer. She had, besides, on her deck, four other guns, one 7-inch rifle, which were to be taken the morning of the escape to the new fort on the middle ground. One of the four belonged to Fort Sumter and had been struck in the rebel attack on that Fort on the muzzle.

Robert, the very intelligent slave and pilot of the boat, who performed this bold feat so skillfully, informed me of this fact, presuming it would be a matter of interest to us to have possession of this gun.

This man Robert Smalls is superior to any who has yet come into lines, intelligent as many of them have been. His information has been most interesting, and portions of it of the utmost importance.

> I shall continue to employ Robert as a pilot on board the *Planter* for the inland waters, with which he appears to be very familiar.[14]

The admiral wanted Smalls in the Union Navy because of his demonstrated abilities, and Smalls was more than willing to serve his country and his people as a navy pilot. Unlike the army, the navy was officially open to blacks, the enlistment of enslaved blacks having been authorized by the secretary of the navy in 1861.[15] However, the navy had an educational requirement that Smalls did not meet: Pilots had to be able to complete the curriculum in naval-training school; consequently they had to know how to read and write. Smalls later admitted that he had a kind owner who had taught him many things and allowed him many privileges, but Henry McKee never taught Smalls to read or write and never allowed anyone else to teach him. However, in an act of collaboration between the services, Smalls was inducted into the U.S. Army, which had no literacy requirements. He was given the rank of lieutenant and assigned to Company B in the Thirty-third Regiment of the U.S. Colored Troops (USCT). The army then detailed him to the navy for such duties as the navy might require.[16]

Smalls served with distinction throughout the war, and the navy greatly appreciated his services. Throughout his service he was not officially in the U.S. Navy, but at the end of the war Congress passed a special law, signed by President Abraham Lincoln, inducting Smalls into the navy so that he could be discharged and receive a navy pension.

Action and Reaction

Newspapers and magazines all over the North hailed Smalls's feat, some declaring him the first hero of the war. *Harper's Weekly* published an illustration of Smalls alongside the *Planter* and declared his capture of that ship to be "one of the most daring and heroic adventures since the war commenced."[17]

The June 17, 1862, issue of the *New York Daily Tribune* printed a verbatim transcript of the *Planter*'s log for May 13, the day of the seizure:

> "Robert Smalls, Pilot; Alfred Gradine, Engineer; Abram Jackson, Jebel Turner, W.C. Thompson, Sam Chisholm, Abram Allston, Hannah Smalls, Susan Smalls, Clara Jones, Arina White, Levina Wilson, David McCloud, 3 small children."
>
> Log: "We leave Charleston at ½ past 3 o'clock on Tuesday morning. We pass Fort Sumter ¼ past 4 o'clock. We arrive at blockading squadron at Charleston Bar at ¼ to 6. We give three cheers for the Union flag once more.

"Articles of Sundry: 4 large c., not mounted, 2 mortars. We arrive at Port Royal, Hilton, on same night about 9 P.M."[18]

John Smalls, the first mate, must have written this log entry, omitting his own name from the list of crew and passengers. This log contains some original information. Until the discovery of this story, it was not generally known by Smalls's descendants or other writers that Clara Jones, Robert Smalls's step-daughter, was a passenger. (Other accounts refer to Du Pont's list of those receiving payments, which does not include other family members.) This official log gives further confirmation of descendants' assertion that Smalls treated his step-children as though they were his own. The reactions of Confederate officials to the seizure of the *Planter* are captured in official dispatches written by Major General John C. Pemberton, Commander of the Department of South Carolina and Georgia (May 13, 1862); General Roswell S. Ripley, Commander of the Second Military District of South Carolina (May 14, 1862); Lieutenant F. G. Ravenel, Ripley's aide de camp (May 13, 1862), and Major Alfred Rhett of the First South Carolina Artillery (May 13, 1862). Ripley placed blame for the loss of the *Planter* on its officers:

> The mischief has occurred from the negligence of the captain and officers of the boat and their disobedience of orders, a copy of which is herewith enclosed, and which had been repeatedly urged upon them. I shall prefer charges against them at an early day and lay them before the general commanding the department.[19]

Yet, in general, these official documents mixed concern for the loss of the *Planter* with excuses for its occurrence. The reaction of the southern press was, however, immediate and outraged. The *Charleston Daily Courier* reported that three of the enslaved persons on the *Planter* belonged to Captain Ferguson, who owned the *Planter* and leased it to the Confederate Navy; one belonged to Mrs. Michael; and one was owned by Mrs. McKee (Smalls). The *Charleston Mercury,* the *North Carolina Journal,* and the *Columbia Guardian* all ran stories.[20] The Confederate authorities also paid an unintentional tribute to Smalls's achievement by offering a reward of $4,000 to anyone who could capture and return him. To a man who had bought his wife and child for $800, the sum offered for his capture must have been a great surprise. Fortunately, no one was ever able to claim that prize.

Most of the southern press denounced the captors of the vessel in the strongest terms, making dire threats if they should be captured and returned. Some of the rage, however, was directed against the white officers who had abandoned the *Planter* on the night of May 12. The *Columbia Guardian* pleaded that the white officers who had left the *Planter* in the hands of its captors "be brought to speedy justice and the prompt penalty of the halter enforced."[21] The *Charleston Daily Courier* wrote that the white community "was intensely agitated" by the news.

There was considerable dispute at the beginning as to who was actually responsible for the seizure of the *Planter*. One rumor was that John Ferguson had taken the *Planter* and delivered it to the Union in order to receive prize money. A variant of this rumor, which had a long life among Ferguson's descendants, was based on the premise that Relyea and Du Pont had been friends before the war. Early in the war Relyea's son was captured by Union forces, and rumor had it that the Relyea had agreed to exchange the *Planter* for young Relyea. Another rumor was that on the evening of May 12, after the officers left and before the *Planter* steamed out of the harbor, two white two men and a white woman had been seen boarding the *Planter* and had never been seen leaving, so they must have taken the ship. Another report said that "no doubt it was not the niggers, but some smart Union agents (spies) who had turned the trick."[22] Still another rumor was that, not Robert Smalls, but another black crew members had brought the *Planter* out of Charleston harbor. According to this theory, Smalls was just another passenger. As various rumors were circulating, however, the Confederate authorities had no doubt that Smalls had led an all-black crew in the capture of the *Planter*.

Military messages were sent all the way up the line to General Robert E. Lee, who ordered that the officers of the *Planter* be appropriately punished. Thus, Relyea, Hancock, and Pitcher were given a military trial. On July 25, 1862, the three officers were brought before a general court-martial in Charleston, South Carolina. Both Captain Relyea and First Mate Hancock were found guilty of "disobedience of orders" and "neglect of duty." Relyea was given three-months imprisonment and fined $500. Hancock was given a lesser fine and prison sentence. Pitcher was found not guilty and set free. On appeal, however, the verdicts were set aside by a higher military court on the technical grounds that the military court that sentenced them did not have jurisdiction over these men because they were contract employees and not members of the military.[23]

The day after the seizure, after extensive debriefing by Union authorities, Smalls and the other men of the *Planter* crew were inducted into the U.S. Army. There is some dispute among scholars as to whether Smalls was actually inducted or always served as a civilian contract employee. Smalls said, however, that he and the other blacks in his party were inducted into the army.

Smalls was now free to visit his mother for the first time since the war broke out. The joyous reunion took place at 511 Prince Street, where Lydia Smalls was now serving as housekeeper for the Union soldiers billeted there.

Du Pont had recommended that prize money be awarded to Smalls and his crew, and the May 20, 1862, issue of the *New York Herald* reported that a bill to that effect had been introduced and passed in the U.S. Senate the previous day:

> The bill provides that the steamship *Planter* and the guns it carried be appraised by a competent board of officers, and that one-half the value there shall go to Robert Smalls and his associates who ran the *Planter* out of Charleston Harbor with the provision that the Secretary of the Navy may invest the same in United States stocks, their interest to be paid to Smalls and his associates or heirs.

Northern public sentiment was expressed in a May 20, 1862, *New York Tribune* editorial:

> the country should feel doubly humbled if there is not magnanimity enough to acknowledge a gallant action because it was the head of a black man that conceived, and the hand of a black man who executed it. It would better, indeed become us to remember that no small share of the naval glory of the war belongs to the race which we have forbidden to fight for us; that one negro has recaptured a vessel from a Southern privateer, and another has brought away from under the very guns of the enemy, where no fleet of ours has yet dared venture, a prize whose possession a Commodore thinks worthy to be announced in a special dispatch.

The same issue of the *Herald* carried the news that the U.S. House had passed Senate bill immediately and it had been sent forthwith for President Lincoln's signature. Enacted on May 30, 1862, the statute stipulated that the value of the Planter and its cargo "be appraised by a board of competent officers" and that one half of its value be divided equitably among "Robert Smalls and his associates who assisted in rescuing her from the enemies of the Government."

The fact that the federal government passed the statute within roughly two weeks after the seizure of the *Planter* is indicative of how appreciative the Union was for Smalls's actions, which gave a huge morale boost to the North.

In a message dated June 7, 1862, New York congressman C. B. Sedgewick expressed his appreciation for the seizure of the *Planter* and noted that consideration should be given to appointing Smalls military governor of South Carolina after that state's defeat. Further honoring the daring of Smalls and his crew, on July 15, 1862, Admiral Du Pont sent the two flags carried by the *Planter* on its capture—the Confederate flag and the South Carolina state flag—to the secretary of the navy for historic preservation.

The *Planter* was appraised at a little more than $9,000, and, as the statute specified, half that amount was awarded to the crew. (It was learned later that the real value of the ship at that time was $70,000.) By August, Admiral Du Pont had distributed the money as follows:

Robert Smalls, Captain	$1,500
John Smalls, (no relation) 1st Mate	$450
Anthony Gridiron [Alfred Gradine], Engineer	$450
J. Samuel Chisholm	$400
Abraham Allston	$400
Gabriel Turno	$400
Abraham Jackson	$400
William Morrison (from the Etowah)	$384
Annie, unattached woman in the party	$100
Lavina, unattached woman in the party	$100
Total	**$4,584**

Years later Congress granted Smalls another $3,500. Smalls put these funds to good use, but while he served his country diligently, he constantly tried through the years to get Congress and the Navy Department to recognize the true value of the *Planter*. During his many defeats in this effort, Hannah reminded him on occasion that his motivation for capturing the ship was never money, but rather the values his mother taught him.

As spectacular as it was, the taking of the *Planter* was not an individual or isolated act. It was propelled by political forces in the nation and the outbreak of the Civil War. The family was also an indispensable support system for the inspiration, motivation, planning, and execution of the seizure of the *Planter*, not just Hannah's plotting with him on the escape plan but also the support of the entire sixteen-member African American extended family that accompanied and assisted him on this journey. This support was expressed most eloquently in Hannah's determination: "I will go . . . and where you die, I will die."

Smalls's mixed family of origin had prepared him in character, attitude, and skills. His family of procreation further inspired and assisted him, and his family of liberation accompanied and aided him. Smalls left a legacy for young people today. He demonstrated courageous commitment to a goal, skill and determination in pursing it, and grace to share the burdens and the laurels with others. These attributes have been passed down through his descendants from generation to generation.

5

Early Duty for the Union Forces, 1862

During his first year with the Union forces, Smalls was assigned several missions, all of which tested and developed his military and political skills. These assignments included a raid up the Stono River in May 1862, a mission to Port Royal in June 1862, a trip to Washington in August 1862, and a promotional excursion to New York in October 1862. The Stono raid drew on his intelligence and his navigational skills and was featured in a report President Lincoln made to a joint session of Congress.

Du Pont wasted no time putting Smalls to work fighting for the Union. Smalls's knowledge of Confederate plans, strategies, and fortifications was valuable. Smalls revealed that most of the troops in Charleston had been moved to Tennessee and Virginia, leaving behind only a few thousand men, and that Coles Island and its batteries, which protected Stono Inlet and the southern flank of Charleston, had been abandoned.

Stono Incursion

This intelligence led to the Union capture of the Stono River region. A message to the War Department from Admiral Du Pont dated May 31, 1862, describes action that took place on May 19, barely a week after Smalls's arrival:

> I have the honor to inform the Department that the gunboats have possession of Stono.
>
> From information derived chiefly from the contraband pilot, Robert Smalls, I had reason to believe that the rebels had abandoned their batteries, and accordingly directed Commander Marchand, the senior officer off Charleston, to make a reconnaissance to ascertain the truth of the report.

> This was done on the 19th instant, and the information proving correct, I
> ordered the gunboats on the next day (being myself off Charleston, on the
> Keystone State) to cross the bar.[1]

Admiral Du Pont had confidence in Lieutenant Alexander S. Rhind as a ship
captain. He placed Smalls and Rhind together for the first time on June 23,
1862, as reported in Rhind's message to Du Pont.

> I enclosed a report of an expedition to Simmon's Bluff, on Wadmalaw
> Sound [River]. I prepared *Planter* for it by building some musket-proof
> bulwarks round her aft and about her machinery. We were piloted up by
> Robert Smalls, and were detained but once, by grounding near Bear Bluff;
> however, the *Planter* was soon hauling us off.[2]

Two days later in a dispatch to Navy Secretary Gideon Welles, Du Pont added
more information on the expedition:

> On 21st instant, with the *Crusader* and *Planter,* and piloted by Robert
> Smalls, he ran up North Edisto into Wadmalaw Sound [River] as far as
> Simmon's Bluff, which is on the mainland. The rebels had an encampment
> there and some artillery, but made no use of the latter. A few broadsides
> from the *Crusader* dispersed the enemy, and Lieutenant Rhind, on landing
> with a company of Fifty-fifth Pennsylvania Volunteers, under command of
> Captain Bennett, met with no resistance. We had no casualties.[3]

The Port Royal Experiment

The landing of federal troops at Port Royal in November 1861 was the first
major Union conquest of Confederate-occupied lands since the war began earlier that year. Within a few days virtually all the two thousand white persons on
these islands fled to the mainland, leaving behind ten thousand enslaved persons and the rest of their property holdings. The federal government quickly
put into place a series of measures to protect and preserve, as well as to benefit
from, these "abandoned lands." One of the more impressive of these measures
was called "The Port Royal Experiment," which has been chronicled by Willie
Lee Rose in her award-winning *Rehearsal for Reconstruction: The Port Royal
Experiment* (1964).[4] Smalls was appointed Du Pont's personal representative to
the Port Royal Experiment, an assignment that took Smalls back to Beaufort
County and introduced him to a network of northern abolitionists, the first
abolitionists he had ever met, who became his friends, companions, and supporters through war, Reconstruction, and post Reconstruction. Among these
new associates were the Reverend Mansfield French, a Methodist minister, who

had come South with the Port Royal Experiment; Laura Towne, a fervent abolitionist from Philadelphia and cofounder of the Penn School in 1862; Rossa Cooley, cofounder of the Penn School; and later Charlotte Forten, a teacher at the Penn School who was the daughter and granddaughter of prominent black abolitionists in Philadelphia. He also met General Rufus Saxton, who oversaw the Port Royal Experiment on behalf of the military. All became allies in the struggle for freedom.

The impetus for Smalls's assignment was that a severe conflict had developed between the northern white missionaries sent to Beaufort County to assist the freed people with education, economic development, and a host of good works and the persons they had come to assist. The northerners had been instructed to help the blacks produce cotton needed by the North for the war effort and for nonmilitary commercial purposes. Local blacks resisted this effort and refused to cooperate. According to historian Eric Foner, "the blacks commenced planting corn and potatoes for their own subsistence but evinced considerable resistance to growing cotton, the 'slave crop,' which had enriched their masters but had not fed them."[5] Laura Towne, who was one of these teachers, wrote in her diary: "The Negro can see plainly enough that the proceeds of the cotton will never get into black pockets."[6] While this attitude and practice might seem reasonable under the circumstances, it was in sharp conflict with the wishes and instructions of the northerners. They appealed to the military for assistance.

Admiral Du Pont sent Smalls to negotiate the situation because Smalls understood the minds of the northern whites and of the local blacks. Moreover, he was bilingual, competent in the English of the missionaries and in the Gullah of the natives. He was instrumental in fashioning a workable compromise, persuading both sides that the natives should be encouraged to produce some cotton for the market and some fruits and vegetables as well. While this intervention did not provide a permanent solution to the conflict, it did enable the two sides to proceed with the planting of crops in the late summer and fall of 1862. Despite initial difficulties, the freedmen and freedwomen were eventually successful and the Port Royal Experiment became a "showcase for freedom."[7] Smalls developed especially fruitful relationships with General Rufus Saxton and the Reverend Mansfield French, both of whom played major roles in Smalls's next assignment from Admiral Samuel Du Pont.

Mission to Washington

Robert Smalls—twenty-four years old, just three months out of slavery, and with no formal education—was now traveling with the elite. In the past three months he had met and worked with accomplished men and women who represented institutions at the highest levels of society. It was already apparent that a major source of Smalls's achievement was his capacity to establish strong and trusting relationships with people who shared his commitment to freedom and were in positions to be of assistance to him.

In halting General David Hunter's efforts to recruit black soldiers, Lincoln had reminded him that only Congress or the president had the authority to deal with slavery. There was a widespread assumption that, after two infractions of national policy, Hunter was about to be removed from his command. An important meeting between Admiral Du Pont and General Hunter occurred on May 29, 1862, after which Du Pont wrote his wife about the high regard he had for Hunter. Offering his support to Hunter, Du Pont also told the general of his high regard for Robert Smalls, who might be of some help to Hunter in this situation.

On August 9, 1862, three months after Hunter's emancipation initiatives had been canceled and three months after the seizure of the *Planter,* Smalls met General Hunter. It was the beginning of a long and fruitful relationship that lasted until after the war and even beyond Hunter's death. Hunter also invited to this meeting General Saxton and the Reverend French.

At this meeting General Hunter restated his belief that it was not only right but also a military necessity to enlist blacks into the Union forces. Hunter had concluded that his military mission could not succeed without black troops, and he doubted that the United States could win the war without them. The ranks of the white volunteers were thinning, and the enlistment of new white recruits had slowed to a trickle. Meanwhile, the Confederates were gaining strength from several major victories over the Union. There was a gathering consensus in the nation and in the military that President Lincoln had little chance of renomination and no chance of reelection in the upcoming November elections unless the Union forces could turn the tide against the Confederacy.

Hunter told Smalls that he had been authorized by Du Pont to send Smalls on a most important and delicate mission. He needed Smalls to go to Washington and perform another service for his country. Hunter's situation was desperate. Not only had the president and the secretary of war called a halt to his efforts to recruit black troops, but also, because of the Union defeat that very day at Bull Run and heavy losses in General George McClellan's Peninsula Campaign, Hunter had been ordered to send some of his dwindling number of white troops to Richmond.

Hunter wanted Smalls to speak with Secretary of War Edwin Stanton and other members of Lincoln's cabinet and to convince them to authorize Hunter's enlistment of black troops. Smalls was astonished but not intimidated. He was willing to do whatever was asked of him to advance the Union cause, but he wondered what he could possibly say to the officials that General Hunter and others had not already said.

Hunter reassured Smalls by reminding him of his capture of the *Planter* and of his success in getting the different factions in Port Royal to work together. Smalls's record in delivering the *Planter* would speak loudly in Washington, Hunter told him, because it would demonstrate that black men could make important contributions to the Union cause. There were two other things Hunter did to reassure Smalls. First, he gave Smalls a written statement to hand to Secretary Stanton requesting authorization for Hunter to enlist black troops. Smalls could then elaborate on the request from his own experience and in his own way. Second, Hunter asked the Reverend French to accompany Smalls to Washington and introduce him to Secretary Stanton.

Smalls was ready to accept this mission. He knew that he had no other choice; he was a soldier and must obey an order no matter how impossible it might seem. Although apprehensive, he was honored to be given such a difficult task. He was also eager to undertake the mission because General Hunter had persuaded him that the war hung in the balance and with it any hope for the abolition of slavery. Being religious, Smalls undoubtedly felt sustained by the same ultimate force that sustained Moses when God commanded him to lead his people out of Egypt. Smalls requested a few days leave to spend in Beaufort with his family, during which his mother and his wife helped him pack and prepare for this journey.

On August 16, 1862, Smalls and French sailed from Hilton Head aboard the steamer *Massachusetts* bound for Washington, D.C. On August 20, 1862, they met with the secretary of war. Stanton was so impressed with Smalls that he arranged for Secretary of the Treasury Salmon P. Chase, the other strong abolitionist in Lincoln's cabinet, to meet with Smalls and French as well. French reported that Smalls regaled Secretary Chase with his story for nearly an hour. A few days later Stanton ushered Smalls and French into a meeting with President Abraham Lincoln. Smalls proposed that, if the president would authorize the enlistment of black troops, he would personally recruit ten thousand black men, "and they will be better soldiers than the present ones because they will be fighting for their freedom." President Lincoln was enthralled with Smalls's recitation on his capture of the *Planter*. At that time the president was wrestling mightily with the question of admitting black troops, having been urged to do so by Frederick Douglass and others. Lincoln expressed his appreciation to and admiration for Smalls, and a few days later he complied with Smalls's request.

When Smalls and French returned to Beaufort, Smalls personally delivered to General Rufus Saxton an order from the president and the secretary of war dated August 25, 1862, authorizing the enlistment of five thousand African American troops, the first unit of black troops officially admitted by Lincoln into the Union army. Smalls set about recruiting blacks for this regiment, which was headed by Colonel Thomas W. Higginson. Smalls volunteered for duty with the regiment, but Admiral Du Pont needed him for further service in the navy. While this regiment never reached its full strength, it functioned with distinction.

Colonel Higginson's February 1, 1863, report to General Saxton gives an assessment of this regiment:

> Nobody knows anything about these men who has not seen them in battle. I find that I myself knew nothing. There is a fierce energy about them beyond anything of which I have read.
>
> No officer in this regiment now doubts that the key to the successful prosecution of this war lies in the unlimited employment of the black troops. The superiority lies simply in the fact that they know the position of the country while white troops do not, and moreover they have peculiarities of temperament, position, and motive that belong to them alone. They show the resolution and the sagacity that a personal purpose gives. It would have been madness to attempt with the bravest white troops what I have successfully accomplished with the black ones.[8]

In forwarding Higginson's report to Stanton, General Saxton concluded, "No one knows better than the traitors now in arms against our government the great element of strength that the cause of liberty and the Union have in the hearts and muscles of these loyal blacks. And finally, in my humble opinion, it would be no misapplication of the best energies of the Government should they now be directed toward the arming and disciplining of everyone that can be brought within our lines."[9]

General Saxton, Secretary Stanton, and perhaps President Lincoln had every reason to be pleased with the order to enlist black troops. Eventually some 285,000 blacks were officially recruited into the U.S. Army. Some say that this particular resource provided the margin of victory for the Union.[10]

Mission to New York

In less than one month after his return from Washington, Smalls was again dispatched to the North, this time on a mission more diplomatic than military. He undertook this journey with the reluctant permission of Admiral Du Pont.

French had suggested to Du Pont that Smalls, Smalls's wife, and the *Planter* be sent to New York to raise support for the war and the cause of abolition. Afraid that Smalls would be "spoiled" by so much attention in the North and might not return, Du Pont wrote his wife on May 30, 1862:

> I took for granted that Robert Smalls wanted to go, but he came to know if he was going to lose his place here as pilot of the *Planter* and confirmed all I thought of this man as being the most superior negro I had ever known. I told him of course he need not go North unless he wished it— that Mr. French was a friend of him and his race and saw some advantages to him personally; if he returned in a month I would take him on again as a pilot. He said then he would go to Mr. French and unless the latter would promise to have him back in three weeks he would not go. . . .
>
> Then I gave him good advice as to his course and conduct while North, in the course of which I said, "Robert, you have seen how the Navy officers here have treated you—They have made not fuss about you, . . . and if you remain as you are now and don't get spoiled by the abolitionists, they will always be your friends."

Smalls responded, "that is the very point—it is because I know this that I have come to see you today; my best friends are in the Navy and onboard this ship."[11]

On September 7, 1862, Smalls, his wife, and their two-year-old son sailed with French to New York aboard the steamship *McClellan.* The September 10 *New York Daily Tribune* rejoiced over Smalls's visit:

> This man, though black, is one of the few history will delight to honor. He has done something for his race and for the world of mankind. If each one of the Generals in our army had displayed as much coolness and courage as he did when he saluted the Rebel flag and steamed past the Rebel fort, by this time the Rebellion would have been among the things that were.[12]

Smalls was so well received in the North that on September 18, 1862, Du Pont got a letter from a Mr. C. C. Leigh of New York, an officer in the National Freedmen's Relief Association, requesting that Smalls be permitted to remain in New York a while longer. Then, on September 26, a letter from the Reverend French arrived making a similar request. On October 23, 1862, after French had returned to Port Royal without Smalls, Du Pont expressed his displeasure in a letter to his wife: "He [Smalls] did not come with him [French] and General Saxton as I supposed he had, at which I was not pleased. We want him here as a pilot.[13]

For Smalls, a highlight of the trip was an October 2 gathering of black people at the Shiloh Baptist Church, whose pastor was the Reverend Henry Highland Garnet, an avid abolitionist. Lincoln had issued his preliminary Emancipation Proclamation on September 22, and there was much jubilation in the city. "A great concourse of the colored people of this city assembled last evening at Rev. HHG's (Shiloh) Church at the corner of Prince and Marion Streets to participate in the ceremonies of a public reception and presentation to RS. . . . The gathering was most respectable in character; nearly all the colored men of NY and Brooklyn were present."[14] The October 3 *New York Times* described Smalls's reception:

ROBERT SMALLS entered the house [with his wife and child] and was received with deafening cheers. A few minutes later, he was presented on behalf of the colored community with a massive and very handsome gold medal, executed by BALL & BLACK of this city. The medal bore on its face a representation of Charleston harbor, with the steamer *Planter* and Fort Sumter in the foreground, and the Union squadron in the distance, and on the reverse side, the following inscription:

"Presented to ROBERT SMALLS by the colored citizens of New York, October 2, 1862, as a token of their regard for his heroism, his love of liberty and his patriotism." ROBERT SMALLS, whose famous escape and personal appearance we have already made familiar, replied in a very modest and touching address, recounting his desperate venture, and expressing the hope, that as he was about to return to his duty as a pilot on the Union fleet at Port Royal, he might yet guide it safely into Charleston harbor. Mrs. SMALLS and her little boy ROBERT were presented and the whole family was greeted with wild and prolonged cheering. The following resolutions were then read by Prof. REATON and applauded to the echo:

Resolved. That the colored people of the City of New York cordially welcome Mr. ROBERT SMALLS, of Charleston, S.C., as a representative of the loyal people, comprising four millions, of black Unionists, now living in the rebel or semi-rebel States.

Resolved. That Mr. ROBERT SMALLS has nobly represented this loyal population.

First: By achieving his own liberty and freedom from the despotism which now broods over the South.

Secondly: By securing the liberty of his wife and children and of those of the crew of his vessel, thereby carrying out most gloriously and promptly the doctrine of immediate emancipation.

Thirdly: In that the act of seizing the gunboat and passing successfully the six forts, which environ Charleston harbor, he developed a capacity for military and naval conduct excelled by nothing which has occurred in the present war and equaled by only a few events in any other war.

Fourthly: By presenting to the Federal Government the valuable prize won by his prowess, he has shown in his own behalf and of those whom he represents a faithful devotedness to the cause of the American Union which ever has and ever will illustrate the conduct of the black citizens of the United States.

Fifthly: Out brother SMALLS has by this one act proven beyond any man's gainsaying the safety, the justice and the easy possibility of the General Government's accomplishing immediate and universal emancipation. The concourse then, amid general good feeling and cheers for Admiral Du Pont, adjourned.[15]

Hannah did not like to travel and did not like public occasions. This was one of only three public excursions Hannah took with her famous husband. The first was the fateful *Planter* voyage and the final one—again in Charleston harbor—was to celebrate the end of the war on April 14, 1865.

The gold medal that "The Colored Citizens of New York" gave to Smalls is now displayed in the U.S. Navy Museum in Washington, having been given to the museum by Smalls's granddaughter. Smalls and his family returned to Beaufort at the end of October on the steamer *Star of the South.* Admiral Du Pont and an aide named Rodgers met Smalls on the streets of Beaufort on October 31, 1862. The aide told Smalls that Admiral Du Pont had been worried that Smalls's "head would be turned" by the attention he received in New York. "It was," Smalls quickly responded. "All the while I was up there my head was turned one way—toward Port Royal."[16]

Hannah was a mother with uncommonly good judgment. She must have taken young Robert Jr. to New York with great reluctance. He was not well. Within a year he had died of whooping cough.

Henry McKee, owner of Robert Smalls and his mother, Lydia Polite, before the war. From the Robert Smalls Collection, courtesy of Helen Boulware Moore

Jane Bold McKee, wife of Henry McKee. From the Robert Smalls Collection, courtesy of Helen Boulware Moore

Robert Smalls House (originally owned by the McKee family) in Beaufort, S.C., as it stands today. From LyBenson Photography Studios, Rev. Kenneth Hodges, photographer

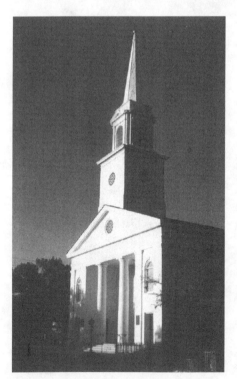

Beaufort Baptist Church, mother church of Tabernacle Baptist, where Lydia worshiped in the years before the war. From LyBenson Photography Studios, Rev. Kenneth Hodges, photographer

ROBERT SMALLS, CAPTAIN OF THE GUN-BOAT "PLANTER."

THE GUN-BOAT "PLANTER," RUN OUT OF CHARLESTON, S. C., BY ROBERT SMALLS MAY 1862.

Smalls and his beloved Planter. *From the Robert Smalls Collection, courtesy of Helen Boulware Moore*

Painting of the SS Planter *by Daniel Dowdey, completed in 2002. From the Robert Smalls Collection, courtesy of Helen Boulware Moore*

Wm. Morrison   **Robert Smalls**   **A. Gradine**
John Smalls

Four members of the crew who brought the Planter *out of Charleston harbor on May 13, 1862. Crew members not pictured include J. Samuel Chisholm, Abraham Allston, Gabriel Turno, and Abraham Jackson. From the Collections of the South Carolina Historical Society*

Attack on Fort Sumter, April 7, 1863, painting by a slave named Dave. Courtesy of Carlin Timmons, Park Ranger, Fort Sumter National Monument

USS Keokuk, *model at Fort Sumter. Photograph from the author's collection, arranged by U.S. Park Ranger Michael Allen*

Eleven-inch Dahlgren gun from the Keokuk, *which fired on Fort Sumter. This gun was retrieved by Confederate forces and currently stands at the corner of East Bay Street and South Battery in Charleston, S.C. Photograph from the author's collection*

Hannah Jones Smalls, Robert Small's first wife, during the early years after the war. From the Robert Smalls Collection, courtesy of Helen Boulware Moore

Elizabeth Lydia Smalls, first child of Robert and Hannah, born in slavery. From the Robert Smalls Collection, courtesy of Helen Boulware Moore

Sarah Voorhees Smalls, second daughter of Robert and Hannah, at about age sixteen. From the Robert Smalls Collection, courtesy of Helen Boulware Moore

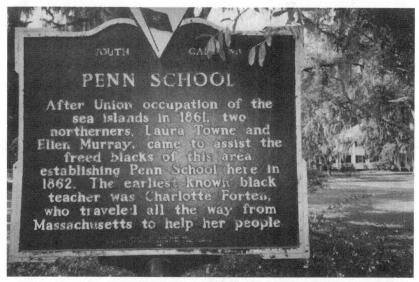

Penn School (right) was established by missionaries from the North for the education of the newly freed persons. From LyBenson Photography Studios, Rev. Kenneth Hodges, photographer

Brick Baptist Church, near Penn School. This church was used for several years as one of the Penn School classrooms. Elizabeth Smalls was one of Charlotte Forten's students in this church. From the author's collection

Tabernacle Baptist Church, where Smalls family worshiped. Some of them are buried in the churchyard. Photograph from the author's collection

Congressman Robert Smalls. From the Collections of the South Carolina Historical Society

African Americans delegates to the South Carolina Constitutional Convention of 1895: Robert B. Anderson, Isaiah Randall Reed, Robert Smalls, William J. Whipper, James Wigg, and Thomas E. Miller. Courtesy of South Caroliniana Library, University of South Carolina, Columbia

*Judge Jonathan J. Wright,
who served on the South
Carolina Supreme Court
for six years. From* Harper's
Weekly, *March 5, 1870.
Courtesy of South Caroliniana Library, University of
South Carolina, Columbia*

*Francis L. Cardozo, elected
South Carolina state treasurer in 1872, 1874, and
1876. From* Frank Leslie's
Illustrated Magazine, *September 26, 1874.
Courtesy of South Caroliniana Library, University of
South Carolina, Columbia*

Annie Wigg Smalls, second wife of Robert and mother of William Robert. From the Association for the Study of Afro-American Life and History. Originally published by Carter G. Woodson in the November 1947 issue of the Negro History Bulletin

Robert Smalls in later years. From the Robert Smalls Collection, courtesy of Helen Boulware Moore

6

Robert Smalls and the USS Keokuk, *April 7, 1863*

When a team of University of South Carolina scholars led by Dr. Cleveland Sellers, director of African American Studies, undertook a study tour of Fort Sumter on September 7, 2000, they expected to learn more about Robert Smalls's handling of the *Planter* in relation to the fort. They learned that and more. U.S. Park Ranger Michael Allen guided the team to the top of the fort, showed them a large replica of the USS *Keokuk,* and described to them what he called "Du Pont's Folly," a Civil War event that also involved Robert Smalls.

While there is much evidence of Smalls's military activities and positions, there is no official record of Smalls's enlistment in the army or the navy during the war. He was always treated and paid as a civilian employee of the U.S. Armed Forces. Years after the war, Congress and the president placed Smalls on the navy pension rolls for the purpose of increasing his pension income.

On April 7, 1863, two days past Robert Smalls's twenty-fourth birthday, Admiral Du Pont launched a massive attack on Fort Sumter and Charleston harbor. Smalls piloted one of the ships. While this mission failed, causing considerable embarrassment to the Union and Du Pont, it was an extraordinary opportunity for Smalls to demonstrate his valor. Unlike some of Smalls's other ventures during the war, his piloting of the USS *Keokuk* during this historic battle has been little noticed by historians. Even Smalls's descendants have rarely mentioned the *Keokuk,* focusing instead on his exploits aboard the *Planter.* Moreover, even when the *Keokuk* is given recognition, Smalls's role as pilot during the ship's first and only combat mission is not often noted.

The story of Smalls and the USS *Keokuk* began as the Civil War had been raging for two years. Despite the Union's superior resources and early optimism in the North, the Union was no closer to winning the war. Two failures were glaring and considerably aggravating: the Union's failure to capture Richmond and Charleston. Abolitionist sentiment in the North had become strong, fortified by Lincoln's abolition of slavery in Washington, D.C., in April 1862 and in the western territories in June 1862; and also by his September announcement that the Emancipation Proclamation would become effective on January 1, 1863. Also influencing the abolitionist view was Lincoln's authorization in early 1863 of the enlistment of black soldiers. Frederick Douglass in the North and Robert Smalls in the South had played key roles in persuading Lincoln to admit black troops into the federal army, and both were busily recruiting blacks to volunteer for service. While each of these actions was a strike for freedom, there is no doubt that all were essentially defensive war strategies designed by Lincoln to shore up northern resolve and to augment the military. Had the prospects for winning the war been bright without these measures, according to Lincoln's own views, they would not have been taken.[1]

In the spring of 1863, with the considerable reinforcement provided by new black troops in the Union Army, renewed determination to capture Charleston prevailed. Earlier, in May 1862, Secretary of the Navy Gideon Welles had written to Admiral Du Pont: "This department has determined to capture Charleston as soon as Richmond falls . . . the glorious achievements of our Navy, inaugurated by yourself, give every reason to hope for a successful issue at this point, where rebellion first lighted the flames of civil war." But Richmond refused to fall according to the Union schedule. By January 1863 the navy decided to wait no longer and prepared to attack Charleston. Secretary Welles sent five additional ships to Du Pont with the following directive: "The *New Ironsides, Passaic, Montauk, Patapsco,* and *Weehawken* have been ordered and are now on the way to join your command to enable you to enter the harbor of Charleston and demand the surrender of all its defenses, or suffer the consequences of a refusal."[2]

Du Pont began to gather his ships and to engage in some local test runs. He added four additional monitors to the ones sent by Welles, to make a nine-ship combat flotilla. By March he considered his ships and men in a state of readiness to carry out Welles's orders. It was by all accounts a formidable invasion plan. The *Charleston Post and Courier* wrote, "In the spring of 1863, the most powerful naval squadron ever assembled under the stars and stripes gathered at Port Royal to attack the Confederate Citadel at Charleston."[3]

The Ironclads

Ironclads were steam-propelled wooden warships protected from gunfire by plates of iron armor. One of the first ironclads, the CSS *Virginia,* was built in 1861 by the Confederates, who produced it by attaching iron plates to the remains of the scuttled Union steam frigate USS *Merrimac.* Although ironclads were used by both sides in the U.S. Civil War, only the Union Navy had at its disposal sufficient industrial resources to build a sizable fleet of them.[4]

There were several different types of ironclads, but the most common ones in the Civil War were monitors and casemate ironclads. The monitor was an armored, steam-propelled vessel with a very low freeboard. Monitors were mounted with a few heavy guns in one or more revolving armored turrets.

Designed by Charles W. Whitney, a colleague of John Ericsson, the USS *Keokuk* represented a first step in the development of composite armor. Crafted in a modified conventional hull form, the *Keokuk* had a keel and a round bottom, with a single screw and rudder located at the sternpost. It was built at the Underhill Ironworks in New York, launched on December 6, 1862, and commissioned in March 1863 under the command of Alexander S. Rhind. This experimental twin casemate ironclad steamer embodied some unusual concepts: her two cylindrical gun towers, each pierced with three gun ports, often caused her to be mistaken for a double-turreted monitor; and its armor of horizontal iron bars alternating with strips of wood as sides and casemates was unusual. At 159'6" in length and weighing 840 tons, the *Keokuk* could travel ten knots per hour.

The armament of the *Keokuk* consisted of two eleven-foot Dahlgren guns placed in the two nonrotating turrets. Dahlgren's soda-bottle-shaped naval pieces were the ultimate refinement in smoothbore muzzle-loaded artillery. The guns were mounted on carriages that swiveled on circular tracks embedded in the wood deck within the turrets. The Dahlgren guns of the *Keokuk* were particularly advantageous over the rifles that armed the Confederate ships. The Union primarily used its ironclads to fight the Confederate ironclads and to bombard their forts and land forces. Dahlgrens had greater smashing power, and their projectiles could be skipped (ricochet fired) over the surface of the water to better ensure a hull hit. Rifle projectiles could not do this; they would either burrow into the water or bounce off it wildly because of their spin. Furthermore, because of the inferior metalwork of the time, rifles burst with distressing frequency. In contrast, no Dahlgrens are known to have burst except in test firing. This was why, following the 1863 attack, the Confederates ran great risks to salvage the *Keokuk's* cannon.

The expedition consisted of four monitors in front and four in the rear of the large *New Ironsides,* where Du Pont had his command post. The lead ship of the fleet was the *Weehawken* under the command of Captain John Rodgers, followed by the *Passaic,* the *Montauk,* and the *Patapsco.* Following the *New Ironsides* were the *Catskill,* the *Nantucket,* the *Nahant,* and, bringing up the rear, the *Keokuk,* commanded by Lieutenant A. S. Rhind and piloted by Robert Smalls. This column of ironclads advanced in accordance with Du Pont's instructions to attack Fort Sumter. So focused was the mission on Sumter that Du Pont ordered the crew not to return the fire from Confederate positions along the way.

The Battle

At about 2:30 P.M. on April 7, 1863, Du Pont ordered the attack to begin. The Confederates proved once again that Fort Sumter could withstand all the firepower the Union was capable of delivering. After three hours of intense fighting, he ordered his forces to withdraw from the engagement.

Du Pont had confidence in and warm admiration for Smalls, who had been selected by Lieutenant Rhind, based on his personal experience with Smalls in previous combat missions on the *Planter* and other ships. It is not difficult to imagine that Smalls's eager anticipation was mixed with anxiety.

While Smalls was addressing an assembly in New York, someone had asked him about the $4,000 reward the Confederates had offered for his capture and return to Charleston. He had responded, "The only way he proposed to return to Charleston was at the head of a Union fleet ordered to capture the city." Now, on April 7, 1863, he had been selected to participate in a massive attack on Charleston. Though he was not at the head of the attack but rather at the end, he was nevertheless glad to be there, assuredly aware that history was being made. It is likely that some of his crew from the *Planter* also served on this mission.

The third engineer on the *Keokuk* during this unsuccessful invasion was a young Jewish lad from New Jersey named Jonathon Manly Emanuel. Some 140 years later, when this author introduced Jonathon's great-grandson Jerry Emanuel to Robert Smalls's great-granddaughter Dolly Nash, they embraced each other as though they were long lost relatives.

The flotilla passed Morris Island without drawing Confederate fire. When it reached Cummings Point, at the narrow mouth of Charleston harbor, however, the Confederate guns were unleashed. Following Du Pont's order, the crews did not return the fire. Their target was Fort Sumter, and they would not be distracted by lesser battles. Following Smalls's route of May 13, 1862, in reverse, they were soon in range of the fort and were sandwiched between it on their left and Fort Moultrie on their right. As the Union flotilla came within range of the two formidable Confederate forts, forces on both islands unleashed a barrage of gunfire from both sides. Both forts had been given ample warning of the attack.

The *Weehawken* moved forward under heavy Confederate fire, with the rest of the squadron strung out behind her and the *Keokuk* bringing up the rear. It became difficult to maneuver the ships in the narrow channel with fire coming from both directions. The *Weehawken,* took a barrage of cannonball fire, and soon her propellers became entangled in Confederate nets. Another ironside veered off course and blocked the other ships behind it. The formation dissolved. At this point, showing bravery and self-confidence, Smalls, who knew these waters thoroughly, asked Lieutenant Rhind if he could proceed forward. Rhind, who had extreme confidence in Smalls, gave his assent.

Smalls's knowledge of the harbor and its currents came into play. He ordered his engineers to pick up speed as he steered the *Keokuk* around the ships in front of him. Within a half hour, the *Keokuk* had moved from the end of the convoy to the head of the line, replacing the disabled *Weehawken.*

By 3:30 P.M., amid the furious Confederate barrage, Smalls managed to bring the *Keokuk* to within striking range of Fort Sumter. Able to reach their target, the gunners of the *Keokuk* shelled Fort Sumter for thirty minutes, while taking heavy fire from the guns on that fort. Smalls reported later that the *Keokuk,* took 90 rounds of fire, with 19 rounds striking below the water line, which made the *Keokuk* eminently sinkable. During this three-hour battle, five of Du Pont's ships took 439 rounds of fire and were severely damaged. In turn, they fired 154 rounds against Sumter.

For an extra measure of bad luck, nature seemed to side with the Confederates that day. The waves were extraordinarily high and rough, causing the ships to toss and turn. Smalls reported later that the wheelman, who sat beside him, was struck in the face by cannon fire and his blood splattered all over Smalls. The barrage damaged Smalls's eyesight for the rest of his life. While he was not blinded, his injury was severe enough to entitle him, years later, to receive a wounded-veteran's pension.

The damaged *Keokuk* began to drift aimlessly with the tide. After about an hour the vessel lurched drunkenly and plunged underneath the waves. With expert handling, Smalls brought the ship upright again, but after nearly an hour of struggle, Lieutenant Rhind noted that the *Keokuk* was no longer seaworthy and ordered Smalls to withdraw the ship from this engagement. Smalls piloted the ship safely to a position of safety off Morris Island, where Rhind and his crew worked through the night stopping holes in the ship.

At 7:30 A.M. on April 8 the task was complete. The *Keokuk* was seaworthy again. Then another strong wind came up, the waves picked up fury, and *Keokuk* sank upright just minutes after the crew had been rescued by another ship.

At high tide only her smoke stack was visible about the water while at low tide her gun turrets could be seen.[5]

The *Nahant's* turret was damaged so that it would not turn; her pilothouse was damaged; and her wheelman had been fatally injured. The *Nantucket* had her port jammed and deck broken. The *Catskill* experienced a heavy blow on deck, smashing woodwork. The *Patapsco's* rifle gun became deranged at fourth fire. The *Passiac's* pilothouse was badly damaged. It seems that the *Weehawken* and *Montauk,* though well hammered, were not damaged.

The *New York Times* of April 17, 1863, quoted the *Keokuk's* paymaster as saying:

> I will not attempt to describe the night of the 7th, or the *horrors* of that afternoon. The *Keokuk* was struck 90 times; more than half of these shots went through the small vessel. It was as one chance out of ten thousand of our ever getting out of the fight. Never before was a vessel under such fire. Over 300 guns must have been playing on us, and that too within 300 yards of Sumter. We were nearer the fort and further up than any other vessel. The men were perfectly awe-stricken. Such was the roil of fire along the sides, that we could scarcely open the ports of the vessel to fire. . . .
>
> When the *Keokuk* was going down, within a short distance of Morris Island beach, the rebels on the island tossed their hats and cheered. They might have sunk us, crowded as we were on a little tugboat, with their batteries.[6]

Another crew member added his account:

> The vessel, it is known, steamed toward the rebel forts last in line of battle; but the fleet once engaged, the *Keokuk,* by her superior speed, and the splendid, daring of her commander [Rhind], ran in toward Fort Sumter and took the fire of that fort at little more than half the distance at which the monitor batteries have received it. Our informant explains this apparently inexplicable movement, so far as it was understood on board. Though the *Keokuk* was deemed the weakest of our vessels, and this fact reasonably accounted for the position which was assigned her by the Admiral, still the officers were restive under the implied restraint and the impossibility of going among the first into battle, and it was determined that when the opportunity offered the *Keokuk* should do her duty.
>
> It should be remarked that the officers and crew, with a natural pride in the vessel as their own, did not share the opinions of some other persons that the *Keokuk* was not a first-class battery and they believed that the conflict

into which they were entering they had an even chance with their brethren on the monitors. . . . "If she proved invulnerable," one of her officers remarked, "we were prepared to fight the rebels at the mouths of their cannon." The excellent capacities of the *Keokuk* for maneuvering also entered into the calculations and the confidence of her commander, in the hazardous but brilliant design, which he had formed and which he and his crew entered on without fear.

Only one member of the Keokuk's crew, Ensign McIntosh, was killed in the battle, and twenty-two men were injured. While the mission had not succeeded in capturing Fort Sumter, none of the officers and men involved in the battle was held to blame. Admiral Du Pont took full responsibility for the failure, writing to General Hunter, "I attempted to take the bull by the horns, but he was too much for us." Du Pont complimented Rhind and his crew: "You did everything that the utmost gallantry and skill could accomplish in management of this untried vessel."[7]

The Confederate Surprise

During the next five days Du Pont dispatched ships and crews to inspect the *Keokuk* by daylight to see whether the ship should be salvaged or destroyed. Finally, he concluded that both rescue of the ship and destruction of it were impracticable and that, since it was rapidly filling with sand, it would be of no use to the Confederates. The *Keokuk* still lies off Morris Island.

While Du Pont gave the *Keokuk* up for lost, however, the Confederates had other ideas. Under cover of darkness they salvaged equipment from the *Keokuk*, most notably the two massive Dahlgren guns, which they turned upon their former owners.[8]

According to Warren Ripley, "A ponderous cannon on Charleston's battery today is the sole reminder of one of the most incredible salvage jobs of the Civil War." The gun located at the intersection of East Bay and South Ferry bears the following inscription: "a monument to a group of Americans who proved that courage, ingenuity and hard work can accomplish what many believed impossible."[9]

For the descendants and students of Robert Smalls and Jonathon Manly Emanuel, this Dahlgren gun is the only physical notice of their service on April 7, 1863, and must serve to remind others that the attributes of intelligence, courage, ingenuity, and hard work are not confined to any one region, race, or religion.

7

Robert Smalls and the
Planter *at War, 1862–1866*

Smalls engaged in some seventeen engagements during the war. Though he piloted various ships, during most of these encounters he was at the helm of the *Planter*. He reported that many of his personal records of his war service were lost at sea during one of his encounters. Some twenty years later, when he was a member of Congress, he wrote to the quartermaster general to acquire an official copy of his record, including his own account of his war service after the sinking of the *Keokuk*.

> On the first of December, 1863, I was detailed as a pilot in the Army and in carrying the *Planter* through Folly Island she was fired upon by the Rebel Battery and was abandoned by Captain Nicholson. I took charge of and carried this boat safely through and General Q. A. Gillmore then Commanding the Department of the South with headquarters on Morris Island made an order to Captain Dutton of the Quartermaster Department that I should be put in charge. On the first of December 1863, I was placed in charge of the boat by an order of Col. J. S. Ellsworth, Chief, Quartermaster of the Department, which position I held until September 1866 when the boat was out of commission at Baltimore.[1]

Three weeks later, on January 3, 1883, the quartermaster general's office replied to Smalls's letter, providing precise information:

> The records of this office show that the name of Robert Smalls is reported by Lt. Col. J. J. Elwell, Hilton Head, S.C. as a pilot at $50 per month from

March 1, 1863, to September 30, 1863, and from October 1, 1863, to November 30, 1863, at $75 per month.

He was then transferred to Capt. J. L. Kelly, A. Q. M. November 20, 1863, by whom he was reported by that officer in the same capacity from December 1, 1863, until February 29, 1864, at $150 per month.

The name of Robert Smalls is then reported by Captain Kelly as Captain of the steamer *Planter* at $150 per month from March 1, 1864, until May 15, 1864, when transferred to the Quartermaster in Philadelphia.

He reported to Captain C.D. Sheridan, G. R. ORUC, W. W. Van Ness and John R. Jennings, Asst. Quartermasters at Philadelphia, as Captain of the *Planter* at $150 per month from June 30, 1864 to December 16, 1864, when transferred to Capt. J. L. Kelly, A. Q. M. Hilton Head, S.C., by whom he is reported to January 31, 1865.[2]

This correspondence confirms Smalls's salaries as pilot and, after December 1, 1863, as captain of the *Planter*. In all probability his $150 per month as captain of the *Planter* made him both the highest-ranking and highest-paid African American in the U.S. Navy.

Smalls's service with the *Planter* continued beyond January 31, 1865—and beyond the end of the war in April 1865—until September 1866, when he was ordered to take her to Baltimore for decommissioning. In addition, a record has also been found that lists specific engagements in which the *Planter* participated from May 31, 1862, until April 25, 1865, two weeks after the war's end:

Engagement at Secessionville, May 31, 1862.
Occupation of Edisto Island, June 3, 1862.
Action on Simmon's Bluff, June 23, 1862.
Affair on Skull Creek, S.C., September 24, 1862.
Affair at Kirk's Bluff, October 18, 1862.
Skirmish at Coosawatchie, October 21, 1862.
Skirmish at Coosawatchie and Engagements at Caston and Frampton
     Plantations near Pocotaligo, S.C., October 21, 1862.
Expedition up St. Mary's River, January 23–February 1, 1863.
Operations in S.C., January 1, 1865.
The Campaign of the Carolinas, December 31, 1864–March 24, 1865
     and April 10–May 28, 1865.
Destruction of Locomotives and Rolling Stock between Sumterville
     and Camden, S.C., April 1, 1865.
Expedition to Camden, S.C., April 5–25, 1865.[3]

Smalls played an integral role in General David Hunter's Secessionville campaign. According to Patrick Brennan, Henry Benham's plan for the assault was presented to Hunter, who approved it "after studying the intelligence estimates provided by Robert Smalls."[4] Brennan described the loading of the Third New Hampshire Volunteer Infantry and the Twenty-eighth Massachusetts Infantry:

> They boarded the now famous *Planter* and were ferried to the Seabrook Island Landing, where the men tumbled ashore.
>
> Armed with Smalls's intelligence and driven by both Benham's desire for action and the shadow of General Thomas Sherman's failure, Hunter determined to march his force in the British footsteps of 1780, hoping to duplicate the English success.[5]

Further Military Duties

Smalls was involved in other campaigns that were not on the list. On May 20, 1863, Smalls led a small flotilla of three gunboats to the entrance of the Stono River, where they successfully carried out an attack on Confederate installations at Stono. The commanding officer of this expedition, Captain E. G. Parrott, reported that the success of this mission was owing in large part "to information derived mainly from the contraband pilot Smalls."[6]

In the next phase of the Charleston campaign, Smalls served as duty pilot at the Union base on Folly Island, where he was assigned to various ships as needed. From April to July 1863 he was part of a team that was preparing for a landing on Morris Island, across from Folly Island, with plans to proceed up the four-mile-long island, shelling the batteries at Forts Wagner and Gregg. This would put them within bombardment range of Fort Sumter, some fifteen hundred yards away. In July, Smalls ferried troops to Morris Island, including members of the famous Fifty-fourth Massachusetts Colored Infantry, led by Colonel Robert Shaw. The attack on Fort Wagner on July 18, 1863, was spearheaded by the Fifty-fourth with Shaw, some of his white officers, and nearly half of his black troops being killed as they tried repeatedly to capture Fort Wagner.[7]

Disobeying a Superior Officer

The next major encounter for Smalls occurred on December 1, 1863, several months after the landing on Morris Island. This mission, on which Smalls again showed extraordinary skill and courage, may perhaps be the most noteworthy event of his entire military service because of his bravery in confronting not only the enemy but also his own superior officer, who faltered in the line of duty.

The *Planter,* with a Captain Nickerson in command and Smalls as pilot, was sent on a mission in the Light House Inlet, near Secessionville, to take rations from Folly Island to the Union troops on Morris Island. The ship came under attack from a Confederate battery at Secessionville. Recognizing the *Planter* as their lost ship, the Confederates tried to hem her in and recapture her, firing from three batteries on a high bluff along the Kiawah River.

The shelling was fierce. The *Planter* was struck repeatedly, but because the shells were coming from such a high bluff, the *Planter* was not hit below the waterline and did not sink. Great damage was done, however, to the ship's upper decks. The shelling was so intense that Captain Nickerson ordered Smalls to beach the ship and surrender.

Smalls was now caught between the proverbial "rock and a hard place"—to surrender or not to surrender. He tried to explain his view of their predicament to Nickerson and shouted, "If we surrender, you—a white man and an officer —will be treated as such. But the rest of the crew are all runaway slaves. If the Confederates catch us, they will show us no quarter." Moreover, Smalls had strong faith in his ability to steer the ship to safety. He hoped that the captain would understand as he again shouted above the fervor, "not by a damn sight will I beach this boat."[8]

It is not known whether Smalls persuaded Nickerson that he could save the *Planter.* What is known is that Nickerson became so frightened that he left his post, ran to the coal bunker, and hid there from the furious Confederate fire. Smalls then took command. He called one of his crew to take the pilot wheel— probably Samuel Chisholm, who had been given that assignment before. Then Smalls ran to the coal bunker and latched the door from the outside so that Nickerson could not get out. Smalls returned to the wheel and steered the *Planter* safely back to Morris Island. There they were met by the department commander, Major General Quincy A. Gillmore. Smalls led Gillmore to the coal bunker and released Captain Nickerson. Smalls then reported to General Gillmore what had happened, underscoring the fact that the captain had deserted his post in the heat of battle.

On that same day Admiral Du Pont dismissed Nickerson from the navy for cowardice and desertion. He then promoted Smalls on the spot to be captain of the *Planter.* Effective that day as well, the twenty-four-year-old Smalls began receiving the salary of $150 per month.[9]

The black crewmen of the *Planter* on this voyage were most likely the same men who had worked with Smalls on the *Planter* when it was in Confederate service and helped him to bring the ship out of Charleston harbor and give it to the Union Navy. Now Smalls had rescued them from a sure return to slavery.

They would follow him anywhere. These were in all probability the men who spread the word in Beaufort that Robert Smalls could do anything!

Robert Smalls had risen to a position and salary no other black man and few white men could claim. In saving the *Planter* he had once again shown his remarkable bravery, ability, and self-confidence. Years later Smalls's son William Robert Smalls stated that one of his father's most important attributes was his bravery. His father, he said, was not afraid of any situation or person.

A few days later Smalls learned from an article in the *New York Times* that, on December 1, 1863, his wife Hannah had delivered their second daughter, Sarah Voorhees Smalls. This was especially welcome news because only a few months earlier the Smalls had lost their only son, Robert Jr., not yet three years old. Every year when they celebrated Sarah's birthday they also celebrated Smalls's promotion to captain of the *Planter*. Through the years December 1 came to represent a strong bond between father and daughter.

Peacemaker

In early 1864 Smalls again attained public recognition. This time, however, it was not for something he did but for another's actions toward him. Smalls was accompanying Brigadier General Truman Seymour in a small boat to the USS *Wabash,* Admiral Du Pont's flagship, in Port Royal harbor. Smalls was no doubt on assignment to see Admiral Du Pont. General Seymour is reported to have yelled to someone on the *Wabash* that "this boy [Smalls] wishes to come aboard." A northern reporter for *Harper's Monthly* overheard this remark and wrote that he thought it was prejudicial and offensive to Smalls, as captain of the *Planter,* to be called "boy." *Harper's* and the *New York Evening Post* ran at least two articles about the incident, both critical of Seymour.

This incident caused quite a bit of embarrassment for Seymour, who denied that he had referred to Smalls in that manner. Ever the gentleman and diplomat, Smalls came to Seymour's defense. In a letter to the *Evening Post,* Smalls wrote, "I must say that from the first day of my arrival within the Union lines, General Seymour has always shown me the greatest regard, whenever in public or private."[10] Seymour later wrote a letter to the paper denying the incident and defending his treatment of blacks generally. These two letters apparently ended the controversy.[11]

Mission to Philadelphia

During one of its many engagements, the *Planter* was so damaged that in spring 1864 it needed to be taken to the Philadelphia shipyard for extensive repairs. Smalls was offered the assignment of delivering the vessel. Since he had never steered a ship through the coastal waters that led to Philadelphia, he knew nothing of the hazardous conditions. However, he did know that the *Planter*, a vessel built for the rivers and lakes, was not ocean worthy. Because he had the additional handicap of not being able to read and write, he could not consult the maps and directions for such a journey. However, being a man of uncommon intelligence and self-confidence—as well as man of devout and prayerful demeanor—Smalls accepted the assignment.

Smalls devised a plan. He asked his superiors for a three-week leave of absence from duty. After some inquiry, he used his own money to hire a white retired naval officer acquainted with the route to Philadelphia to teach him all he needed to know for the journey. Smalls and his instructor labored day and night for three weeks to accomplish this task.

After satisfying himself and his teacher that he knew the route and its hazards, Smalls and his devoted crew set out for Philadelphia aboard the *Planter* on May 10, 1864. They arrived safely at the Philadelphia shipyard on May 13, 1864, two years to the day after they had delivered the *Planter* to the Union.

It was initially thought that the repairs could be completed within a few weeks, but the damage required more than six months' work. During this time, sobered by his recent experience of being given a task for which he was not readily prepared and exercising his lifelong thirst for knowledge, Smalls spent this time wisely. In addition to participating actively as a lecturer in the Philadelphia Anti-Slavery Society, Smalls used his own money to hire two free black teachers to teach him to read and write. He studied with a Mr. Basset by day and a Mr. Cantom by night for six months.[12] In this manner Smalls received his first formal education and learned skills that stood him in good stead for the rest of his life. As part of his education, he also became a lifelong subscriber and avid reader of the daily newspaper.

Charlotte Forten had given Smalls letters of introduction to some of the leading abolitionists in the city. They welcomed him into their midst, and he never tired of addressing groups large and small on his adventures. He gave one memorable address to the general conference of the African Methodist Church in Philadelphia in 1864.[13]

One day Smalls and a seaman walked to the shipyard from their quarters in the city. On their return home it began to rain, so they decided to board the streetcar. The conductor asked them to stand on the open platform in the rain so that two white passengers could be seated inside. At this insult Smalls and his companion got off the streetcar and walked, in the rain, into town. This insult to a national hero became an impetus for the campaign to eliminate racial segregation on streetcars, a cause that was eventually successful.[14]

Once at retreat formation in Philadelphia harbor, Smalls noted that a crew member was missing. On asking his whereabouts, he was told that the man had gone swimming. Smalls looked over the rails of the ship, saw bubbles in the water, and knew that the man was drowning. Smalls jumped into the water and rescued the drowning crewman, and other crew members revived him.

After repairs on the *Planter* were completed, Smalls and his crew left Philadelphia and arrived without incident at Hilton Head on Christmas Eve 1864. Smalls was able to spend Christmas with his family in their home on Prince Street in Beaufort.

Forty Acres and a Mule

Smalls's next assignment kept him close to home. In January 1865, General William T. Sherman and Secretary of War Edwin Stanton held an extraordinary meeting in Savannah with twenty black religious leaders to discuss plans for a settlement of the blacks freed by the Emancipation Proclamation. The historian Ira Berlin has described this meeting as "one of the most remarkable gatherings of the Civil War Era."[15]

The secretary of war asked these twenty leaders a total of twelve questions and was most impressed with the men's wisdom. On his return to Washington, he announced that he could not have received better answers if he had been meeting with the president's cabinet.[16] The *New York Times* reported on the meeting and its aftermath on February 13, 1865:

> Four days after the meeting, General Sherman issued Special Field Order 15, which set aside a large expanse of coastal land, stretching from Charleston, South Carolina to northern Florida, "for the settlement of the negroes now made free by the acts of war and the proclamation of the President of the United States." Each family would be allotted forty acres of tillable ground . . . in the possession of which land the military authorities will afford them protection, until such time as they can protect themselves, or until such time as Congress shall regulate their title.[17]

General Sherman appointed General Rufus Saxton to oversee this settlement program.

According to the program, any time four families desired to settle on and cultivate these lands, each family would be given forty acres, and later a mule was added. This resettlement scheme worked well, and thousands of families were settled and protected on these lands during January, February, and March 1865. Some of the settlements took place in Beaufort County.

After Lincoln's assassination in April, however, President Andrew Johnson discontinued the program. The Republican-controlled Congress passed a law reestablishing the program, but President Johnson vetoed the act, and Congress was unable to override his veto. Secretary of War Stanton and Freedmen's Bureau head General Otis Howard tried hard to resist the president's order, but to no avail. Johnson ordered black families evicted from these homesteads and returned the lands to the whites who had abandoned them during the war. This incident played a prominent role in Johnson's impeachment proceedings.

During the resettlement period Sherman and Saxton called on Smalls to assist in transporting these families from Savannah to their new homes. On February 1, 1865, Smalls entered into a contract with the U.S. Army "for vitalizing and manning the U.S. steamer *Planter*" for the purpose of carrying out this mission. The army agreed to make available to Smalls the sum of $1,937 to accomplish the assignment with the *Planter.*

The Fall of Charleston

In February 1865, Smalls was given another major assignment with the *Planter.* Charleston had finally been subdued by Union forces. Smalls was ordered to transport two black regiments, the Twenty-first U.S. Volunteer Regiment and the now-famous Fifty-fourth Massachusetts Colored Infantry, to Charleston. On February 17, 1865, these black troops were the first Union troops to enter and occupy Charleston. After some four years of heavy Union bombardment and valiant southern resistance, Charleston and Fort Sumter capitulated to these black Union troops.[18] On March 18, 1865, Robert Smalls entered the city triumphantly, his first return since his fateful voyage of May 13, 1862. He had brought General Saxton aboard the *Planter* for a high-level inspection reconnaissance. In Charleston, Smalls was the general's personal escort, and he later took the general on inspection tours of Fort Sumter and Edisto Island.[19]

While General Saxon met with officials, Smalls wandered around the city in which he had grown to manhood. He was saddened by the devastation he saw. The harbor was strewn with burned litter; the buildings were blackened from the fires; St. Michael's steeple had been struck by a shell. The once-fashionable homes he had often strolled by on the Battery were littered with marble and brick, broken chandeliers, and crumpled balustrades. The stable on East Bay above which he and Hannah had started as a newly married couple a decade earlier was gone. The cobblestone streets he had often traveled on his way to work were covered with debris. The splintered door to the Planter's Hotel, where he had his first job, stood ajar, its windows covered with boards. C. Ryan's jail was still there, as was the old slave market on Chalmers Street; they had been damaged only slightly by the Union bombardment.

Word spread quickly that Captain Smalls and the *Planter* had docked at the wharf. By the time he returned to meet up with General Saxton for the trip back to Hilton Head, a crowd had gathered to greet Smalls. They were mostly old friends and acquaintances from the days of slavery and from his work on the docks. Then on the edge of the crowded street Smalls recognized three white men and took General Saxton over to greet them. One was Captain John Ferguson, the former owner of the *Planter*. Another was John Simmons, the sail maker who had employed Smalls on the docks of Charleston. The third white man was the one who had made the original boilers and engines for the *Planter*. Smalls shook hands with these men and introduced them to General Saxton, saying to the general, "these men made the *Planter*, but I put the polish on her."[20]

It was not only the blacks who marveled at Smalls's return to Charleston. In the spring of 1865 the whole nation had its eyes on Charleston and on Smalls. Here was Charleston, a proud city with a proud heritage. And here was Robert Smalls, who represented everything Charleston diehards had said and deeply believed a black man could never be. He was first of all their conqueror. He had finally bested them in war as he could not have done in peace. He was courageous and proud, an American hero who wore his heroism well. He was dignified, soft-spoken, and had a ready smile. He was worshiped by blacks and highly respected by whites all over the nation. Beyond that—with his bounty for turning in the *Planter*, with his high earnings during the war, with the $700 he had put aside during slavery, and with his fine head for saving and investment—Smalls was a wealthy man as well. A white observer said at the time that Smalls was "able to give bread to half the bank presidents and brokers on Broad Street."[21] Moreover, at only twenty-six years old in March 1865, he was already the head of a stable and growing family.

Victory Celebration

After the war ended on April 9, 1865, Robert Smalls, his loyal black crew, and their beloved *Planter* got the opportunity of a lifetime. On April 14, 1865, they were sent on an excursion so filled with honor and symbolism that it rivaled their bold and brilliant voyage out of Charleston harbor on May 13, 1862, three long and bloody years earlier.[22]

The decision was made to have a ceremonial raising of the Union flag over Fort Sumter on April 14, 1865, four years to the day after the flag had been struck. It was a most momentous occasion. Ships from all over the southern commands were prepared for this massive water parade. Generals, admirals, and abolitionists from all over the nation were on hand. President Lincoln was invited and seriously considered attending, but his advisers dissuaded him from coming that deep into the South because of safety considerations. Smalls was disappointed. He had enjoyed his meeting with the president in 1862 and had campaigned for his reelection in 1864. If Lincoln had come to this event, there is no doubt that he would have been riding on the lead boat, the *Planter,* with Smalls, who piloted the *Planter* from Charleston harbor to Fort Sumter along the same route he had taken on May 13, 1862. This time, however, the three decks of the *Planter* were loaded with an overcapacity crowd of three thousand blacks and whites, military and civilians, male and female.

An eyewitness described this voyage:

> Almost central interest, the *Planter,* crowded almost to suffocation upon her three decks with General Saxton's freedmen, revealed her splashing paddles through the broken wheelhouse. Another such motley crew will seldom if ever be seen. Grey-haired old men, whose wrinkles were lighted up with deep but quiet joy; middle-aged men and women of every grade of color possible to Southern civilization, the latter decorated with bandanas and turbans of flashy colors; comely and buxom girls attired in neat chintz; cadaverous and ragged beings holding about them their tattered garments; boys and girls whose jubilation exhibited itself in the most astonishing display of ivory—all huddled together like sheep in a pen, hanging over the gunwales, mounted on the posts, doubled up in furtive corners, peering through the gangways, darkening the wheel-house, upon the top of which stood Robert Smalls, a prince among them, self-possessed, prompt and proud, giving his orders to the helmsman in ringing tones of command.[23]

At one point, Smalls lost control of the *Planter,* which rammed another ship and got stuck in the mud. No harm was done, however, as he was rescued by two other ships.

Attending a reception on a ship full of northern abolitionists, Smalls was described by a reporter as "a stoutly built man, little more than medium height, of intelligent countenance, ready speech, entire self-possession and considerable humor. For more than an hour, he submitted to the most rigid catechism, answering every question with surprising intelligence and frequently with genuine wit of report."[24]

In raising the Union flag on Fort Sumter, General Robert Anderson, who had been a major when he brought it down four years earlier, said, "after four long, long years of war, I restore to its proper place this flag which floated here in peace. I thank God that I have lived to see this day."[25] Then, answering from all the surrounding fortifications—Forts Moultrie, Ripley, Pinckney, Putnam, Johnson, Cumming's Point, and Batter Bee—from every battery that took part in the bombardment of Fort Sumter in 1861 and from all the vessels of war in the harbor came the thunder of mighty cannons in national salute until the "earth shook and trembled."

A passionate and eloquent abolitionist, the Reverend Henry Ward Beecher, who had commissioned an entire ship to bring his Brooklyn congregation, said the last word on the flag. "It is not the same flag," he intoned, "when it went down four years ago, four million people had no flag. Today it rises and four million people cry out, behold our flag! No more slavery!"[26]

They celebrated well into the night. In the early hours of the morning, there was a gathering at the Zion Presbyterian Church, the largest church in the city. The church was filled to capacity, including standing room. A group of blacks carried firebrand abolitionist William Lloyd Garrison to the pulpit on their shoulders. His address was drowned out by the cheering, singing, crying, and shouting throngs.

The day that had begun in triumph ended in tragedy. That very evening President Lincoln had gone to a play at Ford's Theatre in Washington, and was assassinated. When Smalls got the news, he cried, "Lord have mercy on us all."

Farewell to the *Planter*

The long and bloody war had finally come to an end. The Union had no more use for the *Planter* or for Smalls as pilot. In December 1865 the *Planter* was transferred by the U.S. Army to the new Freedmen's Bureau to assist with the resettlement of war refugees.

On June 25, 1866, the army was ordered to transfer the *Planter* to the Treasury Department so that it could be sold. The ship was evaluated and found to be worth $15,000. When the *Planter* was put up at a public auction in Charleston on August 15, 1866, John Ferguson, the ship's former owner, was eager to have her back. However, the U.S. Army would not sell it to him because, even though he had been pardoned, he had been an active supporter of the rebel cause. So Ferguson outwitted the federal authorities.

First, he commissioned a northerner, Charles H. Campbell, to buy the *Planter* for him for $25,000, but the government detected the hand of Ferguson and declined this offer. Having no other bids for the ship, the government disarmed the *Planter* and ordered Smalls to take her to Baltimore for sale on the commercial market. This was Smalls's last trip on the *Planter* and for him a most sentimental journey. On the train back from Baltimore to Beaufort, he said that it was all he could do to keep from crying.

In September 1866 the ship was sold at the Baltimore shipyard to Mordecai and Company for $7,700. Four months later, in January 1867, Mordecai and Company sold the *Planter* to Ferguson. The *Planter* was back in the hands of Ferguson, who considered himself its rightful owner, at a fraction of the price he had originally offered. It is believed by Ferguson's descendants that the Mordecai purchase was a Ferguson ploy.

Ferguson registered the *Planter* in Charleston and put her back into his coastal trade. He was not able, however, to hire Smalls at his prewar salary of sixteen dollars a month or at any other rate. Smalls was now twenty-nine years old, a free man, and a wealthy merchant who lived with his family in their home at 501 Prince Street. Smalls soon became deeply involved in Beaufort politics, which consumed his every waking hour for nearly fifty years.

Ferguson died two years later, while Smalls was a leader in the Republican Party and member of the state legislature. On March 25, 1876, Smalls, then a congressman, read in the newspaper that the *Planter,* while attempting to rescue a stranded ship, had grounded on Cape Island. Before the vessel could be refloated, it was broken up by a storm and lost. Smalls said that when he learned of the *Planter's* demise it was as though one of his own children had died.

PART III

Study War No More

8

In Beaufort after the War

Home, Family, and Community Leadership

After the Civil War ended with the overthrow of slavery, the black population all across the nation was caught up in a frenzy unequaled for another hundred years. This was the day their grandparents had told them was coming because God was just and all God's children are supposed to be free. They jumped for joy, sang, danced, cried, hugged each other, and prayed loud prayers of thanksgiving with special tributes to President Lincoln. And then they went to work. Without waiting for the Thirteenth, Fourteenth, and Fifteenth Amendments to the U.S. Constitution, they set about bringing their families together. They visited plantations looking for relatives and loved ones who had been sold away. They walked long distances to courthouses to have their marriages officially registered. They hastily constructed suitable housing for their families. Then they pursued economic well-being for their families through sharecropping, tenant farming, and whatever other work they could find. High on their priority list was the building of independent black churches to nurture their spiritual strivings and schoolhouses to nurture their educational aspirations. Indeed, it is now widely known among scholars that, despite the cruelties of slavery, that system was not able to crush completely the norms of family life among the African captives. Their memories of family, their preferences for family, and their aspirations, faith, and hope kept the concept of family alive during their 250 years of enslavement.

Thus, after slavery, when the times and conditions permitted, former slaves embraced both the concept and the reality of family. Newly released from involuntary servitude, they knew then what social scientists discovered sometime later: in order to have strong families there must be housing, jobs, and religious and educational institutions that were often structurally indistinguishable but functionally interdependent. It was exceedingly difficult to succeed; freedom did not bring resources. The new president had taken away the forty acres and mule that had been promised to each family. It was difficult to get the cooperation they needed from the white minority and hard to sustain the unity and collaboration needed within their own communities.

During this period the characteristic African American family emerged: a nuclear core of parents and children surrounded often by extended blood relatives and frequently augmented by "fictive kin," persons not related but who acted and were treated as family members. Within twenty-five years after slavery the overwhelming majority, 80 percent, of African American households were husband-and-wife families, often with extended family members and non-family members.[1]

In Beaufort County and the Sea Islands generally, the people had a head start in family formation and community development, largely because of the Union troop protection they had received since November 1861. While Beaufort native Robert Smalls had stronger head start in life and more substantial resources than many freedmen, he too faced the same challenges of building a strong family, with adequate housing, sustained by economic viability and reinforced by strong religious and educational institutions. For the first few years after the war—before black men got the right to vote, launching his political career—Smalls devoted himself and his resources unstintingly to the principal objectives of acquiring an adequate home for his growing family, establishing economic viability for them through entrepreneurship, helping to sustain independent black churches, and launching a series of events to bring education to himself, his family, and the other children in the community.

After the war, he consummated an extended romance with the town and county of Beaufort, South Carolina, that lasted beyond his death some fifty years later. Although he traveled widely in the state, the North, and the Midwest, his head was "always turned toward Beaufort." As a war hero he could have moved to any part of the North he desired; yet he always claimed Beaufort as his home. In return the town and county of Beaufort claimed Smalls then and still claim him today.

The Prince Street House

When Smalls sought a home for his family, he had plenty of money and many fine homes on the market from which to choose. During the war the federal government had levied taxes on properties the planters left behind when they evacuated Beaufort. On the failure of the owners to pay these taxes, the federal government confiscated their properties and sold them at tax auctions for their estimated value. In this manner the house on Prince Street, where Smalls grew up in slavery, came on the market. The DeTreville family had purchased this house from Henry McKee in 1851 and had abandoned it ten years later in 1861, when federal forces captured Beaufort. During the war Union forces used the house as a residence for soldiers and hired Lydia, Smalls's mother, as house-keeper. She lived on the Prince Street property to serve these troops for the years 1861–1863. The DeTrevilles had not been able to keep up the taxes; so, after the Union troops moved out of the house, it was put up for sale along with many other similar homes in the area. Smalls and his mother thought that this house, where they had labored long in slavery, would make a perfect home for his expanding family.

The Prince Street house was auctioned at a tax sale in 1863, valued at $700, and Smalls placed the winning bid of $650.[2] The DeTreville family contested Smalls's ownership of the house in a legal case that was ultimately heard in the U.S. Supreme Court. The court decided in Smalls's favor by affirming the valid-ity of the congressional acts providing for direct taxes on property in occupied territory. This action helped many other black families and whites to purchase homes in this neighborhood after the war. In a similar manner Smalls's friend the Reverend Mansfield French purchased a nearby house owned before the war by the Richard Fuller family. Smalls's black neighbors included the attorney William J. Whipper and his brother as well as Julius Washington.

Smalls and his family occupied the house at 501 Prince Street in Beaufort continually for some ninety years. If we count the sixteen years his mother lived in the house as a slave (1834–1851) and the two years she lived there as a vir-tually free woman serving U.S. soldiers billeted there (1861–1863), it may be said that the Smalls family lived in that house for more than a century, much longer than any other family associated with it. This is why his descendants refer to it as the Robert Smalls house (as does the National Park Service plaque on the surrounding brick wall), though the Beaufort Chamber of Commerce identifies it to tourists as the Henry McKee house. Admiral Du Pont's widow from Delaware visited Smalls in this house in 1868. It was her first personal encounter with Smalls, having known him only from her husband's letters to her during the war. She described Smalls in a letter to a friend as "polite and obliging in manners." She was more impressed with his home, writing. "It is a very pretty place. The house is not large, being surrounded by a lot of consid-erable size, tastefully ornamented with trees and shrubbery and . . . flowers . . . are in good order that you will scarcely find the premises of any other negro in the place."[3] The original structure of the two-story clapboard house, which was built in 1834, has been altered several times, resulting in its current square shape with wings on the north and east sides. It is located on the corner of Prince and North streets. In some records it was listed as 511 Prince Street, but in any event it was always the only house in that 500 block.

Today the south facade of the house is headed by a two-story balustrade piazza that rests on brick foundations with wooden supports. The main entrance, centered in the south front, is approached by a short flight of brick stairs that lead to the narrow, decorated doorway. The piazza is supported by attenuated Doric columns. The gable roof has pediments on both ends and is covered by a lightly decorated pediment.

The house originally consisted of a first-floor central hallway flanked by two principal rooms. The back of the hall led into the center of the three rooms that extended across the back of the house to form a one-story T. Above the two principal rooms were two more of the same size. Thus, from the beginning this house was large on the inside and surrounded by a large yard covering half a city block. In 1850, one year before Henry McKee sold the house to William DeTreville, a third bedroom was added over the center of the T. At the same time a glass transom was added to the entrance. In 1870, seven years after Robert Smalls purchased the house, a second-floor front porch was added and the columns were carried up to the eaves. Ten years later Smalls added a back room to the main floor at the back of the T. In 1910 Smalls had electricity put in the house. The family installed central heating sometime after his death in 1915. In 1950, when the last of Smalls's relatives occupied the house, the supporting pillars of the house were enclosed with old bricks and a lace brick wall was built on the front of the yard. These are prominent features of the house today. Despite all the alterations and improvements, the house maintains the flavor of the original. It is situated on almost a full block and is surrounded by trees, shrubs, and flowers. The house on Prince Street has become a landmark in Beaufort not only because of its architecture but also because the Smalls family lived there. Today, this house, the former homes of Thomas and Richard Fuller (whose house was later the Mansfield French home), and those of Samuel J. Bampfield and William S. Whipper are preserved, and they are beautifully depicted in N. Jane Iseley's *Beaufort*.

The Extended Family

The strong family that Smalls built, supported, and presided over in this house during the early years was his "family of emancipation." It was a characteristic African American extended family. The 1870 federal census was the first U.S.

Figure 8.1   Home, Family, and Community: Robert Smalls's Family of Emancipation Residents of 511 Prince Street—1870

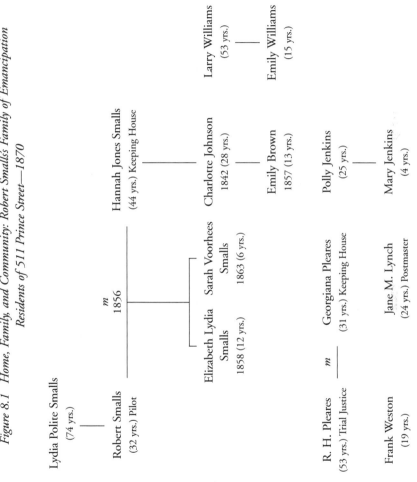

Lydia Polite Smalls
(74 yrs.)

Robert Smalls
(32 yrs.) Pilot

m
1856

Hannah Jones Smalls
(44 yrs.) Keeping House

Elizabeth Lydia
Smalls
1858 (12 yrs.)

Sarah Voorhees
Smalls
1863 (6 yrs.)

Charlotte Johnson
1842 (28 yrs.)

Emily Brown
1857 (13 yrs.)

Larry Williams
(53 yrs.)

Emily Williams
(15 yrs.)

R. H. Pleares
(53 yrs.) Trial Justice

m

Georgiana Pleares
(31 yrs.) Keeping House

Polly Jenkins
(25 yrs.)

Frank Weston
(19 yrs.)

Jane M. Lynch
(24 yrs.) Postmaster

Mary Jenkins
(4 yrs.)

Census since before the war and the first to designate all the members of formerly enslaved black families. All the members of the Robert Smalls household
on Prince Street—adults and children—were enumerated.

At the time of the 1870 U.S. Census, the most senior member of the Smalls
household was seventy-four-year-old Lydia Smalls. This census was the first official record of her age and the first to list her last name as "Smalls." She had
raised Robert in this house when they were both held in slavery. Now she could
preside over the house in freedom without many of the demanding chores of
bondage.

Smalls, now thirty-two years old, was master of the house, son, husband,
stepfather, and stepgrandfather, and he was the primary breadwinner. His invest-
ments and earnings as a pilot, plus political income, enabled him to support his
large family in grand style. He was already a member of the state legislature,
a prominent businessman with property valued at $6,000 and $1,000 in the
bank.

According to his son Willie, Smalls never did any household chores. Those
were done by hired help and other family members. If Lydia was the most
admired member of the family, Smalls was the most feared. He enforced strict
discipline. Hannah Jones Smalls, age forty-four in 1870, was the housekeeper,
the wife of the head of household. They had been married for fourteen years
and free for eight. She provided strong championship to Smalls, produced and
nurtured three children, and made a home for them all.

One child in the family was twelve-year-old Elizabeth Lydia Smalls, who was
already a bright and eager student. Born in slavery, she had been purchased by
her father before the war and accompanied him and her mother on the seizure
of the *Planter*. She was soon sent off to boarding school in the North. Her baby
sister had come to replace her lost baby brother. Now age six, Sarah Voorhees
Smalls had been born on the day her father became captain of the *Planter*. A
sensitive, attractive, and bright child, she had already developed artistic and
musical interests that later blossomed and lasted a lifetime.

Also resident in the family at this time was Hannah's twenty-eight-year-old
daughter, Charlotte Jones, and her thirteen-year-old daughter, Emily Brown.
Charlotte had been left in slavery in Charleston during the capture of the
Planter, while her younger sister, Clara Jones, was taken along. Apparently, at
the time the *Planter* was seized, Charlotte, then twenty years old, was the mother
of a five-year-old daughter and possibly living with the baby's father, a man
named Brown. In 1870 Charlotte lived with the family in their Prince Street
home, assisted her mother with housework, and cared for her child and the
others. Soon thereafter Charlotte married Larry Williams, and they made their
home in a nearby house owned by Smalls.

It is clear from the census report that this family extended far beyond its nuclear members. Fifty-three-year-old Larry Williams and his fifteen-year-old daughter, Emily Williams, were members of this household in 1870. The Honorable R. H. Pleares, a fifty-three-year-old trial justice, and his thirty-one-year-old wife, Georgiana Pleares, also lived with Smalls, as did Dolly Jenkins, age twenty-five, and her four-year-old daughter, Mary Jenkins; twenty-four-year-old postmaster Jane M. Lynch; and nineteen-year-old Frank Weston.

While not much is known about these members of Smalls's extended and augmented family, it is unlikely that they were merely boarders. Some had nuclear alliances of their own, and descendants believe that romantic alliances existed among them as well. They were probably all African Americans, listed in the census as black or mulatto. To accommodate everyone, Smalls added rooms to the house and refurbished the two-room cabin in the backyard, where he and Lydia had slept during slavery. They continued to use the outhouse in the backyard. In its structure this extended nuclear, augmented family very much resembled the family of liberation that accompanied Robert Smalls on the *Planter*'s seizure.

The Henry McKee Family after the War

When Robert Smalls returned from the war, Beaufort was a vastly different place from that he had left in 1851. He and Henry McKee, his former owner, had changed places. Smalls was now free, famous, and a man of financial means, while McKee was destitute. He had lost all his property during the war, including Smalls. But just as the McKees had been kind to him and his mother during slavery, Smalls returned their kindness in full measure after the war. That these two families were able to continue their close relationship under radically changed circumstances was a tribute to both sides, which Smalls's descendants continue to cherish and the citizens of Beaufort continue to honor.

After the war the McKees stayed on in Charleston for a while. On their trips to Beaufort to visit friends, Smalls would meet them at the harbor with his carriage and drive them to their friends' homes. Later he purchased a house with some tillable land for them so they could support themselves. When Smalls was in Congress, he found a government job for the McKees' daughter Jane and recommended a McKee nephew for a position at the U.S. Naval Academy. In Congress he introduced an unsuccessful proposal to reimburse people, including the McKees, who had lost their real estate for nonpayment of taxes. The most notable event occurred after Henry McKee died in 1875, and Mrs. McKee had become old and ill. Smalls then took her into his home and cared for her until her death in 1904.[4] One of the most enduring and endearing stories is about how Smalls took care of Mrs. Jane Bold McKee after her husband died in 1875. William Elliott Jr. reported in a memoir:

> It was said of him, and I believe the story, that when his former owner, Mrs. McKee, came back to Beaufort after the war in great poverty he took her to his house, which had belonged to her and which he had acquired at Direct Tax sale, and gave her the best room in his house, which was a rather fine one. He brought her meals to her, and when she protested that he was now a United States General and a man of prominence and had servants he replied, "Madam, when you were my owner and had power over me you always treated me with kindness and consideration, and now that our positions are somewhat changed, I shall not fail in showing my great respect for you," and continued to bring meals.[5]

Smalls's kindly treatment of the Henry McKee family earned him respect in the white community.

Religion

Religion was a strong feature of family life in the post–Civil War years. During the early years of emancipation, the Baptist religion was the choice of the Smalls family. When the Union forces landed in Beaufort in November 1861, Lydia was an active member of the Baptist Church of Beaufort. As the whites fled the island she joined the other blacks in attending services at the Tabernacle. In 1863 the Tabernacle Baptist Church was officially established with its own pastor, and Lydia continued as a member of this church. When Smalls brought Hannah and the children to Beaufort in 1862, they joined Lydia in attendance at Tabernacle Baptist Church.

Smalls was heavily engaged in military duties and did not settle down to membership in a church until 1865 when, after the war, the whites returned to Beaufort. At that time he joined and became a chief financial supporter of the First African Baptist Church of Beaufort, located a stone's throw from the family's Prince Street home. Descendants say that Smalls was the primary supporter, enabling the purchase of this property from the Beaufort Baptist Church after the war and was personal holder of the mortgage until late in his life. Smalls was also closely associated with the Brick Baptist Church on St. Helena Island, which was affiliated with the Penn School, headed by Laura Towne, a personal and political associate.

Entrepreneurial Base

Another area in which Smalls demonstrated community leadership was in establishing a strong entrepreneurial base in the community. He no doubt learned some rudimentary skills in management from Henry McKee during his early childhood socialization. While growing up on the docks in Charleston, Robert Smalls had developed and enhanced his talent.

During the early years after the war Smalls applied himself vigorously to various business ventures. In addition to entrepreneurial talent, Smalls brought back to Beaufort a considerable amount of wealth. He had the $700 he and Hannah had saved for the final payment on purchasing Hannah, which they kept for themselves. He had been paid $150 a month as captain of the *Planter* during his military service. He had been awarded $1,500 for turning over the *Planter* to the Union. And after the war, he was paid $1,500 per month for piloting the *Planter* on various assignments for the government.

Smalls believed strongly that blacks could and should own and operate successful business enterprises. He led the way with several businesses on Carteret Street, including a general store during the early years after the war. Moreover, Smalls entered into a commercial relationship with Tom Long, a former soldier in the South Carolina black regiment, and others. Calling itself the Star Spangled Banner Association, the group purchased a store in Beaufort and a steamboat to be commanded by Smalls in a commercial coastal service. In order to form this association, Smalls and the others raised $20,000 from local Beaufort residents in shares ranging from $15 to $200. In addition they secured a mortgage of $10,000 on the ship. Unfortunately, while someone else was piloting the ship on one of its voyages, it ran aground on Johns Island. The investors lost a great deal of money. Smalls continued to run his small store.

Between 1866 and 1888 Smalls acquired many properties in Beaufort County, including building lots in Beaufort, a townhouse at Port Royal, and the Lady's Island plantation where his mother had been held in slavery. Smalls must have held some plantation land into the 1890s because his son Willie reported that Smalls took him to view some. In addition to his home at 501 Prince Street, Smalls owned several houses in this neighborhood that he used for housing his relatives and for rental income:

414 New Street, a pink frame house owned and inhabited for twenty-two years by Samuel J. and Elizabeth Smalls Bampfield and now occupied by the mayor of Beaufort;

508 Duke Street, which Smalls built for the craftsmen who worked on his various properties. By 2002 this was the last remaining house in the neighborhood still owned by Smalls's descendants and the only house in the neighborhood owned and occupied by blacks;

708 East Street, at the corner of Hancock Street;

601 Prince Street, the house next door, which he rented to the longtime deputy at the customhouse, Julius I. Washington;

715 New Street, on the corner of New and North streets, a gray house
    with black shutters that was occupied by Smalls's daughter Elizabeth
    and her children for ten years after her husband died;
712 East Street, the two-story, white frame house at the corner of Duke
    and East, which Smalls purchased for his son William Robert Smalls;
501 East Street (no longer standing).

Most of these properties passed out of the Smalls family about 1959, after Elizabeth's death, because descendants had moved to other places.

Among the most impressive ventures Smalls undertook in cooperation with
some of his colleagues was the building and operation of a black-owned railroad
in Charleston.[6] In association with eleven other black men of Charleston and
one white man, Smalls played a leadership role in the establishment of the Enterprise Railroad, Inc. It was authorized by the legislature and incorporated in
1870 with $250,000 in capital subscriptions. By 1874 the railroad had been
constructed. Accommodating passengers and freight, the horse-drawn coaches
ran the breadth of the city and connected with all the railroad stations and all
the major wharfs on the Charleston docks. Richard H. Cain served as president
of the company; William Jerrey was corresponding secretary; and William
McKinlay was treasurer. The only white member of the board was Timothy
Hurley, a prominent Republican. The other black members included Joseph H.
Rainey, Dr. Benjamin A. Boseman, William J. Broadie, J. N. Hayne, Thaddeus
K. Sasportas, John Wright, Henry Maxwell, Lucius Wimbush, Robert Smalls,
William E. Johnston, and Samuel Johnson. The board elected William J. Whip-
per as legal counsel and subscription agent. The railroad operated under black
leadership for a decade, but sometime during the 1880s its operation began to
pass into the hands of a white majority of investors and managers.

Robert Smalls's commitment to black entrepreneurship was expressed not
only in his own personal conduct but in his public policy support as well. Years
later, when he was a member of Congress, he received a letter from R. W. Tyler
asking for his support of a black-owned oil and gas company in Columbus,
Ohio, far from his congressional district in South Carolina. Smalls bought
twenty-five shares in the Wilgara Oil & Gas Company, said he would probably
buy more, and added that other men he knew were interested in investing in
the company. "I assure you," Smalls wrote, "I feel very proud of your organization and shall do all I can to encourage my people to take hold of it." Smalls
added, "It is only one of the enterprises that our people need to stimulate to
greater efforts. As you say, so say I, let the company be exclusively in the hands
of our own people. Let us own every dollar of the stock, and thus demonstrate
our capacity to own and control, and properly manage such a corporation. I am

with you; I congratulate you; I am at your services to do what I can to help you win success, and winning success gives the lie to the oft repeated assertion 'the Negro is a failure in business.'"[7]

Education

When Smalls's son William Robert Smalls was asked what he considered his father's greatest contribution to society, he said without equivocation that it was his father's contribution to education. Smalls's appreciation for and support of education began with himself, extended to his children, then to the newly freed black children of Beaufort, to black and white children of the entire state of South Carolina, and finally to the field of higher education.

In the military Smalls was confronted with the stark reality that his inability to read and write severely compromised his many fine attributes, his personal development, and his desire to bring freedom to others. His first formal education was his hiring of the retired naval officer to teach him how to navigate passage of the *Planter* to Philadelphia in May 1863. His second initiative was hiring two black teachers in Philadelphia to instruct him in the basics of education.

William Robert Smalls recalled his father's work in education:

In . . . [1867], Captain Smalls saw the need . . . for the purchase or erection of a school building for the public education of Negroes in Beaufort. Several private schools had been organized and put into operation by Northern Philanthropy, but his dream was that of public free education. Smalls had made many friends, both white and colored throughout the country. He now sent out his plea on behalf of his people. Traveling at his own expense, he called on his friends. Money was raised because his friends believed in him. Upon his return to Beaufort, he purchased with this money, a large estate with buildings and several acres of ground. This site he deeded to "The Negro Children of Beaufort as a school." The building has since been torn down; a new building has been erected in another spot, and is called Robert Smalls High School. On April 5th each year, his birthday, the town celebrated Robert Smalls's Day, with appropriate exercise at the school and declared this day a holiday.[8]

According to his son, when Smalls returned to Beaufort from the war, he hired a private tutor, Miss Rossa Cooley a Penn School teacher. For some nine months he awoke at 5:00 A.M. every weekday and studied for two hours on lessons his instructor had left for him the previous day. Then the instructor came to his home and tutored him for another hour. At promptly 8:00 A.M. Smalls had breakfast, took a sponge bath, and went off to work. "Breakfast had better be ready," the son said, adding that his father was a stickler for timeliness and showed his irritation if he were unduly delayed.

Smalls's son also reported with justifiable pride the following story: "While in Congress, Smalls was in a debate with Congressman Gritt Bruce, a college graduate, and in reporting on this debate, the daily papers marveled at the fact that Smalls had made fewer grammatical errors than Bruce."[9]

In June 1906 a signal honor was given to Smalls. It was commencement time at Harvard University and as customary, the Harvard Chapter of Phi Beta Kappa was holding its commencement meeting. The president of this chapter at that time was former governor of Massachusetts John D. Long, with whom Smalls had become close friends while the two men were serving in Congress. Learning that his friend was visiting Boston, Long invited Smalls to attend the Phi Beta Kappa meeting. Smalls attended and was called on to address the body. This invitation of an African American who had never had a day of formal education to meet with and address the Harvard Chapter of Phi Beta Kappa was the first and only such case on record in the history of this elite organization.

Smalls often claimed that he owed his education to two sources. One was his faithful reading of the *Washington Star,* to which he began subscribing while he was a member of Congress, when it was a four sheet paper, and to which he continued to subscribe until his death. Smalls's three children, who were well educated and to whom he turned for scholastic guidance and assistance, were the second source of his education. Acting often as private secretaries in the formulation and correction of letters, speeches, and other papers, his children helped him greatly.

One factor was evident in his writing and speaking. As a result of his exhaustive reading, he seldom made a grammatical error. However, when he did make an error, he would see to it that it was quickly corrected, and he never made the same mistake twice.[10]

The next educational priority for Smalls was the education of his children. He personally saw to it that his children—Elizabeth, Sarah, and William Robert —were offered the best education available, and they thrived on it. Elizabeth, attended a school in Beaufort operated by the Freedmen's Bureau. When she was six years old, Smalls enrolled her in the Penn School across the river on St. Helena Island. There her instructor was Charlotte Forten, who taught classes in the Brick Church from October 1862 to March 1864. Forten was the well-educated, refined, and beautiful daughter and granddaughter of prominent black abolitionists in Philadelphia. She had been educated in private schools in New England and was a schoolteacher there when she volunteered to come South on this mission. She was always, however, in quite poor health. After she returned to the North she married into the Grimké family and lived in Washington, D.C.

Elizabeth was an able, eager student who learned her lessons well. Her father questioned her at night on what she had learned that day. Descendants tell the story that once when she told him some fact she had learned, he exclaimed, "Does Miss Forten know that?" "Daddy," she scolded him, "Miss Forten knows everything."[11]

Although Charlotte Forten did not stay long in South Carolina, she continued her association with the Smalls family. Shortly after Elizabeth's twelfth birthday, Charlotte arranged for her to attend Miss Allen's English and Classical School, a girl's finishing school in West Newton, Massachusetts. Forten also arranged for Elizabeth to board with a family Forten knew. Elizabeth took the train home to Beaufort during school holidays. When she graduated at age seventeen, it was just in time for her to become her father's clerk during the first year of his first term in Congress. She went straight from school to his residence at 1017 Twelfth Street, N.W., in Washington, where she helped him with correspondence and speeches.

Smalls's second daughter, Sarah Voorhees Smalls, was educated in the Beaufort school founded by her father, where she later became an instructor. When she was sixteen, Smalls enrolled her in the Minor Normal School in Washington, D.C., now the University of the District of Columbia. She stayed with her father in Washington during that time. She later did further studies at the Boston Conservatory of Music. Sarah lived in her father's and accompanied him to Washington social events for a time because Hannah did not like public life. Sarah became an accomplished schoolteacher, college teacher, piano teacher, and church organist.

After his own education and the education of his children, Smalls gave strong support to the education of other black children in Beaufort County. In February 1867 Smalls joined with other prominent blacks to form the Beaufort County School Board. He was promptly elected chair, even though others had more formal education. Board members included Jonathan J. Wright, who preceded Smalls in the state senate and later gave long and honorable service as a member of the state supreme court; Richard H. Gleaves, who became lieutenant governor and president of the senate; and, later, William J. Whipper, a member of the state legislature and a judge. They purchased the property and established the school at Carteret and Washington streets. It operated as a private school until taken over by Beaufort County about 1893. Later Smalls's daughter Sarah taught there, and his son Willie studied there. In 1925 it was moved and became Robert Smalls High School.

Public Service

Another of Smalls's passions was public service. His leadership following "the great Sea Island storm of 1893" is a poignant example of the dedication that earned the gratitude of his white and black neighbors.

In August 1893, the equivalent of a category-three hurricane hit the South Carolina and Georgia coast at high tide. "By the time the waters ebbed and the winds subsided, 2,000 or more had drowned and tens of thousands were left homeless, hungry, and destitute." Families were decimated, with many losing their children and many surviving children losing one or both of their parents. No relief funds were appropriated by either Congress or the South Carolina state legislature. South Carolina governor Benjamin "Pitchfork" Tillman's slow response to appeals for immediate assistance caused further death and starvation. Some writers have asserted that Tillman was dilatory because the vast majority of the citizens in the path of the storm were black and Republican.[12]

In contrast, Republican Robert Smalls left his post at the customhouse and threw himself into action. He and the mayor were appointed to chair the Beaufort Rescue Mission. Smalls wrote letters to many of his friends in the North, asking for food, clothing and money. They responded generously.

Three weeks after the storm, Governor Tillman invited Clara Barton and the fledgling American Red Cross, which she headed, to come to the area and help.[13] During the nearly one year Barton stayed in Beaufort executing the first American Red Cross hurricane relief and recovery effort, Smalls worked with Barton receiving and distributing food and clothing. They also were aided enormously by Rachel Mather, who was operating the Mather School, a school for black girls.

It has been estimated that after the flood receded, there were some seventy thousand people, mostly black but whites as well, in desperate need of food, clothing and shelter. Not all could be rescued and served but a great many were.[14]

A special report by the South Carolina state senate shows precisely how public service figured in Smalls's career. After noting that Smalls served as a delegate from Beaufort to both the 1868 and 1895 Constitutional Conventions, the report continues:

> Other offices he held included Registrar for Beaufort District (1867); Trustee for a School in Beaufort (1867); Director of the Prudence Fire Engine Company (1870); Member (1873–1876) and Vice President (1874) of the Board of Regents of the State Normal School; and Regent of the State Lunatic Asylum (1874–1877). Long active in the State Militia, he was

a member of the Lincoln Republican Guard (1869); Lieutenant Colonel of the Third Regiment of the First Brigade, First Division (1870–1872); Brigadier General of the First Brigade, First Division (1872–1873); Major General of the Second Division (1873–1877); and Captain of the Beaufort Light Infantry (elected 1879).[15]

Reminders of Robert Smalls
in and around Beaufort Today

There are many reminders of Robert Smalls in Beaufort today. A fifteen-mile stretch of U.S. Highway 170 that leads into Beaufort from the direction of Savannah, Georgia, is called the Robert Smalls Parkway. This parkway was named by the Beaufort County Planning Commission at the request of the alumni association of the Robert Smalls High School in 1989.

Robert Smalls Middle School is a large, modern facility, built in 1984 for about two thousand students of all races. On Boundary Street are the offices of the Beaufort County government. Among them is the Arthur C. Horne Building, formerly Robert Smalls Elementary School. A marker nearby identifies the site of the old Robert Smalls High School, which was located at the corner of Ribaut and Boundary from 1925 to 1984, when it closed to facilitate school desegregation. Alumni still gather every three years.

The dedication of the Robert Smalls Parkway took place at the Robert Smalls Middle School on July 6, 1991. Among members of the Robert Smalls High School alumni present were four great-great-grandchildren of Robert and Hannah Smalls: Helen Meyer Fields, Carolyn Meyer Little, Freddie Meyer, and Charlie Meyer. The mistress of ceremonies was Fulton Terry, a founder of the alumni association in 1951. Margaret Simmons, chair of the dedication committee, announced that "this dedication is the beginning of a campaign to designate Robert Smalls's birthday as a legal holiday in the state of South Carolina."[16] The school's football team, the Generals, brought distinction to the the legacy of Robert Smalls and the state of South Carolina.

Also along Boundary there are two cemeteries (of the three in Beaufort) that have historic significance related to Smalls. First is the small Mercy Cemetery established by the Catholic Sisters of Mercy for blacks displaced by Sherman's march through Georgia. Two settlements were located in the Beaufort area. Many of the blacks were transported from Savannah by Robert Smalls on the *Planter* in January 1865. This venerable cemetery, open to all, has a special family plot: a fifteen-by-twenty-foot section cordoned off from the rest of the cemetery by an iron fence. This is the Bampfield family plot, where ten persons are

buried. Smalls's oldest daughter, Elizabeth Lydia, is buried here with her husband, Samuel J. Bampfield, seven of their eleven children, and an in-law.

Next door to Mercy Cemetery is the Beaufort National Cemetery, located
at 1601 Boundary Street. Descendants of Smalls who are buried here include
Vietnam War veteran Edward Bampfield "Buster" Meyer Jr. (1934–1976) and
Smalls's great-great-granddaughter Laura Simpson Brown (1917–1983). The
Beaufort National Cemetery holds the remains of more than 7,500 Civil War
soldiers, including 4,019 unknown U.S. soldiers and 117 known Confederates.
A total of 1,745 black soldiers are buried there, including 950 who are unknown. Some men buried there were members of the First South Carolina Col-
ored Volunteer Regiment, the first black troops to serve officially in the U.S.
Army by action of President Lincoln. Others buried there were members of the
Second South Carolina Colored Volunteer Regiment; Smalls played a strategic
and instrumental role in the establishment of the Second Regiment, and both
regiments saw action along the Atlantic coast. Also buried here are some men
who served in the Fifty-fourth and Fifty-fifth Massachusetts Colored Infantry
Regiments.

The Tabernacle Baptist Church at 911 Craven Street is Smalls's final resting
place, where he is buried with his two wives and his daughter Sarah. This church
is the oldest continuously operated black church in the city. The churchyard is
also the site of the only statue of Robert Smalls erected in the United States.
A bronze and pewter bust created by artist Marion Etheridge Talmidge was
installed in 1976 during the celebration of the U.S. bicentennial. Michael Boulware Moore, great-great-grandson of Robert Smalls, unveiled the statue and
Governor James B. Edwards issued a proclamation declaring February 22, 1976,
Robert Smalls Day in South Carolina.

Another monument to Smalls is behind the Thomas Law Building at 920
Bay Street, and facing the water is the U.S. Customhouse, where for twenty-
three years Smalls presided as collector of customs for the port of Beaufort.
President Benjamin Harrison appointed Smalls to this position in 1890, after
Smalls's last campaign for Congress was unsuccessful. Nearly two decades ear-
lier, as a young congressman, Smalls had introduced the legislation to create the
Beaufort customhouse.

At 822 Bay Street is the Beaufort Post Office, where Samuel J. and Elizabeth
Smalls Bampfield presided as postmasters. Robert Smalls sponsored the legislation in Congress that established this post office.

At the end of Bay Street stands the two-story, stuccoed U.S. District Courthouse. This was once the site of the Beaufort County Courthouse, where
Smalls's son-in-law, Samuel J. Bampfield, served as clerk of court for more than
twenty years.

The Beaufort Arsenal Museum at 713 Craven Street has both negative and positive connotations for Smalls's legacy. Smalls's mother, Lydia, told her descendants that on the night Smalls was born, a black man was hanged at this arsenal. The arsenal also served as headquarters of the Beaufort Light Infantry unit, organized in 1878 by Smalls, who served as its captain. Now a museum, it contains the desk used by Robert Smalls as collector of customs.

The Beaufort County Library at 311 Scott Street, across the street from the arsenal, is a vital institution for preserving Smalls's legacy. The holdings on Smalls, including books, photographs, letters, newspaper clippings, and speeches, are impressive and growing.

Beyond Beaufort

Across the Beaufort River is Lady's Island, where Smalls's mother was born on Ashdale Plantation and where Smalls owned a plantation after the war. Nearby on Dr. Martin Luther King Drive is the Penn Center Historic District. Founded in 1862 as the Penn School, where Laura Towne and other northern "Gideonites" taught, this was the first major organized school for newly freed African Americans. Robert Smalls became an active collaborator with Towne and, later, Charlotte Forten.

A short distance from Beaufort is Parris Island, home of the U.S. Marine Corps recruitment and training facility. Established through legislation introduced and shepherded through Congress by Smalls, the facility includes the Parris Island Museum, which contains an extensive collection of documents, photographs, and maps depicting Smalls's life, shown to us by museum director Stephen R. Wise.

Smalls's descendants and the citizen of Beaufort County continue to memorialize Smalls in a manner not yet demonstrated in the two other South Carolina cities where he left his mark: Charleston and Columbia. There are strong indications, however, that by the time of the one-hundredth anniversary of his death in 1915, his image will be seen in these two cities and others as well.

9

Mr. Republican

Smalls's Political Leadership during Reconstruction, 1868–1877

Political democracy was a stranger to South Carolina during the first two hundred years of its history, while chattel slavery reigned supreme. Only after the Civil War were black men granted the right to vote that white men had. Even then, it was not automatically or easily accomplished. While Andrew Johnson served out Lincoln's term, he sanctioned the program of Presidential Reconstruction, which kept blacks in near slavery under a different name. Although the Thirteenth Amendment abolishing slavery was passed during Johnson's tenure, he publicly espoused and created policy to support the interests of southern whites and to block voting rights for blacks. It was not until the Republican-majority Congress overruled Johnson and began the program of Congressional Reconstruction that the reality of emancipation came alive for the state's black majority. This congressional leadership, which impeached Johnson and passed legislation over his vetoes, adopted the Thirteenth, Fourteenth and Fifteenth Amendments to the U.S. Constitution, which granted citizenship, due-process rights, and ultimately voting rights to black men. Congress also passed a far-reaching series of civil rights acts. When General Ulysses S. Grant was elected president in 1868, the federal government was firmly placed on the side of freedom and reconstruction of the South.

In 1865, during Presidential Reconstruction, South Carolina adopted a constitution for the purpose of reentering the union. Approved by President Johnson, this constitution returned white men to power with no provision for black participation. South Carolina sent to Congress a delegation that was all male, all white, and principally composed of former Confederate officers and advocates. Congress refused to seat this delegation and demanded that a new state constitution be enacted acknowledging the right of black men, as well as white men, to vote. The landmark convention, constitution, and elections of 1868 were the results.

Out of this setting Robert Smalls rose to political prominence. His background and the influence of Abraham Lincoln also made him a lifelong and extremely active, influential Republican.

The demography of South Carolina favored Smalls's political ascendancy. At the end of the war South Carolina had a population consisting of 400,000 blacks and 275,000 whites. Moreover, 30,000 blacks in Beaufort County constituted an overwhelming majority of better than 80 percent of the population. This was a major source of Smalls's political support.[1]

If the Fifteenth Amendment to the U.S. Constitution guaranteeing black males the right to vote was his platform, the Republican Party—the party of Lincoln and emancipation—was his vehicle. Indeed, Smalls was a founder of the Republican Party in South Carolina at a meeting in 1867, involving thirty-five other blacks and three whites. While both the Fifteenth Amendment and the Republican Party eventually failed him, he never deserted them and never lost his faith in representative democracy as a means of sustaining life, liberty, and the pursuit of social justice.

The 1868 Constitutional Convention

The U.S. Congress ordered that for southern states to reenter the Union each state had to hold a constitutional convention with both black and white men voting. Prior to the South Carolina convention two strategic meetings, which Smalls attended, took place. On March 21, 1867, the Union League met in Charleston. The predominantly black group called itself a "Union Republican" convention and drew up a proposal to submit to the future constitutional convention. Then they called a larger meeting of Republicans at which they called for a radical-reform constitution that would, among other measures, guarantee the right to vote to all adult males. At another Charleston meeting in late May, some fifteen hundred to two thousand mostly black men ratified the platform that had been drawn up in March. In July 1867 most of these reforms were adopted by a more broadly representative Union Republican State Convention meeting in Columbia. Sixty-four of the eighty delegates at the July meeting were blacks from nineteen of the state's thirty-one counties; only sixteen delegates were white. At this meeting Smalls was elected Beaufort County's representative to the Union Republican Party's Central Committee and was appointed voter registrar for Beaufort County.

Meanwhile, military authorities established voting procedures for the Constitutional Convention. To be eligible to vote, each person had to sign an oath that he had not served in the Confederate military or otherwise engaged in rebellion against the Union. Many whites, although not a majority, were thus disqualified.

Smalls was diligent in enrolling large numbers of Republican voters, black and white. In September 1867, when registration was completed, there were 127,761 persons registered to vote on the convention referendum in South Carolina. Of these, roughly 63 percent were black and some 37 percent were white. In twenty-one counties blacks constituted a majority of registered voters, and in ten counties whites held a majority. In Beaufort County registered black voters outnumbered registered whites nine to one.

Elections were held on November 19 and 20 to determine the fate of a constitutional convention. Simultaneously, voters were asked to select their representatives for the proposed convention. Altogether, 124 delegate positions were apportioned among the counties on the basis of registered voters.

The vote was overwhelmingly in favor of holding the Constitutional Convention. Of the nearly 128,000 registered voters, 71,000 actually voted; 42,000 whites, following the advice of Democratic politicians, boycotted the election. Of the 71,000 voting, some 69,000 voted for the convention. Because of the Democratic boycott, most of these delegates elected were Republicans. Robert Smalls was prominent among them.

The Constitutional Convention began on January 14, 1868, in Charleston. Of the 124 delegates assembled, 76, a clear majority, were black, and 48 were white. The Beaufort County delegation was made up of two whites, Reuben G. Holmes and James D. Bell, and five blacks, Robert Smalls, William J. Whipper, Landon S. Langley, Jonathan J. Wright, and Francis E. Wilder. After more than two hundred years of governance by white men, interracial government had begun in South Carolina. Neither white nor black women had yet won the right to vote. While some denounced the convention as unconstitutional, black-controlled, and composed of ignorant men, the *Charleston Daily News* reported that the black members showed "remarkable moderation and dignity."[2]

When Governor James L. Orr addressed the convention on January 17, he urged attendees to pursue moderation and reported that the white-run government had left the state with debts of $5.5 million, primarily in general and railroad bonds, and had only $54.24 in the state treasury. The delegates followed Orr's advice and dropped some radical proposals, such as land confiscation and women's suffrage. They avoided revenge against former Confederates and urged Congress to restore their civil rights, which had been taken away by the federal government, provided that each subscribed to a loyalty oath.[3] Moreover, at the request of General Robert K. Scott, assistant commissioner of the Freedmen's Bureau for South Carolina, the convention made it clear that no further land would be distributed to the former slaves, unless they purchased it.

A state-funded program, the South Carolina Land Commission, established 654 homesteads during its first two years. And after 1876, under the direction of Secretary of State Francis L. Cardozo, fourteen thousand black families and a lesser number of white families were settled on homesteads purchased by the state and sold to the families on favorable terms. No other southern state had such a program. After the Democrats took control again in 1877, the program was canceled and many black families, unable to pay newly imposed mortgages, were evicted from their homesteads.

Smalls was active and influential at the Constitutional Convention. He was appointed to the finance committee, but his major contribution was in the field of education. He proposed that the convention adopt a resolution providing for "a system of common schools . . . to be open without charge to all classes of persons."[4] The resolution was passed. The legislature later approved it, and the state had its first public schools. After meeting for sixty-two days, the convention adjourned on March 17, 1868, having laid the groundwork for a modern constitution and a representative government for the state.

Back in Beaufort, Smalls campaigned hard for the constitution, for the statewide Republican slate, and for a seat in the state house of representatives. Seventy-two percent of voters approved the constitution, and the entire state-level Republican ticket was elected. The Democrats, who had abandoned their boycott and tried to woo black voters, won only 6 of the 33 senatorial and 14 of the 124 representative positions. Congress accepted the constitution and declared South Carolina entitled to congressional representation once the state ratified the Fourteenth Amendment. The amendment was ratified on July 7, and on July 9, 1868, South Carolina was readmitted to the Union.

That day Robert K. Scott was sworn in as the first Reconstruction governor of South Carolina. Smalls strongly supported Scott, who won most of the Republican black voters and a minority of white votes. Smalls later had occasion to regret and to withdraw this support from Scott, but only and always in support of another Republican. Scott was handicapped in his governorship. He was becoming increasingly addicted to the opium he used to counter the pain of a war wound. In addition, he had contracted a disability that enabled him to read only one word at a time. More seriously, his conduct in office caused him to be accused of personal corruption.[5] On July 24, 1868, General Edward R. Canby, the federal commander, turned over all his authority to the state officials. This new Reconstruction government lasted nine years. In 1877 the Democrats by violence and intimidation recaptured the South Carolina government. Smalls, however, continued active political leadership from his base in Beaufort County for another twenty years.

Black Political Leadership in South Carolina during Reconstruction

South Carolina had the distinction of having two blacks elected to the office of lieutenant governor. Richard H. Gleaves and later Alonzo J. Ransier were elected to this post and presided over the state senate. Francis L. Cardozo was elected secretary of state and later state treasurer. Henry E. Hayne succeeded Cardozo as secretary of state. South Carolina had the only black elected to the state supreme court, attorney Jonathan J. Wright. Two men were elected to the state land commission: Robert C. De Large and Henry Hayne. South Carolina also had two blacks serve as speaker of the house: Robert B. Elliott and Samuel J. Lee—a distinction the state shared with Mississippi.

South Carolina blacks were at the forefront on several measures. During Reconstruction, South Carolina had the largest number of black officeholders of any state. In the U.S. Congress, South Carolina led all states, northern and southern, with eight black members. South Carolina black congressmen were not only the most numerous but they served longer and were more active in national Republican Party affairs than blacks in other southern states. The eight black congressmen from South Carolina during Reconstruction were:

Richard Cain (1825–1887), served 1873–1875 and 1877–1879;
Robert C. De Large (1842–1874), served 1871–1873;
Robert B. Elliott (1842–1884), served 1871–1874;
Joseph H. Rainey (1832–1887), served 1870-1879;
Alonzo J. Ransier (1834–1882), served one term 1873–1875;
Robert Smalls (1839–1915), served 1875–1879, 1882–1883,
     1884–1887;
Thomas E. Miller (1849–1938), served 1889–1891;
George Washington Murray (1853–1926) served 1893–1895,
     1896–1897.

During his time in office Murray was the only black congressman in the nation. Alabama and Mississippi had three congressmen each. Florida, Georgia, Louisiana, and North Carolina had one each. Only Mississippi had two blacks who served in the U.S. Senate: Hiram Revels and Blanche K. Bruce.

Smalls's Political Career

During his long career, Smalls served in five broad political arenas. In each of these, he rose from the bottom to the top in responsibility and influence. And while he faced enormous obstacles in each of them and often failed to reach his goals, he never faltered in his efforts, doubted his own capacity, or lost faith in the political system and the economic system that sustained it.

The first arena was the Republican Party. Smalls became a Republican when Lincoln won his first election in 1860. As organizer and leader of the Republican Party in Beaufort County and as frequent chair and vice chair of the state political convention, he made his mark. All Republican candidates for governor sought his support. He seldom missed a national convention, and no Republican candidate between Abraham Lincoln in 1864 and William Howard Taft in 1912 campaigned without Smalls's active support.

Although he was elected as a delegate to the 1864 Republican National Convention, which renominated Lincoln, Smalls could not attend because of military duties. He did attend Replication National Conventions in 1868, 1872, 1876, 1884, 1888, 1892, 1896, 1900, 1904, and 1908. He skipped the convention in 1880 because of differences with President Rutherford B. Hayes. He missed only one other, in 1912, because of a severe illness.

Smalls campaigned for Republican presidential candidates in the North and the Midwest. At the 1884 convention in Chicago, Smalls "stood up in the chair and his rotund person was the target for the eyes of thousands in that vast assembly." Another account, by his usual critic the *News and Courier,* said that "he made a good speech, which was [as] well received by whites as by blacks."[6] Smalls was sought after by whites, with many requesting to be introduced to him.

During the early years of Reconstruction, Beaufort's city government was controlled by white Democrats held over from the past, but by 1873 the mayor, police force, and magistrates were black, and the "celebrated former slave Robert Smalls dominated local politics."[7] Perhaps the zenith in black political representation in the state occurred in 1870, when blacks elected half the eight statewide officers and all three congressmen from the state, as well as placing Jonathan J. Wright on the state supreme court.

Smalls in the State Legislature

The 1868 General Assembly consisted of a majority of blacks in the house of representatives, where seventy-eight blacks and sixteen whites were seated. In the state senate whites held the majority, with twenty-four whites and nine blacks. House members and the governor, served two-year terms, while senators served four-year terms.

In his first legislative session Smalls was active in debates to pass the state budget, to establish and fund public schools, to ascribe duties of judges and other officials, and other matters. One of his duties was voting for and election-eering for candidates to be appointed by the legislature to the U.S. Senate. At that time both U.S. senators elected by the legislature were white. Here Smalls threw his support behind his friend the Reverend Mansfield French. French could not muster a majority although Smalls stuck by him for six ballots. Finally, on the seventh ballot, he voted for Frederick A. Sawyer, who served from 1868 to 1873. Smalls introduced legislation to create county solicitors to work with circuit solicitors. He requested and received support for the pilots in Port Royal and Charleston harbors, his old associates.

Smalls was especially proud of his election to the commission to establish and maintain a system of free common schools. He was a member of the house committee investigating voter intimidation and killings during the 1868 elections in the Third Congressional District. The committee met from late March through August 1869. Its members traveled through four counties and took eight hundred pages of testimony. The legislature, however, did not act on the commission's report. Later Smalls was appointed to a three-member committee of the General Assembly to look into payment of some $7,500 to a private attorney retained by the earlier committee. Smalls's committee found and certified that the attorney did no work, but again the legislature took no action. As a member of the Committee on Mines, Smalls introduced a bill to grant a monopoly to two private companies for mining phosphates from the state's rivers and streams. Governor Scott vetoed the legislation, but it was passed over his veto.

The civil rights measures passed by the Congress over the president's veto and passage of the Fourteenth and Fifteenth Amendments of the U.S. Constitution caused a great deal of jubilation among black leaders and abolitionists. In Washington, Frederick Douglass, still the undisputed leader of black people, exclaimed, "I seem to myself to be living in a new world."[8] By 1870 the necessary thirty states in the union, including South Carolina, had ratified the Fifteenth Amendment, providing black men the right to vote nationwide. Smalls could not contain his elation. Always eloquent at times such as this, he introduced a resolution in the state legislature on February 2, 1870, which read in part:

> Whereas, thirty states of the American Union have ratified the Fifteenth Amendment to the Constitution of the United States; and whereas this action of the American people fixes our government firmly on the side of right, and makes it a beacon light to the nations of the earth, and our flag

the emblem of liberty, and the aegis of every citizen beneath its fold through-out the length and breadth of our land and the world over, and whereas, it is eminently proper that this great event should be hailed with joy and thanksgiving; therefore: Be it resolved . . . that, as an expression of our deep sense of gratitude to the Almighty God for this victory of right, and in honor of this event, His Excellency, the Governor, be requested to set apart a day of Thanksgiving and prayer immediately after the official notice of the ratification has been promulgated.[9]

In South Carolina, as in other southern states, federal civil rights measures were widely ignored by the white authorities. By 1867 the Ku Klux Klan had spread to South Carolina and unleashed a reign of terror and violence against black citizens, especially those who sought to exercise their voting rights. Not content just to pass resolutions of support, Smalls used his increasing legislative skills to forge ahead in the interest of social justice. In 1869 he called for the use of force, if necessary, to implement the Civil Rights Act of the U.S. Congress. He could not, however, get the support of the legislature. In the following session he introduced a bill to enforce "by all means possible" the Civil Rights Act "and secure to the people a republican government in this state." The bill was read and referred to the Judiciary Committee, where it died.[10]

On local issues Smalls was more successful. He was a strong advocate for the vigorous enforcement of the Homestead Act, which provided homes and farms for landless people. Enforcement of this act had been hampered by the attitudes of white sheriffs and other officers in some locations, who were more sympathetic with the creditors than the debtors. Smalls introduced a bill to punish officers who interfered with the implementation of the Homestead Act, and he was successful.

Smalls pushed for austerity in government spending. He successfully opposed a resolution to allow the speaker an increase of four dollars to his regular per diem. He opposed the payment of per diem to members who were granted leaves of absence for business, and he urged that no per diem be paid to members or employees during adjournment. In the 1869 session he called for the regulation of fees for probate judges, clerks of the courts, trial lawyers, justices of the peace, and other public officers.

Smalls also sought local reform. Observing discord between the Beaufort town council, controlled by white Democrats, and the new county government with its black Republican majority, Smalls stated that fighting hampered the economic and social development of the area. He introduced a measure in the General Assembly establishing a commission to study the issue. The measure passed, and Smalls was appointed to the commission. The commission's study and Smalls's report demonstrated how the contentious situation hampered economic development. Smalls later reconciled the two factions through his mediation.

Smalls introduced several successful resolutions for Beaufort County. The county seat was moved from Gillisonville to Beaufort, and a new voting precinct was established in Beaufort. He was also successful in persuading the legislature to levy a special tax for restoration of the Beaufort County jail and courthouse.[11]

In 1870, true to his focus on economic development, Smalls obtained a franchise from the legislature for the Beaufort Railroad Company, in which he was an investor, to build a railroad from Port Royal to Beaufort, a project planned since 1857. By 1873 the railroad was completed and not only provided needed transportation but also offered employment for blacks and whites.[12]

During the 1870 election season, Governor Scott declared for renomination and reelection, causing a split among the Republicans. The Democrats, called Conservatives, took advantage of this split. They nominated Richard B. Carpenter, a Republican from Kentucky, as their candidate for governor and a Conservative for lieutenant governor. They then declared themselves the Union Reform Party, dedicated to cleaning up the corruption charged to Governor Scott. This enticed a few blacks to their cause, including Richard Harvey Cain, a prominent Charleston clergyman and journalist. But Smalls, a loyal Republican, supported Scott. He believed that Republicans could and should undertake necessary reforms.

Smalls succeeded in his support of Scott and in his own election to the S.C. Senate. The Beaufort County Republican Club delivered 6,142 votes for Scott as opposed to 999 for Carpenter. Smalls defeated his Democrat opponent, winning by a 4,000-vote margin.

Smalls in the S.C. Senate

At the end of the 1869–1870 session of the state legislature, while Smalls was serving as a member of the lower house, he was elected state senator from Beaufort County to fill the unexpired term of Jonathan J. Wright, newly elected to the state supreme court. In the election for the state supreme court, Smalls had supported Wright's opponent, attorney William J. Whipper. When Wright won and vacated his senate seat, Smalls won it handily.

In the state senate, Smalls was elected by his colleagues to important committees dealing with claims, mines, printing, and penitentiary. As chair of the Printing Committee, Smalls nominated Josephus Woodruff for another term as clerk of the senate, a position that worked closely with the Printing Committee.

During his first term in the state senate, Smalls entered the controversy surrounding phosphate mining in the state. Phosphate-mining companies were exploiting public lands without making sufficient contributions to state revenue. Senator Daniel T. Corbin, who was president of one of the companies, refused to recognize the rights of the state in such enterprises. Smalls took up the issue, introducing a strongly worded resolution condemning the phosphate companies for not paying royalties. He called on the senate to appoint a committee of five members to investigate and report on the matter. Smalls was appointed as one of the members, and the committee recommended that a state inspector of phosphates be named with duties defined by law and with authority to enforce his decisions. By 1876 the attorney general could report that "full collection [had been made] of all royalties due the state from mining companies."[13] Phosphate mining became a major source of employment for black men, particularly in the winter months after the harvest.

In 1872 Smalls was called on to address charges of corruption in the Republican Party. He received a warning letter from his good friend General Rufus Saxton, who was then stationed in the North:

> When you brought the *Planter* out from Charleston . . . you knew where lay the torpedoes on the right, and the shoals and rocks on the left, you knew where the channel was deep and sailed into it. You held your helm, and soon the *Planter* was safe and you were free. The ship of [the] State of South Carolina is now in stormy waters, your rights are in danger. The rocks and shoals, torpedoes and hostile guns are ignorance, intemperance, immorality, dishonesty and corruption in high places. The beacon lights ahead are honesty, purity, virtue, intelligence, the schoolhouse and the church. Keep her helm steady toward these, and soon the ship shall glide gently by the breakers into the peaceful waters of freedom.[14]

After leading the annual militia parade celebrating Emancipation Day on January 1, 1872, Smalls took the opportunity to reply publicly to Saxton. When the crowd was gathered for his address, Smalls "dismounted from his horse, climbed to the speaker's stand, and solemnly read Saxton's letter to the assembled crowd." Then, admitting the existence of corruption, Smalls said, "I differ with you that the Republican Party should be responsible for the action of a few men who have prostituted their high official position to the robbery of the state treasury. In any event, the electorate will throw the rascals out in the 1872 elections." He pledged to fight for reforms and promised the people that

> the reputation I gained in bringing out the *Planter* I do not intend to sully by my actions as a member of the state legislature. . . . As well as I knew the

beacon lights in the time of the *Planter*, I know the beacon lights now, and the channel that leads to honesty, virtue, purity and intelligence, and I trust that I may ever be found working with those who are anxious to guide the ship of state of South Carolina from the dark and troubled waters in which she is now, safe past the rocks, torpedoes and hostile guns of ignorance, immorality and dishonesty in high places into the calm and placid waters of that harbor where religious, social, moral and political purity reign supreme."[15]

Corruption rampant under Governor Scott worsened considerably under Governor Franklin Moses. At a meeting of the 1874 Republican State Convention, presided over by Smalls, the party refused to renominate Moses and instead turned to Daniel Chamberlain, a white, northern-born graduate of Harvard and Yale who had served in Moses's cabinet. They also adopted a reform platform. In general, Chamberlain was a distinct improvement over Moses. His administration has been characterized as "both hard working and honest."[16]

A Second Term for Senator Smalls

In November 1872 Smalls was sworn in for a new four-year term as senator from Beaufort County. He was at the height of his political power, and there was talk of his running for statewide office. One newspaper reported that "it is understood that Senator Smalls will receive the regular nomination for Adjutant and Inspector General, a position he has earned by organizing the only efficient regiment of militia in the state.[17]

During the 1872–1873 sessions Smalls responded to the need for investigating corruption. He introduced a resolution calling for an investigation of the $1 million in pay orders apparently misappropriated by the General Assembly and called for a suspension of payments until the investigation was completed.

At the August 1872 Republican State Convention, a great dispute erupted over who should be the candidate for governor. After much controversy and deliberation, Smalls nominated Circuit Judge Samuel W. Melton to oppose Moses within the party. Moses won the nomination, and in a unifying move Melton became the nominee for attorney general. Melton was nominated as a Republican even though, in league with reformers, he had in 1870 renounced the Republican Party. Both Moses and Melton won the election.

In February 1874, a private "taxpayers convention" met in Columbia to protest the failed Moses administration. The convention charged in part that 1,872 parcels of land were forfeited to the state for taxes and that public-printing costs were outrageous. The Republicans did not ignore the convention and appointed a committee of twenty-four of its leaders to investigate the charges. Senator Smalls was one of the appointees. They found that corruption did indeed exist in the Moses administration and denounced it.

For his Beaufort County constituency, Smalls introduced bills to incorporate the Beaufort Horse Drawn Railroad Company and the Port Royal Hydraulic Cotton Press Company. He continued to support local economic development. As a disciple of Booker T. Washington, Smalls believed that the viability of the black community depended on blacks becoming landowning farmers. In Beaufort County, however, in the mid-1870s the federal government still held vast portions of land, confiscated for nonpayment of taxes. This generally unculti-vated land contributed much to the economic distress of the region.

In 1873 Smalls introduced a resolution asking the state legislature to instruct the state delegation to the U.S. Congress "to use their immediate and most earnest endeavors to secure the passage of a bill that would return the land to the local economy." The resolution was passed by both houses and forwarded to the delegation in Washington. Nothing happened until Smalls was elected to the U.S. Congress the following year.[18]

While in the state senate Smalls helped form a cooperative called the Beaufort Manufacturing and Improvement Company. Among his associates were Alfred Williams, W. J. Whipper, J. Douglass Robertson, David Thomas, N. B. Myers, Francis E. Wilder, James Crowfoot, George Holmes, and other blacks. The purpose of the cooperative was to manufacture cotton-seed oil and pro-mote related business enterprises. It had the authority to build roads and wharves in connection with its business. In March 1872 Smalls introduced a bill granting a charter to this new company. Unfortunately, the project was slow getting off the ground. By 1876 when the Democrats took control of the gov-ernment, all black-owned initiatives were stopped.[19]

Smalls in Congress

In 1874 Smalls was elected U.S. congressman from Beaufort County. He served five terms between 1875 and 1886. During this time he lost two elections to white Democrats: to George Tillman in 1878 and to William Elliott in 1886. On three other occasions he stood aside in favor of other Republicans: E. M. Mackey in 1882, Thomas Miller in 1888, and George Murray in 1892.

Smalls arrived in Washington on December 6, 1874 for the opening of the Forty-first Congress, dressed in one of his Prince Albert suits. He secured a two-bedroom apartment on Second Street in the District of Columbia and was joined by his elder daughter, Elizabeth.

During his first term Smalls did not speak often on the floor but was a most effective legislator. One of his first actions was to enter an ongoing debate about the proposed location of a southern navy base on the Atlantic. Smalls had promoted the qualities of Port Royal, South Carolina, since his early service in the South Carolina legislature. When he arrived in Congress, however, two Georgia ports had been selected as candidates, and their merits were being debated.

Smalls entered these deliberations with his customary thoroughness and vigor. He undertook studies designed to show that Port Royal should be considered. He gathered impressive data showing that it was a superior location and introduced a bill to that effect. With his bill passing both houses of Congress, Smalls delivered a major military and economic resource to his state.

Smalls devoted himself to securing a federal appropriation to improve the port. While the navy estimated the cost at $50,000, Smalls, a watchdog against government extravagance, reviewed the recommendations and persuaded the navy that $40,000 would suffice. His bill passed with little debate.[20]

He also introduced a bill requiring the federal government to return to the state unused land that had been confiscated for nonpayment of taxes. The bill passed, enabling blacks and others to purchase land at very low cost. In consequence by 1890 blacks owned three-fourths of the land in Beaufort County. At that time blacks constituted nearly 80 percent of the population and nearly the same percentage of registered voters.[21]

During this time, Governor Chamberlain got into serious trouble with black leaders. In an effort to solidify his support among white Democrats, he refused to sign the commissions of William J. Whipper and Franklin J. Moses Jr. for the Charleston judgeships to which the General Assembly had elected them. This brought to a head Chamberlain's conflict with black Republicans. Whipper was black, and Moses was white. Of the two men, Whipper drew the particular ire of the governor. A flamboyant, northern-born, highly educated lawyer and planter, Whipper admitted to having been a gambler in the past but had been reformed through a religious conversion. Still, on the basis of this past gambling admission, Chamberlain publicly denounced Whipper and blocked his appointment. Whipper's ascension to the bench would be "a horrible disaster," the governor exclaimed, "that would imperil the civilization of the Puritan and the Cavalier." The Democrat editor of the *News and Courier* chimed in that the election of these men to judgeships by the legislature suggested "a heinous plot to Africanize South Carolina, and to make it a Black Republic."[22] Whipper and Moses could not assume their judgeships over the governor's veto. This action infuriated the black Republican leadership, and strong sentiment rose for deserting the governor at the next election in favor of a fusion ticket.

However, an 1876 incident known as the Hamburg Massacre hardened black sentiment against the Democrats, and Chamberlain's denunciation of this violence softened black sentiments toward him. The event occurred in

Hamburg, South Carolina, across the river from Augusta, Georgia. At a July 4, 1876, centennial celebration by a black militia group led by Doc Adams, two white farmers arrived on the scene and demanded that Adams disperse his men so the two white men could pass through. Harsh words were exchanged. Adams eventually ordered his men to part and allow the whites to pass. Even so, the next day the farmer appeared before Judge Prince Rivers and demanded Adams's arrest. Rivers and Adams were black Republican leaders in this small town, Union Army veterans, and friends. Adams criticized the judge for hearing the case, whereupon Judge Rivers cited Adams for contempt of court and ordered him to stand trial on July 8.

On the day of the trial Adams's black militia gathered in the town, as did a large contingent of armed white men. Former Confederate general Matthew C. Butler, the area's most prominent Democratic politician, ordered Adams to disarm his militia. Fighting broke out between the militia and the armed white men. General Butler again ordered Adams to disarm his men, but the forty-member detail instead retreated to their barracks. General Butler then went into Augusta and returned with reinforcements: a cannon and hundreds of armed white men on horseback.

As night fell, the outnumbered and outgunned black militiamen tried to flee from the scene but were followed. Hamburg's black marshal was mortally wounded, and twenty-five militiamen were captured by Butler's men. One white youth was killed. Later, at about 2:00 A.M., five of the captive militiamen were murdered in cold blood. Butler's men then ransacked the homes and shops of the town's black citizens. Butler denied that he had ordered the executions but condoned them nevertheless.

This was too much even for Governor Chamberlain, whose earlier words and actions might be said to have encouraged such wanton violence against blacks. Chamberlain denounced the atrocity in the strongest terms. He wrote to one correspondent, "If you can find words to characterize this atrocity and barbarism, your power of language exceeds mine."[23]

Smalls demanded and received a congressional inquiry. Chamberlain called for a grand jury investigation. In August the grand jury indicted seven men for murder and named several dozen accessories. After the Democrats took over the legislature in the fall elections, however, all these men were acquitted.[24] And Butler was elected by the legislature to a seat in the U.S. Senate.

This incident and the reactions surrounding it doomed any chance that Chamberlain would be able to put together a fusion ticket with Democratic and Republican supporters. In the fall the Democrats nominated one of their own, the popular Wade Hampton. Although Hampton spoke of ending violence, which he said Chamberlain was not able to control, and promised to improve race relations, only one prominent black Republican to crossed over to support him. That was Martin R. Delaney, who expressed support for the Democratic Party's strong commitment to business and economic development. Smalls and most other Republicans endorsed Chamberlain. When the Republican State Convention met after fractious discussion over the governor's policies, they narrowly renominated him, but only after he agreed to accept two of his severest black Republican critics on the state ticket for lieutenant governor and attorney general.

With the Hamburg Massacre in mind, Smalls introduced an amendment to a bill designed to transfer army troops from the infantry to the cavalry and send them to provide security for the Texas frontier. His amendment would provide that "no troops should be drawn from South Carolina as long as the militia of that state peacefully assembled are assaulted, disarmed, and taken prisoners, and then massacred in cold blood by lawless bands of men invading that state from the state of Georgia."[25] Smalls was referring directly to the Hamburg Massacre and the role played by Butler, whom Smalls, without identifying by name, characterized as "one of the most malignant of the unreconstructed rebels."[26]

Introduction of this amendment brought Smalls into dramatic confrontation with two able, experienced white Democratic opponents of Reconstruction: Samuel Cox of Ohio and Congressman Charles Hooker of Mississippi. The exchanges on the floor of the House were bitter. In supporting his amendment, Smalls read from a South Carolina constituent's letter describing the Hamburg Massacre. The writer said that this report contained "facts, which I vouch for entirely, and are not distorted in any degree. It's plain unvarnished narration of painful and horrible truths."[27]

Smalls's reading of this letter was dramatic and touching, causing Cox to rise and challenge Smalls. Several Democrats shouted from the floor, requesting the name of its writer. Smalls refused to divulge the name, stating that he could vouch for its authenticity. Smalls stated, "I will say to the gentleman, if he is desirous that the name shall be given in order to have another Negro killed, he will not get it from me." He received great applause in the House for this response. This exchange drew Cox into the debate. Considered the leading intellectual and wit of Congress, Cox attacked Smalls. Smalls might vouch for the author of the letter, he said, but who would vouch for Smalls? Immediately Smalls answered, "A majority of 13,000," eliciting applause and laughter. Cox then launched into a long diatribe against the black Republican government of South Carolina, quoting from James S. Pike's *The Prostrate State* (1874) as evidence of its government corruption. After he had read a few pages, Smalls interrupted him to ask, "Have you the book there of the city of New York?" The House rocked with laughter, and Cox found himself at a loss for words. Later a New York Republican pointed out that nothing in South Carolina equaled the record of Democrats' extravagance and dishonesty in New York.[28]

Charles Hooker accused the black Republicans in South Carolina of promoting race war. He then asserted, "there was no friend of the colored man more sincere and more honest than he who was his master when the relations prevailed of master and slave." He continued, stating that "in other states blacks were forming Democratic organizations." At this Smalls rose to shout angrily "that is not so." He continued, "The colored people never voted the Democratic ticket except under intimidation."[29]

When the debate had concluded and a vote was taken, Smalls's amendment was approved. Moreover, President Grant, for whom Smalls had actively campaigned in South Carolina and in the Midwest, promised to send additional troops to South Carolina if they were necessary to keep the peace.

Smalls introduced a bill for the federal government to compensate South Carolina for its use of the Citadel at Charleston since the end of the war and to return this valuable property to the people of South Carolina. This and other measures introduced by Smalls were passed.

Smalls did not, however, win all his initiatives. A bill was introduced to reorganize and economize in the army and, in effect, to discontinue the black-only regiments. Smalls introduced an amendment designed to protect blacks from such a fate, but it was defeated.

By the time Congress adjourned in August 1876, Smalls had every reason to be satisfied that he had represented his state, his party, and his race well. To continue this work he had to win a second term. It was to that task and to the election of other Republicans, black and white, including candidates for governor and president, that Smalls turned his considerable talent and energies.

The 1876 election was crucial for Republicans not only in South Carolina but also throughout the nation. Smalls presided over the Republican State Convention.

In the past two years Governor Chamberlain had lived up to his promises of reform. He was popular among Republicans and even among some Democrats. In addition, Democratic-leaning newspapers supported a coalition to back Chamberlain's reelection. The state convention, managed by Smalls, renominated Chamberlain for a second term. The Democrats named Wade Hampton, a Confederate hero, as their candidate for governor and backed a slate of other white men as well. The ensuing campaign was fraught with record levels of violence and fraud on both sides.

Eager to use his military experience and commitment to public service, Smalls had joined the South Carolina State Militia shortly after the war. In 1869 he enlisted in the Lincoln Republican Guard, whose Charleston location required him to commute for exercises. Members were drawn principally from Charleston, Beaufort, and Columbia. Calling itself the "African Turners," the company included black men who rose to high positions in Republican politics: the Reverend Cain, Cardozo, Wright, Whipper, De Large, and Ransier. The unit marched into Charleston on July 4, 1868, under arms, bringing up the rear of an almost all-black parade.

Smalls received an officer's commission in 1870 and was made lieutenant colonel of the Third Regiment (First Brigade). He held this position for two years. In December 1871, Governor Scott appointed him brigadier general of the First Brigade. In his capacity as commander of this brigade, Smalls got the opportunity to review the Third Regiment at an Emancipation Day ceremony in Beaufort on January 1, 1872, the occasion on which he read General Saxton's letter about corruption in the legislature. In 1873 Smalls was appointed major general of the Second Division.

In the spring and summer of 1876, Governor Chamberlain gave Smalls a special assignment, which arose from a long-running dispute between black rice workers and their white planter employers. Workers on several plantations near the lower Combahee River and the Ashepoo River disputed the contracts they were forced to sign shortly after the war. In the spring and summer of 1876, the dispute came to a head. When harvest time came in August, some of the day workers, as contrasted with contract workers, went on strike because of low wages and working conditions. Not only were their wages too low to sustain their families, but they also objected to workers being recruited from outside the area. Another grievance was payment in plantation scrip rather than cash. The scrip could be spent only at company stores and not used to pay other bills, including taxes or doctor bills. The workers demanded, at least, to be paid in cash.

This situation was particularly embarrassing to Governor Chamberlain, who was courting support from both blacks and whites. When violence broke out between strikers and would-be new workers, local whites—fearing that the local militia and law enforcement agents could not handle the situation—appealed to the governor for intervention. Distrusting the primarily black local militia, whites created armed posses, under the guise of rifle clubs, to break up the riots. This in turn caused further tension. There were somewhere between forty and sixty armed white men on horseback confronting hundreds of unarmed but determined black strikers when the governor received an appeal to prevent a bloody race riot.

On August 23, Governor Chamberlain dispatched General Smalls to the scene. He also sent along Lt. Governor Richard H. Gleaves, who was also black. Their assignment was to bring calm to the situation. The strikers were determined to stand by their demands and block those attempting to take their jobs. Local whites welcomed the intervention by Smalls and Gleaves and hoped that they could persuade the strikers to go back to work. The strikers, on the other hand, did not welcome these emissaries from the governor. Indeed, one of the black strikers was reported to have said that "if Robert Smalls attempted to interfere with them they would tie him up and give him one hundred and fifty lashes on his big fat ass."[30]

Smalls spent the first day sizing up the strikers and the white posse. The next day he reported to Chamberlain that there were some three hundred armed striking workers. Even though he recognized some as members of the militia, they did not carry their weapons. He reported also that "the presence of forty to sixty mounted white men, armed with Spencer rifles, sixteen shooters, and double-barreled shot guns, did much to alarm and excite the strikers."[31]

By the time Smalls arrived, seven strikers had reportedly whipped two strike breakers. The local trial judge brought charges against the seven and ordered them to submit to arrest. When they refused the judge's request, a group of armed white men ordered them to turn themselves in. They again refused.

Smalls, who was unarmed, addressed the men in their Gullah language. As commander of the state militia, he then asked them to surrender. When they went to do so, the judge could not be found, so Smalls ordered the men to walk fourteen miles and surrender to the Beaufort sheriff, which they did. They stayed in jail overnight and were released for time served. The planters agreed to pay the men their wages in cash, and they all returned to work.

Smalls won his bid for reelection, but Chamberlain lost the governorship to Wade Hampton in a close race that was long contested. This election and the seating of a white Democratic majority in the state legislature signaled the end of Reconstruction in South Carolina. Reconstruction ended in the other ten southern states around the same time with the simultaneous election of Democratic governors and Democratic majorities in their state legislatures.

Among the achievements of the Reconstruction government was the opening of the University of South Carolina to black and white students alike in 1873.[32] One of the early black undergraduates was Hannibal B. Kershaw, who in 1879 became the first black graduate of Grinnell College in Iowa.[33]

While women could not vote or hold office during Reconstruction, they did take part in this political revolution. Educators Charlotte Forten and Laura Towne were prominent in the movement. At one rally an organized group of black women physically attacked white male Democrats. At another rally a woman asked Smalls what wives should do if their husbands planned to vote for Democrats. He is reported to have said: "Tell them they will have to find another bed to sleep in."

IO

They Tried to Cut Him Down

The Trial of Robert Smalls, November 9, 1877

Autumn 1877 was a watershed in the life of Robert Smalls. On October 6, 1877, during his first term in Congress and while Congress was in session, police arrested Smalls at his home in Beaufort. He was charged with having accepted a bribe four years earlier, when he was a member of the state senate. In short order he was arraigned, indicted, tried, found guilty, and sentenced to serve three years at hard labor in the state penitentiary.

Smalls's conviction caused great distress to his family and friends, members of the declining Republican Party, and blacks all over the state. It also caused an uproar on the floor of Congress and throughout the North, where Smalls was held in high esteem.

Meanwhile South Carolina Democrats were as jubilant over the conviction of Smalls as they were over their gaining control of state government after the 1876 elections. Both events were interrelated. For nearly ten years Smalls had been the point man in the Republican Party. Opposition to him from Democrats and the daily press was often personal and visceral. This conviction was the only serious blemish on Smalls's record in more than fifty years of dedicated public service, hanging like a dark cloud over his many public achievements during the rest of his long life.

The judgment widely shared among his descendants, informed persons today, and his family and attorneys at that time was that Smalls's arrest and conviction had little to do with what Smalls did, or was accused of having done, in the state senate in 1873. He was tried for his seizure of the *Planter* in 1862, for having served the Union, and for his successful leadership in politics, government, and business since the war.

Specifically, Smalls's arrest and conviction were a consequence of the flawed 1876 elections at the national and state levels. These results included the ascendancy of Rutherford B. Hayes to the presidency, Wade Hampton's election as governor of South Carolina, and the Democratic take over of the General Assembly and state judiciary.

Smalls was an active participant in the national and state elections of 1876. On election night he had reason to believe that out of a hard-fought and highly flawed campaign had come, once again, victory. At the national level Rutherford B. Hayes, the Republican for whom Smalls had campaigned, lost the popular vote to Tilden, but won the election. In the governor's race Smalls's candidate, Daniel Chamberlain, won a majority of the votes cast and was legally considered governor. Much to his personal delight, Smalls won a bitter fight against Democrat George. D. Tillman for election to his second term in the U.S. Congress. Two of his friends, J. H. Rainey and R. H. Cain, were reelected to the U.S. House of Representatives. This meant that South Carolina's five-member delegation to Congress was again biracial and majority black. Smalls's good friend Francis L. Cardozo won his third statewide election as state treasurer.

Remarkably, however, when the dust settled from the 1876 election, Smalls and his cause had lost the governorship, both houses of the state legislature, the state judiciary—and the support of the president they had helped to elect. The 1876 elections marked the end of Reconstruction, the beginning of a long eclipse in the political and civil fortunes of African Americans, and the end of the Republican Party in South Carolina. Historian Walter Edgar has characterized the 1876 election as "the return of the old order," when the white elite who had ruled the state during slavery returned to power with a determination to reestablish slavery in every way but in name.[1] This force swept across the South, carrying blacks and Republicans out of power and sweeping Smalls into trial, conviction, and jail. (He was eventually pardoned.)

Target Congressman Robert Smalls

The trial of 1877 was the second Democratic assault on Congressman Smalls. In the fall 1876 elections, Democrats tried diligently to prevent Smalls's reelection. In a district with an overwhelmingly black population, with registered voters two-to-one in favor of Republicans, and with Smalls the most popular and powerful politician in the district, Democrats put forth a white candidate, George D. Tillman. Brother of Ben Tillman, George was little known in the district but had powerful family connections statewide. In the end all means fair and foul had failed, and Smalls was overwhelmingly reelected to his second term. Tillman contested the election results to no avail. The Democrats in Congress saw no reason to take up Tillman's challenge until toward the end of the term and then ruled in favor of Smalls. When Congress ruled for Smalls, George Tillman took it with grace and humor, congratulating Smalls, "with whom I am glad to say, I always get along pleasantly." While commending the Republicans who supported Smalls, Tillman chastised the Democrats for abandoning him in favor of Smalls.[2]

Unbiased in serving his constituents, white as well as black, Smalls even introduced a private bill to the benefit of Edgefield's postmaster, Lacon R. Tillman, a relative of his political opponent.[3] However, this was only the beginning of Smalls's encounters with the Tillmans, which became increasingly acrimonious.

Compromise of 1876

How did the election of Republican Rutherford B. Hayes in 1877 have a negative impact on Robert Smalls's career? As an elected delegate to the 1876 Republican convention in Cincinnati, Smalls was appointed to the convention's rules committee, which governed the order of business of the convention.[4] He led the biracial South Carolina delegation in support of the successful nomination of Hayes, former Republican governor of Ohio. Democrats selected Samuel J. Tilden of New York. Smalls campaigned for Hayes in the North and in South Carolina. While both these candidates were considered to be moderates who believed in reconciliation between the North and the South, the fact that Hayes was Republican, following in the footsteps of Lincoln and Grant, gave him the edge with northern and southern black voters. Smalls was disappointed when Hayes lost a majority of the popular votes cast in that election. However, though Tilden won the popular vote, the election deadlocked in the Electoral College, where Tilden won a plurality but was one vote short of the absolute majority required. This meant, according to the Constitution, that the winner of the election had to be decided by the House of Representatives with each state delegation casting a single vote.

When the presidential election was held in the House of Representatives, Smalls cast his support to Hayes; however, support for the two candidates was evenly divided in the House, which was unable to declare a winner. Months of negotiations ensued. In an effort to resolve the matter, the House named a special elections committee to decide the outcome, but this committee was also equally divided. After a while the southern Democratic forces proposed a resolution, which came to be known as the Hayes-Tilden Compromise. The southern Democrats agreed to throw their support to the northern Republican Hayes (and against their own Democratic candidate Tilden), thus making Hayes president of the United States. Their provision was that Hayes would use his authority as president and commander-in-chief of the armed forces to withdraw federal troops from the South.

Congressman Smalls was distressed by the proposed compromise. He desperately wanted Hayes to become president and had no doubt that Tilden would support the Democratic South in every way to overturn Reconstruction, including removal of federal troops. Hayes, Smalls prayed, being a Republican and heir to the mantles of Grant and Lincoln, could be counted on to uphold the Republican platform.

After three months of deadlock and delay, events moved swiftly. On March 4, 1877, Hayes was sworn in as president, and on March 9 Smalls took a delegation of prominent black Republicans to the president's office to plead for the continued occupation of federal troops in the South. Frederick Douglass had already called on the president, and Booker T. Washington had also urged Hayes not to withdraw the federal troops. The Smalls delegation—which also included J. H. Rainey, R. H. Cain, J. J. Wright, and several other South Carolina Republican leaders[5]—had campaigned for Hayes in South Carolina and had been successful in carrying the state for him. The president met with Smalls's delegation for some forty minutes, thanking them for their support and congratulating them on their reelection. Then, urging Hayes not to withdraw the federal troops from the South, the delegation explained that this action would give Democrats free reign to gain control of state governments, overturn Republican victories, and negate the results of the Civil War and Reconstruction. Hayes promised to consider their views before taking action, but he had already made a commitment to withdraw federal troops from the South. This was not the last time that Smalls was disappointed in the actions of a Republican president, but there could hardly have been another Republican betrayal so destructive of the well-being of black people and democracy in the South. Since it was not in Smalls's nature to quit, he had no choice but to continue the Republican fight for justice, which had been crippled by its own Republican leader.

Dual Governorship in South Carolina

The South Carolina gubernatorial election also damaged Smalls and paved the path to his trial and conviction. While the closeness of the presidential election had led to no selection of president for several months, the bitter election in South Carolina had resulted in two governors over much the same period. After the 1876 elections Chamberlain clung to the governor's office, to which he claimed to have been reelected. Meanwhile, General Hampton proclaimed that he had been elected governor and proceeded to exercise certain gubernatorial prerogatives.

Smalls was intimately involved with the governorship of South Carolina. He had been a principal organizer of the Republican Party of Beaufort County, and no Republican could have been elected governor without Smalls's support or without backing black leaders in their pursuit of other statewide offices. Thus, Smalls bore some responsibility for the corruption emanating from the governor's office, particularly during the terms of Scott and Moses.

Daniel H. Chamberlain was of a different sort. He was more qualified than his predecessors, more committed to the principles of freedom and equality embedded in the Republican Party, and endowed with strong moral integrity. He was a genuine reformer.[6] As perhaps the most powerful leader in the state Republican Party, Smalls had supported Chamberlain. By the 1876 elections Smalls and Chamberlain had formed a formidable personal and political partnership. They campaigned extensively for Hayes for president, for Chamberlain for governor, and for Smalls and other Republicans for Congress. Perhaps what held Smalls and Chamberlain together was their commitment to the principles of the Republican Party—a commitment to which many of their colleagues paid only lip service. Indeed, in 1874 Chamberlain—with the active support of Republican leaders, including Richard Gleaves, Francis L. Cardozo, and Smalls —had launched a campaign against corruption within the party, which the press and some Democrats welcomed with surprise and enthusiasm. Some Democrats even talked of supporting Chamberlain or not fielding a Democratic candidate against him.

Smalls's support for Governor Chamberlain's campaign is reflected in a resolution of the Beaufort Republican Party. When the *Beaufort Tribune* accused county treasurer George Holmes of misconduct in office, Republican Party officials came to his defense, passing a resolution that Smalls, as party chair, forwarded to Chamberlain. The resolution was introduced by Thomas E. Miller —later congressman, state legislator, and the first president of South Carolina State University—about whom not a single charge of corruption was ever sustained. The resolution shows strong support for their fellow political leader and, even more noteworthy, strong support for Governor Chamberlain's campaign to root out corruption.

Campaign in Edgefield

The Edgefield County campaign demonstrates how Smalls and Chamberlain supported each other and the Republican Party in the face of personal and political peril. On August 12, 1876, Smalls left Washington and joined Chamberlain in Columbia for campaigning.[7] The next day they took a train to Edgefield, "the heart of red shirt country." Completing the final leg of the trip by carriage, they were constantly heckled by red shirts, Wade Hampton's paramilitary force. At the meeting site, where some fifteen hundred, mostly black, Republicans gathered, Smalls and Chamberlain also encountered several hundred white Democrats who had come to heckle them. The Democrats demanded that their leaders be given equal speaking time. To keep the peace and out of a sense of fairness, Chamberlain agreed. The governor spoke first amid constant heckling. The Democrats circled the platform, keeping back many of the Republicans. The governor spoke of reconciliation, honesty in government, and the right of suffrage for all men. He urged the crowd to listen to both sides, which would reaffirm their duty to come to the polls and vote for the Republicans.

Then General Matthew C. Butler spoke for the Democrats while his associate Martin W. Gary stood by in support. Butler denounced the governor and the Republicans with incendiary language. He denounced Smalls for saying on the floor of the U.S. Congress that Butler was a leader of the Ku Klux Klan and then shouted: "I dare him to open his lips on this stand today."[8]

Smalls rose and approached the platform. The denunciations became louder and more hostile. "Kill the damned nigger" was heard frequently. Amid the commotion, the platform collapsed. Smalls and Chamberlain retreated to the village, where the crowd followed them, but they were not allowed to speak. As Chamberlain and Smalls boarded the train for the return to Columbia, the red shirts who had followed them to the station, some boarding the train, shouted epithets at Smalls in particular.

While Smalls and Chamberlain were sitting side by side, one of Chamberlain's aides handed Smalls a pistol, which he was entitled to carry as militia major general and commander. Smalls laid the pistol on his lap, where it stayed during the trip back to Columbia.

After a few days in Columbia, Smalls took the train to Beaufort on August 16, 1877. He was met at the station by black and white supporters along with Allen's Brass Band, which he had organized and funded. They all gave him a rousing welcome.[9]

Return to Edgefield

After a few days of rest and planning, Smalls was back on the campaign trail, and Edgefield was high on his list. Though Edgefield was a stronghold of the Democrats, Smalls had carried the county in his first election for Congress. He

had not relished the experience of having been run out of town a few days earlier and vowed, "I shall return."

This time when Smalls returned to Edgefield, he went without Chamberlain. He was accompanied by some state militia officers. Butler and Gary were
again on hand as were many armed white men. This time, however, there was
no violence or personal confrontation, and Smalls spoke to the people who had
come to hear him. Later, when asked in a congressional committee why he
returned to Edgefield, Smalls stated that he felt honor- and duty-bound to do
so. He wanted to show the voters that he was not afraid and to encourage them
not to fear turning out to cast their ballots for the Republican ticket.[10] By showing up as a congressman and militia commander surrounded by loyal troops,
Smalls demonstrated that he could protect his supporters in their quest for
political expression.

General Hampton Becomes Governor

When President Hayes was inaugurated in March 1877, the South Carolina
governorship was still in dispute. The election of Chamberlain, who claimed a
majority of votes cast, had been certified by the Republican-controlled election
commission. He had refused to vacate the governor's office, and federal troops
had been assigned to protect him. General Wade Hampton, claiming to be the
properly elected governor, was pressing his case for recognition and acting in
certain respects as though he were governor.

Both Chamberlain and Hampton appealed to the president for recognition
as the legally elected governor. In an effort to be conciliatory to the South,
Hayes invited first Chamberlain and then Hampton to come to Washington
and discuss the matter with him.

After consulting with both men, President Hayes executed what might be
called a "double whammy." First, he decided to recognize Hampton as governor. Then on April 3, 1877, he ordered all federal troops to withdraw from
their posts in South Carolina, including the statehouse and governor's mansion,
and return to their barracks. That order sounded the death knell for Reconstruction. Without federal-troop protection, the fragile democracy could not
stand. General T. W. Grant carried out the order on April 10, 1877.[11] The jubilation this action brought to white South Carolina was matched by the gloom
it brought to the state's blacks. It created a breach that only began to be closed
a hundred years later.

After having staunchly resisted what he considered the illegal and violent
machinations of the Democrats for six months, Governor Chamberlain gave up
his fight. On April 11, 1877, he surrendered the governor's office to Hampton,

rode with his family to the depot, took a train to the North, and never returned to South Carolina.

At the same time Democrats also gained control of the South Carolina legislature for the first time since the state was readmitted to the Union. The Republican president's withdrawal of federal troops, the ascendancy of a Democratic governor, and the Democrats' capture of both houses of the legislature and then the judiciary signaled the end of Reconstruction in South Carolina.

Removal of Associate Justice Jonathan J. Wright

Smalls was not alone in being targeted for removal from high office. State supreme court justice Jonathan Jasper Wright and state treasurer Francis L. Cardozo also suffered legal persecution and political bullying.

Born on February 11, 1840, in Pennsylvania, Wright was one of six children born to Samuel Wright and his wife, Jane. Samuel Wright had gone North from Maryland as a runaway from slavery on the underground railroad. The family settled in Springfield, Pennsylvania, and joined the Springfield Presbyterian Church. Jonathan was trained in private schools to prepare for the bar exam. However, because of racial bias in Pennsylvania at that time, he was not allowed to take the exam and, instead, became a schoolteacher.

Wright came to South Carolina in April 1865 as a teacher for the black Union soldiers. He settled in Beaufort. A year later he returned to Pennsylvania, where in 1866 he passed the state bar, becoming the first black attorney licensed in Pennsylvania. In January 1867 he returned to Beaufort County, where under Smalls's political influence he became active in education, as well as legal and political work. Recruited by Smalls into the Republican Party, Wright was elected along with Smalls and others to the 1868 state Constitutional Convention as a delegate from Beaufort County. Then in the first free General Assembly elections, Wright was elected the sole senator from Beaufort County; Smalls was elected to the house, as was attorney William J. Whipper, also from Beaufort and Smalls and Wright's close political colleague.[12]

When Wright and Whipper both sought election to the state supreme court, Smalls, as a friend of both candidates, faced a dilemma over which one to support. He decided to support his House colleague Whipper. Among the many ironies of the period is that, if Smalls had been successful with his candidate for the court, Smalls would not have been elected to the state senate or as chair of the Committee on Printing because Wright would have retained his senate seat. During the joint session of the legislature, when their nominations were being considered, it is said that the two candidates sat side by side and chatted amicably during the speeches and voting.

Wright won the election handily, getting seventy-two votes to Whipper's fifty-seven with five going to other candidates. Wright's election margin showed that he received votes from senate and house members, Republicans and Democrats, and blacks and whites. For the next six years on the state supreme court, Wright lived up to the confidence that had been placed in him across these various lines of demarcation. During his tenure he wrote some ninety-four decisions, an impressive 90 percent of which were cited in later opinions by the courts. None of Wright's decisions has ever been overruled.

After the Democrats took control of the legislature in 1877, they moved quickly to force Wright from office. On April 14, 1877, three days after taking office, Hampton sent Wright a letter demanding that he resign. In an effort to clean house, Hampton sent similar letters to other Republican officeholders. At first Wright refused to resign on the grounds that the term to which he had been duly elected by the legislature had not yet expired and that he had done nothing to dishonor his office. Both facts were true, uncontested, and irrelevant. In swift reaction to Wright's refusal to resign, the house on May 1, 1877, appointed a five-man committee to investigate him. Ten days later, on May 11, the committee issued its report. Wright's honorable record, his nonpartisanship on the bench, and his upright personal conduct were so evident that the only negative example the committee could report was that Wright had been accused of "drunkenness." No proof was presented; none was necessary. The committee gave Wright no opportunity to respond to its finding. The committee, the legislature, and the governor had made up their minds and did not wish to be distracted by matters of fact, truth, or justice.

In consequence, on June 6, 1877, four months before Smalls's arrest, the Democrat-controlled house voted to impeach Judge Wright by a vote of seventy-five to twenty-three, without even extending him the privilege of testifying in his own defense. The resolution of impeachment was passed on to the Democrat-controlled senate with a recommendation for confirmation and thus Wright's expulsion from office.

Like Governor Chamberlain before him, Justice Wright bowed to the political and physical force that had overtaken him. In August 1877, after four months of defiance, Wright sent a letter to the governor stating that he would resign his office effective December 1, 1877. Hampton accepted the resignation with a conciliatory note to Wright. Later Hampton appointed Wright to a minor post in his administration, and Wright supported Hampton for reelection in 1878. Wright lectured in the North for a while, but his heart belonged to South Carolina. He settled down to the practice of law in Charleston and taught law courses at Claflin College in Orangeburg, South Carolina. Hampton once visited Wright in Orangeburg and had dinner with him, causing a stir in both black and white communities. Wright died on February 19, 1885. In his will he left his considerable property to his law students at Claflin College and to his siblings in Pennsylvania.

The Purge of State Treasurer Francis L. Cardozo

In 1877 the state treasurer, Francis L. Cardozo, became the next high-profile black Republican to fall victim to Democratic governor Wade Hampton and the Democratic legislature. Cardozo was removed from office in a most disgraceful and humiliating manner.

Born in Charleston on January 1, 1836, to a free black mother, Lydia Williams, and a Jewish father, Isaac Nunez, a customs official in Charleston, Cardozo was always identified as an African American. His parents sent him to schools for free black children operated by other free blacks in Charleston before the Civil War. Later they sent him to the University of Glasgow for three years of study, then to further study at Edinburgh and London. When he returned to Charleston in 1864, he was described as the most learned man in Charleston, black or white.[13]

After the war, Cardozo was a founder and the first superintendent of the Avery Institute for African American students. In the first election under the 1868 Constitution, he was elected secretary of state. He left South Carolina in 1871 to serve briefly as professor of law at Howard University in Washington, D.C. He returned to South Carolina in 1872 and was elected state treasurer, the second highest office in the state. Cardozo was reelected in 1874 and again in 1876.

While in Columbia serving as state treasurer, thirty-eight-year-old Cardozo entered the University of South Carolina School of Law in 1873 and graduated with his law degree in 1876. In Cardozo's graduating class, there were six other blacks and two whites. The year before there had been three blacks and two whites, and the previous year only one black and four white law students graduated.

Governor Hampton wrote to Cardozo on April 14, 1877, demanding that he resign. Cardozo replied that he had just been reelected to his third term as state treasurer and refused to resign. Then the Democratic Joint House/Senate Investigating Committee brought charges that Cardozo had committed eight counts of fraud in the handling of his official duties.

Like Chamberlain and Wright, Cardozo realized that his case, if not his cause, was lost. He submitted his resignation to Hampton on May 1, 1877. Despite his resignation, however, he was indicted on eight charges of illegalities in the performance of his duties. A judge dismissed seven charges, but Cardozo was tried in Richland County on the charge "that he conspired to issue fraudulent pay certificates." His defense attorney was Samuel W. Melton, the brother of a former law professor who had taught Cardozo in law school. The prosecutor was the new Democratic attorney general, James Conner.

The trial began on November 1, 1876. Cardozo was charged on one count of misuse of his office as state treasurer.[14] The chief witness against Cardozo was former Republican speaker of the house Samuel J. Lee, who was also black. Lee testified under oath that he had conspired with Cardozo to issue the fraudulent pay certificates. He admitted that he had made an arrangement with state authorities to testify against Cardozo in exchange for not being prosecuted himself. A second witness against Cardozo was Josephus Woodruff, former Republican clerk of the state senate, who swore that he witnessed the transaction that Lee described. Woodruff, charged with several crimes, had fled South Carolina to avoid prosecution. He was extradited and given immunity in exchange for his testimony against Cardozo and Smalls.

Smalls sat in the courtroom throughout Cardozo's trial. Cardozo was convicted, and his sentence was suspended pending his appeal to the state supreme court. The court refused to hear the case. He spent several months in jail over the next two years until he was pardoned by Governor William L. Simpson, who succeeded Hampton. Simpson pardoned Cardozo in an agreement between the state and the federal governments to drop charges against some Democrats for election fraud and participation in the Hamburg Massacre.

After his release from jail, Cardozo left the state he had served so well and faithfully. He returned to Washington, D.C., where he had previously taught at Howard University. He took a job at the U.S. Treasury Department and served six years until 1884, when Grover Cleveland became president and dismissed him. Cardozo withdrew from politics and legal work and returned to education. He was principal of a Washington high school for more than a decade. Later, the school was named for Cardozo.

The Trial and Conviction of Robert Smalls

The October 6, 1877, edition of the *Charleston News and Courier* newspaper blasted this headline across its front page: "Robert Smalls, the former senator from this county, and now claiming to be congressman from this district, was arrested today and taken to Columbia"[15] Smalls was arrested at his home on Prince Street in Beaufort by state police on the morning of October 6, 1877, while his ailing mother, Lydia; his wife, Hannah; his children; and other relatives and supporters stood by in agony. They were with him because he had prepared them to expect his arrest. He had assured them, however, that he would not be convicted. Smalls surrendered promptly and went stoically with his captors.

The officers handcuffed him, taking him by carriage to the railroad station and from there by train to Columbia. They arrived in Columbia around noon of the same day. From the depot they took him by carriage to the Richland County Courthouse, where Judge J. Q. Marshall was waiting for them. Smalls's able and well-respected attorney, Samuel J. Melton, who had been waiting at the station, accompanied Smalls to his arraignment. The state attorney general and prosecutor read an indictment that a county grand jury had returned under seal in response to a report of the Joint House and Senate Investigating Committee. The judge ordered Smalls to return to court for the preliminary hearing on October 8, 1877. Melton persuaded the judge to release Smalls on a $5,000 bond.

On October 8, the attorney general called Smalls's sole accuser, Josephus Woodruff, who swore under oath that he had given Smalls $5,000 in 1873 in payment for Smalls's support of a House and Senate resolution to award a printing contract of $350,000 to Woodruff's Republican Printing Company. Smalls was then chair of the Senate Printing Committee and had substantial authority to influence the printing contract award.

Judge Marshall ruled that there was sufficient evidence to seek an indictment. He released Smalls on another $5,000 bond. Smalls returned to Beaufort and visited with his family for a few days while conducting further discussions with his attorney. Then Smalls took the train to Washington, where he arrived on October 15, just in time to be sworn into his seat for the second session of the Forty-fifth Congress.

Smalls did not have to wait long before being interrupted by news from South Carolina. On October 22, 1877, the grand jury, on the basis of Woodruff's testimony alone, brought in an indictment charging Smalls with receiving a bribe in 1873 while he was a member of the state senate.

Smalls took a leave of absence from Congress and returned to Columbia to work with his attorney and others preparing his defense. He arrived in time to observe the trial of his friend Francis L. Cardozo.

An Indictment Is a Conviction

Smalls reported that after his indictment and before his trial, John R. Cochrane, a Republican known to Smalls, visited him as an emissary from Hampton and the Democrats:

Mr. Cochrane, the Chairman of that great investigating committee appointed by the Legislature of South Carolina, said to me, "Smalls, you had better resign." "Resign what!" "Resign your seat in Congress." "What," said I, "the seat the people elected me to!" "Yes; you had better resign, because if you don't they are going to convict you." Said I, "I don't believe that, sir. I am innocent and they cannot do it." "Well," said he, "bear in mind that these men have got the court, they have got the jury, and an indictment is a conviction." I did not believe it, but I tell you those gentlemen taught me it was so. And it was so.[16]

Moreover, Smalls reported that the Democrats offered to pay him $5,000, which he refused.

To help Melton in his defense, Smalls hired another attorney, Richard B. Carpenter, who had impeccable credentials and a spotless reputation. In 1872 Carpenter had been a candidate for governor on the Conservative Party ticket. In 1873, as a judge, he had dismissed charges against Smalls in another case for lack of credible evidence. That case was brought under Republican rule and based on evidence also provided by Josephus Woodruff, then clerk of the senate and a political ally of Smalls.

Jurisdiction

Smalls's trial began on November 7, 1877, in the Richland County Court of General Sessions, Judge C. P. Townsend presiding. Melton moved right away that the trial be moved from the Richland County court to the federal district court. He argued that as a U.S. congressman, Smalls was entitled to have his case heard in federal court. The judge called a recess to consider this motion. Two days later he ruled against it, and the trial resumed. Melton then introduced another motion with affidavits arguing that Smalls should not be on trial at this time because Congress was in session. Pointing out that, as a congressman, Smalls was required to be on duty in Washington carrying out his federal responsibilities, Melton argued for a delay until the session concluded. Attorney General James Connor and prosecutor Leroy F. Youmans argued vigorously against Melton's motion. Judge Townsend ruled against it and ordered the trial to begin. This became a major issue on appeal.

The Jury

The twelve-man jury consisted of seven black and five white men. Smalls testified later that he knew all these men. One juror, William J. Martin, was seated by the judge against Melton's objection, even though Smalls still had left a preemptory challenge, which allowed him to object to and bar any juror without cause. This also constituted a major issue on appeal. As further assessment of the jury, Smalls pointed out that all five white men and two of the blacks were Democrats. Moreover, he argued that all twelve on this jury had worked for and voted for General Wade Hampton in the fall 1876 gubernatorial election. Some scholars have sought to make much of the fact that the jury was predominantly black. But apparently, whatever proclivity they might have had to favor Smalls, the political situation and fear outweighed not only racial pride but also a sense of fairness and justice. Smalls's assertion is only one of several questions about the impartiality of the jury, as his attorney argued vigorously on appeal.

Prime Witness: Josephus Woodruff

As the trial got under way, the prosecution called to the stand Josephus Wood-ruff, who repeated his earlier testimony under oath that on January 19, 1873, he had given Robert Smalls a check for $5,000 to secure Smalls's support in the printing contract award. When asked how he came to remember so precisely giving this check to Smalls, Woodruff produced what he said was his diary and proceeded to read to the jury from the text, which stated that on January 19 he delivered the check for $5,000 to Senator Smalls.

There were several problems with Woodruff's testimony. One was that the diary he produced was not written in standard English, standard shorthand, or any other language but in markings that Woodruff had made up and that only he could read, understand, and interpret. Therefore neither Smalls's attorneys, the judge, the jury, nor anyone else could read the diary entry. Despite Melton's objections, Judge Townsend allowed Woodruff to read from the diary to refresh his memory and then read it to the jury, and he allowed all this testimony to stand as evidence.

Another problem with the testimony was that Woodruff read from his diary that the check had been written on the South Carolina Bank and Trust Company, where Woodruff had an account. He produced several canceled checks he had written. The one dated January 19, 1873, was written as follows: "Pay to cash, or bearer, five thousand dollars." Attorney Melton objected that the check was not written to Smalls at all and had not been endorsed by Smalls or any-one else. Nothing about the check connected it to Smalls or the South Carolina Bank and Trust Company, "to which my client, the defendant, was and is a stranger." Smalls did not have an account at that bank and would not have made a deposit there. Woodruff responded that he wrote the check in that way to be cautious and protective of Smalls, knowing that Smalls or anyone could cash the check. He insisted that he handed that check to Smalls on that date.

Yet another issue that caused considerable stir was that the check was dated January 19, 1873. Melton pointed out that in 1873 January 19 fell on a Sunday and wondered how Smalls had deposited it on the same day when both the senate and the bank were closed. Woodruff responded that he knowingly dated the check for January 19 and gave it to Smalls on Saturday the eighteenth because he was not sure his balance in the bank was sufficient on that day to cover it. Woodruff could not explain why, if his balance was not sufficient to cover the $5,000 check on Saturday, January 18, it would be sufficient to cover it on Sunday the nineteenth when the next business day was not until Monday, January 20.

The prosecution next called to the witness stand Lawrence W. Zealy, an employee of the South Carolina Bank and Trust Company, to verify Woodruff's assertion that Smalls had deposited the check on January 18. Zealy produced a slip of paper, containing a handwritten note dated January 18, which read: "Deposited by Hon. Robert Smalls, $5,000." There was no place for Smalls's or Woodruff's signature on the deposit slip. A handwritten "AW" on the deposit slip was interpreted to mean Woodruff had written the check on his account at that bank and that on the same day it was deposited by Smalls. Though the check was dated January 19, the bank had honored it on January 18 because Woodruff's account was sufficient to cover it. The bank could not produce the actual canceled check. Nor could it produce an account in Smalls's name or a deposit.

How then did they account for this deposit slip written in pencil and dated January 18? On cross-examination, Zealy admitted that he did not write the deposit slip. He said it was written by another bank employee, a Mr. Jacobs, who had worked as a cashier at the bank in 1873. Zealy further testified that Jacobs did not come to testify in this case because he had been fired by the bank. Melton learned that Jacobs was still alive and still in the United States, so he could have been called to testify. Moreover, Zealy revealed that Jacobs had been charged by the Democratic investigating committee with at least four criminal acts of perjury and had left the state as a fugitive from justice. Despite vigorous questioning by Melton, Judge Townsend allowed all Woodruff's and Zealy's testimony to stand and to be considered by the jury.

Smalls's attorney pointed out that the joint resolution, which Woodruff said he bribed Smalls to support with his payment on January 18 had already been approved by the legislature on December 16 with Smalls voting in favor. How could a person be bribed to take an action that he had taken a month earlier? To constitute a bribe, the payment would need to have been agreed on before the resolution vote. Woodruff testified that even though his payment to Smalls occurred a month after the vote to approve the resolution, he had actually promised Smalls before the vote that if Smalls supported it, he would give Smalls

$5,000. Woodruff could not explain why it took him so long after the vote to pay his obligation. Melton thought that this sworn testimony, like others before, was less than convincing and without verification. Still Judge Townsend let the testimony stand.

The Verdict

The case went to the jury on November 10, 1877. Despite the holes in the testimony, Woodruff's unsavory character, Zealy's unreliability, and the excellent defense put on by Melton and Carpenter, the jury returned the following day with a verdict of "guilty as charged." According to one report, Smalls was stunned with disbelief. On hearing the verdict, he stood in his place and glared at the judge for nearly sixty seconds. There was jubilation among the Democrats and the press, however.

Melton was sure that the case put on by the prosecution was not strong enough to justify a conviction, referring to "the uncorroborated testimony of an admitted felon." Smalls was more direct, saying that he had been convicted "by the testimony of a self confessed thief who admitted under oath that he had been granted immunity from trial because he had promised the prosecution to testify against me."[17]

A $10,000 Bribe Offer

After the trial and before the sentence, Smalls received another emissary from Hampton and the Democrats, a newspaper editor from Aiken, whom Smalls identified as Mr. Drayton. Smalls recalled the conversation:

> He came to me and said, "Smalls, we don't want to harm you. Get out of the way. We know you were kind to our people just after the surrender, and Governor Hampton says he doesn't want to injure you. We want this government, and we must have it. If you will vacate your office we will pay you $10,000 for your two years' salary." Said I, "Mr. Drayton, where did you get this money to give me!" Said he, "Smalls, don't you ask that. We have got the money. The people of South Carolina have paid in 10 percent on their taxes to perpetuate the Hampton government and we intend to have it." Said I, "Sir, if you want me to resign my position you must call meetings all over the Congressional District and get those people who elected me to pass resolutions requiring me to resign, and then you can have the office without a penny. Otherwise I would suffer myself to go into the penitentiary and rot before I would resign an office that I was elected to on a trumped-up charge against me for the purpose of making me resign."

Smalls continued, "Make me resign when I am innocent; make me resign when the only testimony against me is that of a self-confessed thief."[18] By now Smalls had gotten accustomed to this verdict, and was already planning his appeal all the way to the U.S. Supreme Court.

The Sentence

On November 26 Judge Townsend announced the sentence: "Three years with hard labor, in the state penitentiary." Smalls was sent to the city jail, where he remained for three days until his release on bond pending an appeal before the state supreme court. On December 3, 1877, Smalls returned to Washington and resumed his congressional duties.

After the Trial

Smalls's attorneys wasted no time appealing his conviction. They moved for an arrest of judgment before Judge Townsend, which was denied. They petitioned for a retrial, which was also denied. Giving up on receiving any measure of justice from Judge Townsend, they turned their attention to preparing their appeal for the state supreme court. There were six principal elements in the appeal to reverse Townsend's judgment.

1. The Trial Court was without jurisdiction and authority in this case in that Smalls was a member of the U.S. Congress and the court erred in refusing to transfer the case to the federal district court.
2. The jury rendering the verdict in this case was not a legal and competent jury in that one juror William T. Martin was seated in a manner, which denied Smalls his right to preemptory challenge.
3. The first, second, third, fourth and fifth counts of the indictment were fatally defective for the reasons given, and more specifically: Because the court erred in denying the defendant his right of preemptory challenge.
4. The court erred in permitting the witness Josephus Woodruff to refresh his memory by reference to a book purporting to be a diary written in phonographic characters peculiar to the witness and of his own invention and allowing them to be transcribed by the witness and read to the jury.
5. The court erred in admitting into evidence the books of a private corporation known as "The South Carolina Bank and Trust Company," (to which this defendant was and is a stranger) and permitting entries therein, in the handwriting of the assistant book keeper, (Lawrence W. Zealy) to be read and shown to the jury as evidence competent to prove, as against defendant, that payments were made by the said bank, on account of the

said Woodruff, and a deposit made to the credit of this defendant, of like amount, and the precise dates of such transactions, although it was in evidence that such transactions were not had with the assistant book keeper (Zealy) or within his personal knowledge; although nothing appeared to connect the transaction had with the said bank and Woodruff with the transactions with the said bank by this defendant; although the person with whom the transactions are alleged to have occurred (Jacobs) is alive.

6. The court erred in admitting in evidence a slip of paper, said to be in the handwriting of one S. F. Jacobs, an officer of the said bank, containing a date, the name of the defendant (Smalls); and the figure $5,000, written in pencil, as evidence to prove that at such date this defendant did deposit the sum of five thousand dollars in the said bank by way of check; although it was proved that the said S. F. Jacobs is alive, and nothing was proved to connect this defendant with the said paper, or to refer the said paper to any transaction between this defendant and the said Woodruff. (Signed:) Melton & Wingate.

Despite the uproar that Smalls's arrest, trial, and conviction caused in Washington, at the end of January 1878 a committee of Congress, after a study of the matter, reported that his trial did not violate his privileges as a U. S. Congressman. In April 1879 Smalls's appeal was finally heard by the South Carolina Supreme Court, which rejected all his claims, thus upholding his conviction. Smalls took his case to the U. S. Supreme Court, which accepted it and placed it on the docket for later hearing. Melton arranged for Smalls to speak directly with Chief Justice Morrison Remick Waite, who encouraged Smalls to testify personally when the case was argued. Smalls's grounds were essentially that the trial in state court was in violation of his rights and privileges as a member of the U. S. Congress. Smalls was eagerly looking forward to appearing before the Supreme Court, which was permitted at that time. Smalls expressed considerable disappointment, therefore, when President Hayes made a deal with the government of South Carolina while Hampton was still governor (before his election to the U. S. Senate) to void the prosecution of South Carolina Democrats charged in political corruption and violence in the 1876 federal elections and the Hamburg Massacre and other criminals in exchange for pardons issued by the governor of South Carolina to Smalls, Cardozo, and Carpenter. In accordance with this agreement, Governor Simpson on April 23, 1879, granted full pardons to Smalls and Cardozo. Carpenter had already been pardoned by Governor Hampton.

McKee Support

While Smalls preferred a Supreme Court reversal of his conviction to a governor's pardon, there was strong support in the state for a pardon. Preeminent
among Smalls's supporters at this time was the McKee family, who had owned
him during slavery and who had been assisted by Smalls since the war. Thomas
G. White, M.D., of Beaufort joined with Smalls in soliciting the assistance of
one McKee descendant. W. B. McKee, chief clerk of the Receivers Atlantic and
Gulf Railroad in Savannah, Georgia, expressed much admiration for Smalls.
McKee made a dispassionate, statesman-like appeal to Hampton to grant executive clemency or pardon to Smalls:

> believing that there are extenuating circumstances in this case so far as I
> understand it, I must cheerfully and willingly say before you the following
> facts in connection with the life of Smalls, which I trust may have some
> weight in the scales of justice. Robert Smalls belonged to my father's nephew
> John McKee. He was raised in our family as a houseboy, always proved him-
> self intelligent and of a kind disposition. Upon my cousin marrying, he
> took Smalls with him. I then lost sight of him until the end of the war.
> When two weeks after its close, I visited my native place being taken sick
> there, convalescing was sitting on the porch of the store of a gentleman in
> Beaufort. When Smalls, then Captain of the *Planter,* met me and greeted
> me with all the welcome that he would have extended me in the days of our
> boyhood when we played together. Noting that I had on a confederate gray
> jacket, he said to me there have been paid off today in term five regiments
> of Negro troops and if you go out in that town dressed that way you will
> experience fear. Then in the most delicate way, he asked if I would permit
> him to present me with a citizen's gift, which I was glad to accept and which
> I believe gave him more pleasure to purchase. He extended to me many
> other kindness during my short stay in Beaufort and has continued to exer-
> cise them; one instance upon his election to Congress offering me the ap-
> pointment in his gift to the Naval Academy for my brother. I know of my
> own knowledge that he has extended not only kindness but substantial aid
> to the widow and children of his late Master, and to many other citizens of
> the town in which he was born and who have returned there since the war.
> All these kindly acts go to show that there is nothing of malice in his dis-
> position and that he is not the bitter opponent of the white race that some
> would believe him. His crimes look like errors of judgment and perhaps
> want of education and the result of the effect of association with those with
> whom he has been politically united. I trust that you will pardon me for
> writing at such length but feeling a kindly interest in Smalls and sensible of

the many acts of kindness that he has extended me, I feel that I could nor sit silent if my voice could aid him in his day of trial.[19]

Dr. White's effort to get a pardon for Smalls highlights the postwar relationships among the McKees, the Whites, and the Smalls. Another aspect of W. B. McKee's letter is his identification of John McKee as his father's nephew. This means that John McKee had an uncle in his same age range who had at least one child in Smalls's age range. Since W. B. McKee reported that he and Smalls were playmates, this tells us that in growing up in the McKee household, Smalls had available to him not only John and Henry McKee's children but a wider range of extended kin as well, all of whom were in the position to extend kindness, friendship, and fraternity. Despite the fact that they had fought on opposite sides, these two young men in their early thirties could sit and reminisce about the old days when they were young and played together.

This letter also confirms how gracious, generous, and helpful Smalls was to the McKee family and other whites who returned to Beaufort. This would include Smalls's efforts in Congress to pass legislation reimbursing the property owners in Beaufort who lost their homes during the war. It also includes Congressman Smalls's "unsolicited" effort to get an appointment in the U.S. Naval Academy for W.B. McKee's son. In his characterization of Smalls as "without malice" and "not the opponent of the white race as some would believe him," McKee echoed, the strongly held views of Smalls's descendants and some historians. Regardless of the effect on Hampton's decision, the McKee letter reveals the depth of mutual affection between these two branches of this complex family.

The Press

The newspapers could not bring themselves to be generous in Smalls's victory or kindly toward him in his defeat. The anti-Smalls and anti-Republican press enjoyed a field day at Smalls's expense for nearly two years after the trial, while the action of the state supreme court was anticipated on all sides. An article by T.G.W. in the July 15, 1878, issue of the *Charleston News and Courier* demonstrates that even in its anti-Smalls diatribe, it could reveal the strong support and adulation Smalls received from his constituents. It also shows Smalls's magnanimity toward Governor Hampton. Referring to Smalls as "Beaufort's Brown Idol" and as "the convict Congressman addressing his 'dusky' constituents," the paper covered a Republican meeting at Brick Church, St. Helena Island, in Beaufort County:

The redoubtable Congressman Smalls was next called upon, and took the stage amid the vociferous cheers of an adoring multitude. It is perfectly astonishing to witness the increasing influence of this negro. He seems to possess the confidence of his race to a degree that no other negro can hope to attain. The men, women and children seem to regard him with a feeling akin to worship.

His speech was mostly directed to a vindication of himself from the charges made against him by the investigating committee. He stated to his constituents that since he last met them upon this post he had been tried, convicted and sentenced to the penitentiary. That his case was now before the three judges of the Supreme Court of the State, that at any time he would not be surprised to hear that the judgment of the lower court had been affirmed. That in deference, however, to the tribunal on whom his fate depended he would have to say they are all good men, that doubtless their decision would be right, but that in the event of an unfavorable decision against him he would rely upon an appeal to a higher tribunal, and that therefore, he did not apprehend he would reach the penitentiary before he would have the opportunity of speaking to them again and frequently. "Thank God" from a voice in the crowd. He referred to the administration of Governor Hampton, at which he expressed himself satisfied, and stated that he should abstain from speaking as favorably of him as he felt for fear that his motives might be misconstrued, and that he be accused of cringing to the powers that be. He referred to the just and liberal conduct of the Governor which had recommended him to the confidence of the people and believed that if he continued to be surrounded by fair supporters that his course would continue to demand the respect which was being accorded it by adherents of both political parties. He told his hearers that the Governor had made a speech recently at Blackville which for fairness and liberality of expression was worthy of the immortal Sumner, and that he (Smalls) could not doubt his (Hampton's) sincerity in view of the fulfillment of many of the pledges he had made before his election.

He (Smalls) considered the coming campaign as the most important for the future of the Republican Party in the State, and advised a steady adherence to the Straight-out Republican nominations.[20]

Later in the meeting Tom Hamilton asked to speak but met with "considerable opposition" because he had supported the Democrats in the last election. Smalls, however, asserted that Hamilton should be allowed to speak, and because of Smalls's influence, Hamilton was allowed to do so.

Smalls's appearance at this meeting was vintage Robert Smalls, strong in defeat with optimism for the future. He was a master communicator to his political base, with solid fealty to the Republican Party yet conciliatory in relations with the Governor Hampton.

Conclusion

They tried to cut down Robert Smalls with the trial of 1877. Who were they? They were chiefly Wade Hampton and the white Democrats who took over state government after the elections of 1876 dislodged the predominantly black Republicans. But Hampton and his crew had a great deal of help from others, including white Republicans eager to incur favor or avoid prosecution by the Democrats. They had the support of key black Republicans and other blacks high and low who helped to prosecute Wright, Cardozo, and Smalls. They especially had the support of a violently resurgent Democratic-led reign of terror over the state, the Republicans, and the fragile black citizenry. Yet, despite all this power, force, and intimidation, they could not have tried and convicted Smalls without the active support of Republican president Rutherford B. Hayes and his withdrawal of federal troops from South Carolina. All these forces and factors came together in a virtual crescendo to sweep the Republicans and blacks out of power and to land Smalls in jail.

Thus, the results and the aftermath of the 1876 elections and the subsequent end of Reconstruction converged on Smalls. Did they succeed? Of course they did. They cost him large sums of money to defend himself in state courts and to defend his challenged congressional seat, on top of his regular expenses in support of his family in Beaufort and his living arrangements in Washington. More important still they succeeded in creating a cloud over his reputation and years of legal uncertainty as to his status and his freedom. Moreover, this trial and conviction hung like the sword of Damocles over his political future. It was a major cause of his defeat in the 1878 elections, along with dissension in the Republican ranks between black and white Republicans and among blacks. Much of Smalls's political luster had been dissipated by the 1878 elections. He was not alone. The other two black Republican congressmen from South Carolina also lost their seats to white Democrats, making the South Carolina delegation to Congress all white for the first time in a decade.

But if Smalls was cut down a few pegs by the trial and conviction of 1877, it was not a total rout. They did not rob him of his dignity; his spirit of adventure; his self confidence; his belief in the principles of the Republican Party; his ability to earn, save, and invest substantial properties; his deep religious beliefs; his sense of humor; or his capacity to form positive relations and patterns of cooperation with whites as well as blacks of high and low status. The trial and conviction did not rob Smalls of the deep respect and admiration the people of

Beaufort County held for him. As a consequence, even though he was frequently embattled, he remained the leader of the Beaufort County Republican Party, leader of the crumbling state Republican Party, and a perennial delegate to national Republican Party conventions. Moreover, after his 1878 defeat, Smalls returned to Washington for three more terms in Congress.

PART IV

After Reconstruction

II

Consummate Politician, 1877–1889

The Election of 1878

The election campaign of 1878 was a repeat of the violence, intimidation, and fraud of 1876. Smalls lost his seat in Congress to the white Democrat George Tillman despite the fact that the district was still overwhelming black and Republican. Smalls spent the next two years pursuing business and community service, and planning for his renomination to run for Congress against George Tillman in 1880.

By 1878 the Democrats had succeeded so well that at the Republican State Convention, no candidates were nominated for governor or any other statewide office. In Beaufort County, however, the Republican Party was still strong. The party nominated county officers, and Smalls was nominated for his old seat in Congress. It was a hard-fought election campaign filled with violence, intimidation, election fraud, and internal dissension among black and white Republicans. Indeed, one writer has argued that the death of the Republican Party in South Carolina was not primarily the result of Democratic insurgence but rather the consequence of conflict and dissent among black and white Republicans.[1]

At a Republican rally in Blackwell on October 11, 1878, Smalls was prevented from speaking by a band of twelve mounted red shirts. At another rally in Gillisonville, a similar attack was threatened. Black men readied themselves to repel the men, but Smalls restrained them. When the Democrats demanded half the speaking time at this rally, Smalls disbanded the meeting. Smalls and his supporters were then fired on as they took cover in a nearby store. When word got out that Smalls was under attack, black men with loaded guns came to rescue him and his party, so the red shirts rode away.[2]

Despite such violent opposition Smalls easily won renomination. However, he was defeated by Tillman in the general election. Smalls returned to Washington to complete the rest of his congressional term. During this session Smalls introduced two bills. One, which changed the boundaries of the customs offices in Charleston and Beaufort, passed by voice vote on January 7, 1879. Smalls's second bill was a measure to provide assistance to the McKee family and others who had incurred losses when the government took ownership of their property in the direct-tax legislation and sold it for profit to the U.S. Treasury. This was Smalls's second effort to benefit the McKees and other whites who had lost their property; he had introduced a similar bill during his first term in Congress. Even though this bill also failed in the House, it demonstrated Smalls's eagerness to serve all his constituents, not just black ones. This made him quite popular among whites in Beaufort County.

The Election of 1880

In the election of 1880 George D. Tillman again won the vote in the district. But this time Smalls contested the election in the House of Representatives. After extensive debate and political warfare, the Republican-controlled House decided late in the term, on June 19, 1882, to seat Smalls instead of Tillman. It had taken the House more than a year and a half to make its decision. Thus Smalls's third term as congressman was very brief, and he soon had to turn his attention to reelection.

Smalls still worked for his district. Enormously popular and highly respected in Congress, he successfully introduced a bill to erect a customhouse, a post office, and other federal government buildings in Beaufort.

The Election of 1882

In the election campaign of 1882, three candidates filed for the Republican nomination for Smalls's seat. Because the districts had been gerrymandered to create a new white district next door, Beaufort District was even more overwhelmingly black and Republican and was referred to as the "Black District." The Democrats fielded no candidate for Congress in this district.

The three candidates who filed for the Republican nomination were Robert Smalls, another black Republican named Samuel J. Lee, and a white Republican named E. M. Mackey, who was married to a black woman. This was a major challenge to Smalls's leadership. At the beginning of balloting at the nominating convention, Mackey received fifteen votes; Lee received fourteen; and Smalls got ten. A candidate needed a majority of the votes cast to be nominated.

On the thirty-fifth ballot there was no change, despite fierce politicking among the delegations. Smalls's low showing was in part a result of the fallout from his conviction and pardon. Not only were black Republicans split and no longer overwhelmingly supportive of Smalls, but also the chair of the convention declared that he could not back Smalls. Still, Smalls stayed in the race for ballot after ballot. If at any time he had withdrawn, either Lee or Mackey would have been nominated.

On the two hundred forty-seventh ballot Smalls decided to break the deadlock. He and Mackey agreed that in the event of a deadlock the one with the lower number of votes would throw his support to the other. Smalls ultimately withdrew in favor of Mackey, who was nominated on the next ballot. Lee bolted the convention and ran for Congress on an independent ticket. He lost overwhelmingly, however, to Mackey.

The *News and Courier* of Thursday, September 28, 1882, described the processes that gave Mackey the nomination:

> The chairman was then proceeding to announce the election when Sam Lee took the floor, and at the close of a long and bitter denunciation of Mackey said that on his personal responsibility he would state that the nomination of E. W. M. Mackey had not been fairly or honestly made; and that to make the statement plain "that he had bribed C. C. Robertson to vote for him, and that he held the proof of that statement in his hand." This brought Robertson to his feet. Arising from his seat he walked rapidly over to Lee and was about to assail him when he was held by some of Lee's friends until he could be quieted down. The Berkeley delegation were all on their feet violently gesticulating and a row was imminent, when, by the interference of Smalls and Mackey, a partial peace was secured and Lee was allowed to go on with his speech."[3]

Mackey was elected in November 1882 with no Democratic opposition and took his seat in Congress in December. However, he died before the end of his first year, and Smalls was elected to his old seat in Congress.

Smalls had a busy and effective session. Among his most memorable acts was his introduction of a bill to add fifty dollars a month to the pension of General David Hunter's widow, Maria Hunter, apparently without her knowledge. The bill passed both houses of Congress but was vetoed by President Grover Cleveland, a Democrat. Smalls's speech criticizing the actions of the president was memorable and revealed his views on a variety of issues. He remarked that he and Congressman James E. O'Hare of North Carolina were the only two blacks left in Congress "to represent upwards of seven million people."[4]

The Election of 1884

In the 1884 campaign Smalls was renominated to run for Congress. The Democrats nominated white Confederate veteran and attorney William Elliott Sr.
The state had been gerrymandered by the Democrats into seven districts, the
seventh being the only one where a black majority of voters existed and the only
one where the Republican Party was still dominant.

William Elliott Jr. provided a personal perspective on that election, in which
Smalls defeated William Elliott Sr.:

> It was, I think, in the campaign of 1884 that General Wade Hampton came
> to Beaufort to address the citizens. . . . He made a vigorous attack on Gen-
> eral Robert Smalls who was then opposing my father for Congress in the
> "Black District" containing Beaufort. He referred to Smalls's conviction of
> bribery after the 1876 overturn of the carpetbagger-negro government. I
> think he called him a "convicted felon." Smalls jumped from his seat with
> an umbrella top, advanced to the edge of the crowd and, with the sweat
> popping from his face, vigorously denied the charges, and called on Hamp-
> ton to certify to his innocence, since Hampton had signed his pardon.
> Hampton cited the political reason that induced the pardon. Smalls then
> said, "General Hampton, what about the charge that you defrauded a widow
> in Mississippi? I do not make the charge, but it has been made." General
> Hampton listened with entire composure and when Smalls had finished,
> raised his right hand and with great impressiveness replied, "I swear before
> God I have never defrauded any widow in Mississippi or elsewhere, nor any
> person, man or woman in my life; and the man who makes the charge
> against me, or sponsors it, is a slanderer and a liar." Smalls replied, "Remem-
> ber I said I did not make the charge." "But you sponsored it," said Hamp-
> ton, and the incident closed.
>
>   My father regretted that General Hampton had made the attack on
> Smalls for Smalls had conducted a decent campaign.[5]

William Elliott Jr. also provided a description of Smalls's arrival at the event at
the head of the Washington Light Infantry, of which he was captain: "The uni-
form of this company was blue with white trimmings and the plumes of the
helmets were white feathers. General Smalls (for he was a real United States General) was short and very fat, and when he rolled rather than walked down Bay
Street, one could not but think of a comet revolving through space. This company was generally led by Allen's Brass Band—a really excellent band then led
by Roper, the porter of the custom house."[6]

The Election of 1886

In the 1886 elections, the Democratic Party pulled out all stops at both the national and state levels to prevent Smalls from returning to Congress. In addition, from Washington, Senator Wade Hampton brought word that President Grover Cleveland was personally interested in defeating Smalls. Cleveland was offended by Smalls's extended attack on him for vetoing Smalls's bill to increase the pension for Maria Hunter, widow of General David Hunter, for whom Smalls felt a special affinity. The Democrats again nominated William Elliott Sr. Because the Republicans were split along color lines, Elliott won the election by a safe vote margin.

Smalls contested the election in the House. Sponsored by Henry Cabot Lodge, Smalls was permitted to speak for himself, and he was eloquent. But it was already ten years past the end of Reconstruction in the South, and in the North the mood had turned against black advancement. Smalls lost the election in the House.

The Elections of 1888, 1890, and 1892

Out of elective office, Smalls had plenty to do. He was still leader of the fractured Republican Party in Beaufort County. He tended to his family, business, and community service. He also geared up to run again for Congress. But at age forty-nine this happy warrior was persuaded to stand aside and support the nomination of his protégé, Thomas E. Miller. Ten years younger than Smalls, Miller was a highly respected state senator, and Smalls campaigned actively for him. Miller was elected to Congress.

In 1890 Smalls was again nominated, but his challenge to William Elliott Sr. for his seat in the House of Representatives was not successful. This election marked the end of Smalls's congressional career.

In 1892 George Murray won election to the House by a narrow margin. In 1894 he was renominated and lost to William Elliott Sr., but he successfully contested the election and served from June 1896 until the end of the term. He was the last black congressman from South Carolina until a hundred years later, when the Honorable James E. Clyburn was elected as a Democrat, reflecting the shift in the political parties' appeal to black voters.

Finale

By the late 1800s Robert Smalls was a familiar figure in Washington. A short man, he had grown heavier with the years and favored Prince Albert suits, top hats, and high-button shoes. His first wife had died in July 1883, and after her death his companion at capital functions was his younger daughter, Sarah. His other daughter, Elizabeth, had married and was running her own home. In 1890 Smalls wed Annie Wigg, a teacher much nearer his daughters' ages than his own. Two years later she bore him his last child, William Robert Smalls.

Collector of Customs

At the conclusion of his congressional career, Smalls moved into another phase of his active life. In 1889 he received a presidential appointment, subsequently confirmed by the Senate, to be collector of customs at the Port of Beaufort. He had campaigned hard for Republican president Benjamin Harrison in the 1888 elections, and he was appointed as a reward for his loyal support. He was easily confirmed by the Senate even though there was active competition for this position and opposition to Smalls. He brought together a strong cadre of Democrats and Republicans in high offices to support him and delivered to the president a most persuasive petition on his own behalf.

Harrison announced Smalls's appointment on June 13, 1889, and he was confirmed by the Senate on January 25, 1890. The white Democratic senators from South Carolina, George Tillman and John L. McLaurin, did not object to Smalls's confirmation. He had a long, distinguished career in this post, while continuing his active participation as a Republican political leader and functioning as a local businessman. He held office under Republican and Democratic presidents and was confirmed by Democratic- and Republican-held Senates until June 1913—with one exception: for the 1894–1898 term he was not reappointed by the Democratic president.

Smalls's office was a two-room suite in the customhouse. Generally, he had one or two deputies and six or seven workers. The position paid $1,000 per year plus 3 percent of all receipts up to $3,000. He was, therefore, quite well paid.

He was also well respected in this position by Republicans and Democrats alike and especially by the local businessmen, who benefited from the port trade. In 1906, when he went to Washington to petition for reappointment, he was met at the train station by messengers who told him that his reappointment had already been made and confirmed. In 1910 Beaufort Democrats joined in recommending him for reappointment.

At the end of his long and competent service, he was reappointed in 1912 by Republican President William Howard Taft for whom he had campaigned. However, he was not confirmed by the Republican-controlled Senate because, for the first time, the two senators from South Carolina had actively opposed his nomination. By now Smalls was in very bad health.

Between May 1912 to March 1913 Smalls produced a barrage of letters, mainly to his friend Whitfield McKinlay in Washington, pleading reappointment to just one more term as collector of customs. His health was failing, and his daughter Sarah was also ill.

In his May 11, 1912, letter to McKinlay, Smalls asked him to urge Congress to reappoint him on May 13, because it would mark the fiftieth year since he seized *Planter,* adding: "I have a very strong petition on file, signed by members of both political parties, so there can be no valid reason for any opposition to my confirmation. There is no Democrat of any prominence in this place, who has not signed the petition."[7]

Smalls wrote to McKinley again a week later complaining of ill health but still eager to advance his cause:

> I am not at all well; my limbs bother me from my knees to my feet, from numbness, but I am able to get about just the same.
>
> When you see Sen. Smith I wish you will extend to him for me my thanks and appreciation for his interest in my confirmation.[8]

Five days later, however, Senator Knute Nelson, chairman of the Senate Commerce Committee wrote to Smalls.

> The Senators of your state having objected to your confirmation in your nomination, according to custom [your request] was referred to a subcommittee and that subcommittee has not yet reported to the full committee. I will have the matter looked after as soon as possible. Senator Simmons of North Carolina is chairman of the subcommittee.[9]

Senator Nelson's letter signaled an end to the matter. Though Smalls was not yet ready to halt his fight and continued to write letters through September 1912, he was not reappointed. Booker T. Washington sent Smalls a letter expressing his disappointment. Washington had assumed that Smalls would hold that position by appointment and confirmation for as long as he wanted. In his response to Washington, Smalls summed up his career in the customhouse and his political life as well.

> I felt gratified to know that I have lived and so conducted my office, with the assistance of my competent deputy, Julius Washington, for all these years and have not had a single complaint, either of the transactions of the collectorship or of my deputy. During the twenty odd years I have held the position of collector, I have succeeded to so manage affairs that when I leave it, I will do so with credit to myself, my family and the race. When we go

out of office we go clean. So when the excellent history of the Tuskegee [Institute] and the Negro shall be written, the Customs House at Beaufort, while conducted by colored men, can be easily attached to the top or bottom for whatever inspiration it may be to the race."[10]

Business at the customhouse in Beaufort had declined, and the Port of Beaufort closed after Smalls left. Maritime business was transferred to Charleston.

Robert Smalls at his desk in the customhouse during the last decade of his life. From the Robert Smalls Collection, courtesy of Helen Boulware Moore

Desk used by Smalls as collector of customs, now in the Beaufort Arsenal Museum. LyBenson Photography Studios, Rev. Kenneth Hodges, photographer

Elizabeth Smalls Bampfield in her wedding gown. From the Robert Smalls Collection, courtesy of Helen Boulware Moore

Samuel J. Bampfield as a young man. From the Robert Smalls Collection, courtesy of Helen Boulware Moore

Joseph Bampfield Jr., father of Samuel J. Bampfield. From the Robert Smalls Collection, courtesy of Helen Boulware Moore

Judith Robinson Bampfield, mother of Samuel J. Bampfield. From the Robert Smalls Collection, courtesy of Helen Boulware Moore

Elizabeth and Samuel J. Bampfield's surviving children. (Two died in infancy.) From the Robert Smalls Collection, courtesy of Helen Boulware Moore

First African Baptist Church in Beaufort, where Robert Smalls was a member and where his funeral was held. From the author's collection

Memorial bust of Robert Smalls by Marion Etheridge, in Tabernacle Baptist Churchyard. Photograph from the author's collection

Elizabeth Smalls Bampfield (seated second from left) surrounded by her nine surviving children on her eightieth birthday. From the Robert Smalls Collection, courtesy of Helen Boulware Moore

William Robert Smalls, son of Robert Smalls, with family in 1948. Front row: Michael W. Grigsby (grandson) and Linda M. Grigsby (granddaughter). Second row: William Robert Smalls, Annie (Anne) Smalls Grigsby (daughter), Martineau "Marty" Smalls (wife), Wendell Grigsby (son-in-law). From the Collection of Linda Grigsby

William Robert Smalls and his wife, Marty, celebrating their wedding anniversary in 1963 aboard a Holland Cruise Lines ship. From the Collection of Linda Grigsby

Dolly Davidson and her brother, Edward Estes Davidson, the only children of Edward and Janet Bampfield Davidson (granddaughter of Robert Smalls). From the Robert Smalls Collection, courtesy of Helen Boulware Moore

Edward Estes Davidson, who served in the U.S. Navy during World War II. From the Robert Smalls Collection, courtesy of Helen Boulware Moore

Dolly Nash sharing the legacy of Robert Smalls at the Confederate Relic Room and Museum. Photograph from the author's collection

The author with Dolly Nash, whose great-grandfather Robert Smalls was pilot of the Keokuk *in the Union attack on Fort Sumter (April 7, 1863), meeting Jerry Emanuel, whose great-grandfather Jonathon Manly Emanuel was third engineer of the* Keokuk *on that occasion. Photograph from the author's collection*

Jones family historian Furman Franklin Williams, age ninety-four, at the 2000 family reunion in New York. Williams is the great-great-grandson of Hannah Jones Smalls. Photograph from the author's collection

U.S. Army transport ship Major General Robert Smalls *at its christening April 21, 2004. From LyBenson Photography Studios, Rev. Kenneth Hodges, photographer*

Robin Moore, daughter of Helen and Robert Moore and great-great-granddaughter of Robert Smalls speaking at the christening of the Major General Robert Smalls, *April 21, 2004. From the Robert Smalls Collection, courtesy of Helen Boulware Moore*

Robert Smalls III, grandson of William Robert Smalls, at the christening of the Major General Robert Smalls. *Photograph from the author's collection*

Helen Stinson Greenlee and Helen Boulware Moore, great-granddaughter of Robert Smalls, at the christening of the Major General Robert Smalls. *From LyBenson Photography Studios, Rev. Kenneth Hodges, photographer*

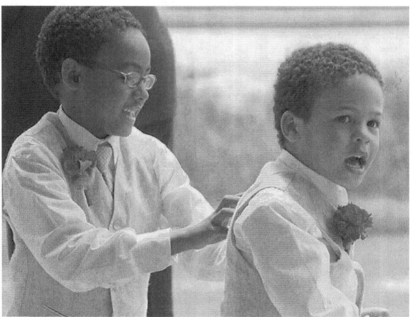

David and Lucas Moore, children of Michael Boulware Moore and great-great-great-grandchildren of Robert Smalls, at the christening of the Major General Robert Smalls. *From LyBenson Photography Studios, Rev. Kenneth Hodges, photographer*

Anne Smalls Grigsby, daughter of William Robert Smalls, with grandson Michael and granddaughter Linda. From the Collection of Linda Grigsby

Robert Smalls Middle School on Robert Smalls Parkway in Beaufort today. Photograph from the author's collection

12

Robert Smalls and the
Constitutional Convention of 1895

The 1890 election of Benjamin R. Tillman, younger brother of George D. Till-man, as governor marked a political and cultural revolution in South Carolina's Democratic Party. A self-confessed and well-known antagonist to the rights, privileges, and humanity of black people, Ben Tillman was a dominant political leader, who became a U.S. senator in 1894.

The South Carolina Constitutional Convention of 1895 was called at Till-man's urging. The purpose was to amend the state constitution to deny black people the right to vote, a right that had been guaranteed by the Fifteenth Amendment and the state constitution of 1868. The Constitutional Convention of 1895 was a bookend to the 1868 convention. While the 1868 convention had ushered in biracial political democracy for adult males in the state, the 1895 convention closed that chapter in South Carolina and U.S. history.[1]

The convention called for delegates from all the counties of the state, apportioned loosely by population size and generally by white-male voting strength. Beaufort, the only county to survive the white Democratic purges since 1877, elected five black Republican delegates. Georgetown elected one black and two white delegates. Robert Smalls and William J. Whipper were the only black Republicans who served as delegates to both the 1868 and 1895 conventions. At the 1868 convention the twenty-nine-year-old Smalls was in the majority both as a black man and a Republican and had been launched on a successful political career. By 1895, however, he had lost his seat in Congress and his majority status. There were only 6 black Republicans elected and seated at the 1895 convention with 156 white Democratic delegates, 113 reformers and 43 conservatives.[2]

When Robert Smalls left Beaufort for Columbia, he left behind a community in which he was respected and well regarded. His work as customs collector continued under the able leadership of his deputy and next-door neighbor, Julius I. Washington. The people of Beaufort had again expressed their pride in Smalls by electing him as a delegate. While he was not in the best of health, his condition was not bad enough to cause him to forgo this honor. Although it was not the first or last time his struggle for political democracy took priority over all else, this time his family was also unwell. For this reason and because of the dangers presented by the convention, Smalls asked his friend Julius Washington to guard his family. His wife, Annie, and daughter Sarah were ailing, and his son Willie was but three years old. Smalls left a loaded shotgun in the upstairs closet and, for the first time, traveled with a handgun in his pocket. Violence against and intimidation of blacks who might seek to vote had reached a fever pitch under Ben Tillman's leadership.

The Convention

The convention opened in Columbia on September 10, in the South Carolina house of representatives. Robert Aldrich, the temporary chair of the convention, set the theme as follows: "The Convention of 1868 was the fruit of the Reconstruction Acts, which were notoriously unconstitutional. . . . That Constitution was made by aliens, Negroes, and natives without character, all the enemies of South Carolina."[3]

The 162 delegates comprised 113 white reform Democrats led by Tillman, 43 conservatives Democrats led by William C. McGowan, and 6 black Republicans led by Smalls. The Beaufort Republicans were James Wigg, Thomas E. Miller, Isaiah R. Reed, William J. Whipper, and Robert Smalls. Georgetown County sent three delegates, one of whom, Robert B. Anderson, was black and Republican. These were able, experienced, and economically stable men who had all played important roles in Reconstruction government, in the Republican Party, and in their communities. All the other delegates were white Democrats. Both white delegations were pledged to create a constitutional ban on black voting without jeopardizing white voters. If Smalls was David in this fight, Ben Tillman was surely Goliath. While the black delegates were treated respectfully for the most part, they were not assigned to the most important committees, and the convention rules required that ten delegates must vote in favor of a resolution for it to be considered. Even so, the black delegates were given wide latitude and support for presenting their case in debates, resolutions, and voting, which they generally lost overwhelmingly.

The permanent chair, Governor John C. Evans, ruled that eleven delegates would be appointed to each of the working convention committees. Senator

Ben Tillman was appointed chair of the most important, the Committee on the Rights of Suffrage, and no black members were named to it. The black Republicans were appointed to the following committees:

Isaiah R. Reed—Eminent Domain
Robert Smalls—Militia
W. J. Whipper—Amendments
Thomas E. Miller—Engrossed Resolutions and Ordinances
James Wigg—Miscellaneous Matters
R. B. Anderson—Impeachment.

Rights of Suffrage

The Committee on the Rights of Suffrage had the most work, the most resolutions presented, the most public (newspaper) coverage, and the most controversy. Though no black members were appointed to this committee, several participated actively in its deliberations and its final report. Also, George Murray, though he was not an elected delegate, used his position as a member of Congress to speak out against the antisuffrage aims of the convention.

During one of his addresses to the convention, Senator Tillman declared, "the question of suffrage and its wise regulation is the sole cause of our being here." In his opening remarks, Governor Evans appealed to the conservatives and reformers to band together for a common purpose: "We have seen that white men can divide, and it is your duty, in view of such division, to so fix your election laws that your wives, your children and your homes will be protected and Anglo-Saxon supremacy preserved."[4]

The Democratic majority's challenge was to fashion a constitution that would disenfranchise as many black men as possible and enable as many white men as possible to vote, without coming into conflict with the Fifteenth Amendment. It was easily agreed that the solution lay in two measures, literacy and property ownership. The challenge was how to develop literacy measures that would bar illiterate and literate blacks from voting while permitting illiterate and literate white men to vote. To craft a property requirement that would accomplish the same purpose was the second challenge.

The six black delegates fought fiercely, ably, and honorably, earning the reluctant admiration of the whites, who nonetheless voted in lockstep against them. Two important and personal perspectives on the participation of these black delegates have long been buried in obscurity. One is by Sarah V. Smalls, daughter of Robert Smalls, and the other by Mary J. Miller, wife of Thomas E. Miller. Their compilations of black delegates' speeches are an important contribution to scholarship.

In her pamphlet Sarah Smalls included "such parts of the new Constitution have been selected as affect the colored people, together with the speeches made thereon by my father Robert Smalls; several editorials from leading newspapers; also a few of many letters received by him from all parts of the country congratulating him for the manly spirit displayed by him and the other colored delegates, whenever the rights of their race were in jeopardy." And, she wrote:

> Indeed, it may have been an object lesson, planned by the all-wise God, to teach the naughty, boastful sons of Carolina that there are Negroes capable and amply qualified in every respect to protect themselves whenever it becomes necessary to do so; that those few representatives of the race were but a very small part of the rising host that time and education are bringing forward day by day in spite of lynching, caste prejudice or any methods used against them.[5]

In the introduction to her collection Mary Miller wrote:

> In the name of white supremacy, the editors and orators of the South (and the North in part) have taught the nation to believe that the presence of the Negroes in the South means the destruction of progress and pure government. The nation never knew that the South did not want a suffrage plan that would eliminate the ignorant and incompetent vote. The nation never knew until this convention convened that South Carolina wanted a legalized, fraudulent election machinery. And as the six Republicans of that body, by their acts and speeches, taught the nation the true object of the majority of the late convention. . . . [6]

Miller went on to explain that Smalls and James Wigg had proposed "suffrage plans that eliminated the ignorant vote" while still allowing literate blacks to vote, but only the six black delegates voted in favor of them. Indeed, Miller noted, the true sentiment of the white delegates was voiced by a Mr. Henderson, from Berkeley, who said: "Talk about adopting a suffrage plan that will secure a fair and honest election is the talk of a child. If you put anything in the Constitution that will require fair and honest elections, Negroes will be elected from my county, for there are more Negroes who can read and write than there are white men in the county of Berkeley." Then, Miller added, "Senator Tillman admitted on the floor of the convention that for a while at least it is necessary to drink from the poisoned chalice the dregs of fraudulent elections."[7]

Yet, Miller also recorded the positive response the six blacks received from their fellow delegates and from the press. For example, a Mr. Burn from Darlington said that the Beaufort delegates have acquitted themselves with the highest credit to their race. . . . They have, with consummate ability, given the history, marshaled the facts and statistics favorable to their side. They have displayed splendid argumentative abilities, keen sarcasm and telling humor, which does credit to them individually and as representatives of their race. Between the lines the truth begins to shine, What oppressed people, denied the opportunities for the cultivation of good manners, the refining influences of civilization and religion, ever sent a delegation anywhere who, in their deportment, in their powers of reasoning, in their rhetorical ability, in their knowledge of the laws of the land, the common law, the statutory law and the constitutional law, both state and national, could surpass in ability that colored delegation from Beaufort.[8]

Miller quoted an October 31, 1896, editorial from the *Columbia State,* which spoke of the "strong" Beaufort County delegation, "amply able to present the cause of their race with logic and eloquence" and called Miller and Wigg "exceptionally good debaters." She also quoted from the October 27 issue of the *Columbia Register,* which said, "Abler representatives the colored people could not have had if the state had been raked over with a fine tooth comb"—and singled out Miller for praise. Finally, she quoted from the November 2 *Sumter Watchman and Southern:*

The way Miller, Smalls, Wigg and Whipper, the Negro delegates from Beaufort have been bullyragging the Constitutional Convention for the last few days on the suffrage question is too ludicrous for anything. These Negroes have decidedly the best of the situation, and so far have had altogether the best of the argument. They have the bulge on the convention and there is no dignified way out of the dilemma into which the majority of the convention has been forced. We never expected to see the day that four Negroes from Beaufort would stand up in a body like the one sitting in Columbia and ask for an educational and property qualification of the suffrage and have the request denied. Is all the talk about the rule of the intelligent and superior race all buncombe? These Negroes may not be sincere in making the request, believing that it would not be granted and hoping to make political capital out of the matter, but their sincerity or insincerity is not germane to the subject; the request itself is all that the convention has to consider, and this request is right and it should be granted. And educational and property qualification will solve the problem of suffrage in South Carolina by eliminating the votes of the ignorant and irresponsible of both races.[9]

As Miller pointed out, these "comments are all from Democrats," not Republicans or other allies. "They show in what regard their acts are held."[10]

Resolutions on Suffrage

On the third day of the convention, several suffrage resolutions were introduced, read, and referred to the appropriate committees for consideration. H. C. Patton introduced "a Resolution for the Regulation of Suffrage in the state of South Carolina," setting forth qualifications for voting that were generally consistent with the "Mississippi Plan" and with the Senator Ben Tillman's publicly stated views, both of which rested on property and literacy requirements. Patton's resolution required every applicant for voter registration to be male, at least twenty-one, and "a legal resident of the state and country for two years"; he also had to have paid a one-dollar-per year poll tax and all other taxes for the current and previous years; he

> must be able to read the Constitution in English
>
> must be able to print and sign his own name; or
>
> shall own property in the amount of three hundred dollars;
>
> shall have been in active service on behalf of the late Confederate states of America; and shall be from a lawful line of descendants of a person who engaged in such service.[11]

Several other suffrage resolutions offered minor variations.

Robert Smalls's Suffrage Plan

On the sixth day of the convention, Monday, September 16, Robert Smalls offered his suffrage plan.

> Sec. 1. In all elections by the people the electors shall vote by ballot.
>
> Sec. 2. Every male citizen of the United States of the age of twenty-one years and upwards, not laboring under the disabilities named in this Constitution, without distinction of race, color or former condition, who shall be a resident of this state at the time of the adoption of this Constitution, or who shall thereafter reside in this state one year, and in the county in which he offers to vote sixty days next preceding any election, shall all be entitled to vote for all officers that are now or hereafter may be elected by the people, and upon all questions submitted to the electors at any elections provided further, That no person while kept in any alms house or asylum, or any of unsound mind, or confined in any public prison, shall be allowed to vote or hold office.

Sec. 3. It shall be the duty of the General Assembly to provide from time to time for the registration of all electors.

Sec. 4. For the purpose of voting, no person shall be deemed to have lost his residence by reason of absence while employed in the service of the United States, nor while engaged upon the waters of this state, or the United States or the high seas, nor while temporarily absent from the state, or removing from one house to another or from one place to another in the same precinct.

Sec. 5. No soldier, seaman or marine in the army or navy of the United States shall be deemed a resident of this state as consequence of having been stationed therein.

Sec. 6. Electors shall in all case, except treason, felony, or breach of the peace, be privileged from arrest and civil process during attendance at elections and in going to and returning from the same.

Sec. 7. Every person entitled to vote at any election shall be eligible to any office, which now is, or hereafter shall be elective by the people in the county where he shall have resided sixty days previous to such election, except as otherwise provided in this Constitution or the Constitution and laws of the United States.

Sec. 8. The General Assembly shall never pass any law that will deprive any of the citizens of this state of the right of suffrage, except for treason, murder, robbery, or dueling whereof the persons shall have been duly tried and convicted.

Sec. 9. Presidential electors shall be elected by the people.

Sec. 10. In all elections, state and federal, there shall be but one ballot box, and one ticket for each party or faction thereof, with the names of all the candidates thereon. There shall be three commissioners of election for each county and three managers for each polling precinct, not more than two of whom shall be of the same political party.

Sec. 11. In all elections held by the people under this Constitution the person or persons who shall receive the highest number of votes shall be declared elected.[12]

Smalls's resolution was a powerful, well-designed attack on the very purpose and sentiments of the convention. Section 2 embraced the spirit of the Thirteenth, Fourteenth, and Fifteenth Amendments and the 1868 Constitution, without jeopardizing the fair and equal treatment of white male voters. Section 6 reflected his experience and observations of abuse particularly by Democrats during and since Reconstruction.

Thomas E. Miller's Speech

Miller was one of the few remaining blacks in the legislature. An attorney, he
had a great deal of respect from the audience. His eloquent, lengthy speech,
which went on for several hours, spread over two days, pointedly described the
true purpose of the convention:

> After a residence of more than 250 years with love and affection for the
> government, after having borne our part in every struggle and answered to
> every call, after having proven to the world that we are conservative in
> thought and action, lovable in our natures, forbearing towards our oppres-
> sor, living under and by the laws, at all time, we are confronted at this hour
> the noon day of peace and unity in the nation, the noon day of prosper-
> ity and hope, the noon day of this magnificent existence of ours with this
> proposition to disfranchise the common people; to take from them the
> dearest right, the right to vote. Oh, Mr. President, why is this to be done?
> Is there anybody here who can or dare deny that the sole purpose for which
> this convention was called is for the disfranchisement of the common peo-
> ple, and the Negro more especially? If there is such a person I ask him to
> read the speeches of the leaders who forced this convention upon us against
> the will of the people, and they will all be convinced that the only thing for
> which this convention was called is for the disfranchisement of that class of
> people, whose chief lot has been toil, toil, toil. With no hopes but to toil!
> . . . He will be convinced that this convention was called to disfranchise the
> Negro in every walk of life and the poor white boy who edits a newspaper
> in which he speak fulsomely for the greatest of all misnomers and southern
> bug bears-white supremacy. There is no hope for him, though he wields an
> eloquent pen, if he is poor. His forefathers may have come here, and, like
> the Negro, spilt his blood, shed his tears, and toiled to plan this magnifi-
> cent tree of liberty, but if this monstrosity becomes the law, there is no hope
> for him but to toil and grovel in poverty, because for the want of $300,
> though an educated Caucasian, he is no better off than his ignorant brother
> in black skin.
>
> Why do they say that the Negro must be disfranchised? Is it because he
> is lawless? No! Is it because he is riotous in the discharge of the right of
> suffrage? No! They answer, "Because his skin is black he should not vote.
> Because his skin is black he is inferior. Because he did not fight for the bal-
> lot he should not have it. Because we were a conquered people and were
> conquered by the National Government, in the name of the Negro, he shall
> not vote."

Miller noted that black Americans "have fought in every Indian war, in every foreign war, in every domestic struggle by the side of the white soldiers from Boston commons and Lake Erie to the Mississippi valley and the banks of the Rio Grande," mentioning specifically that in the American Revolution the "first drop of blood . . . was shed on Boston commons by a Negro slave, Crispus Attucks." Then he addressed the fears of southern whites, saying:

> The Negro will never by any act of his seek to destroy white supremacy. He is non-obstructive; he is the best element of conservative citizenship in the south. Onto his hands is the keeping of peace and happiness of the southern people. But the Hon. Geo. D. Tillman says that the south is a conquered province.
>
> The majority of you blame the poor Negro for the humility inflicted upon you during that conflict, but he had nothing to do with it. It was your love of power and your supreme arrogance that brought it upon you. You are too feeble to settle up with the government for that old grudge. This hatred has even centered upon the Negro, and he is the innocent sufferer. But, sirs, we are here. We intend to obey every phase of law that you may legislate against us. We intend to continue to love and forgive you for what you are doing to us. We intend to remain here and cause the south to blossom anew by our toil and suffering. . . .
>
> . . . The Negroes do not want and would not have social equality, but they do want to cast a ballot for the men who make their laws and administer the laws.

Miller also spoke of the class issue: "Pass this law, and you disfranchise all the laboring people, white and black, unless you so administer this law, which is the avowed intention of your leaders, so as to discriminate against the Negro. Such a discrimination, Mr. President, will be a nullification of the Fifteenth amendment."

In defending the Reconstruction government against charges of corruption, Miller continued as follows:

> We were eight years in power. We had built school houses, established charitable institutions, built and maintained a penitentiary system, provided for the education of the deaf and dumb, rebuilt the jails and court houses, rebuilt the bridges and re-established the ferries. In short, we had reconstructed the state and placed it upon the road to prosperity, and, at the same time, by our acts of financial reform transmitted to the Hampton government indebtedness not greater by more than $2,500,000 than was the

bonded debt of the state in 1868, before the Republican Negroes and their white allies came into power. . . .

Because there had been robbery and fraud and perjury during a part of the time of Negro domination as it is called, it must not be thought that all Negroes were dishonest. Because Tweed and his gang had been corrupt, that did not signify that all of the men who put Tweed into office were corrupt. Because white Democrats voted solidly for and by their votes, elected the most corrupt judge (Thomas J. Mackey) that has ever disgraced the judicial system in South Carolina, why should the white people of our state be pronounced as venal as that arch scoundrel?

He ended his speech by calling for "peace and good feeling between the two races," but concluded "Peace! Peace! Peace! Happiness and prosperity, and the hope for a brighter day seems withered!"[13]

James Wigg's Speech

After Miller finally took his seat, delegate James Wigg then took the floor and made a another long speech in support of Smalls's amendment, telling white delegates that, "if in a spirit of passion and caste you elect to turn a deaf ear to the voice of reason and experience, and blindly abrogate to yourselves rights which you do not justly possess, striving to turn backward on the dial of time the shadow that marks the advancement of liberty and equal rights, you will be guilty of a tremendous blunder, and will ruthlessly reopen issues long since thought to be closed and wounds which good people everywhere hoped had been healed." Wigg warned them:

> You have declared your intention to solve for South Carolina the so-called Negro problem, and to sever at a single stroke the Gordian knot of the suffrage by disfranchising as many Negroes as possible, so as to make it impossible for him by any force of circumstances of wealth or intelligence to outvote the white people and control the destinies of the State. . . .
>
> White supremacy, you say, must be secured, by honest means if you can, by dishonest means if you must. To this, I believe, every white delegate here stands pledged. Beneath this yoke, humiliating as it is, each one of you had to pass; to this pledge each one of you had to subscribe before you could have the privilege of being counted as a delegate to this convention.

Wigg then questioned why the interests of black and white South Carolinians were considered so different:

> The doctrine so persistently taught that the interests of the Negro and Anglo-Saxon are so opposed as to be irreconcilable is a political subterfuge;

a fallacy so glaring in its inception, so insulting to Providence, so contrary to reason and logic of history, that one can scarcely refrain from calling in question either the sanity or honesty of its advocates. . . .

The edict has gone forth that for the preservation of white supremacy, the negro must be disfranchised to such an extent that it shall be forever impossible for him to outvote his white brother, whether he shall exceed him in intelligence or not. To accomplish this result you are urged to trample under foot every law, human or Divine, to set at defiance every Christian and patriotic sentiment which honorable men are accustomed to hold dear.

Then Wigg addressed the poll-tax provision, asserting that it discriminated against poor people of both races. He contrasted the white proposal with that offered by Smalls and the rest of the black delegation:

The committee offers you white supremacy with white degradation. We offer the supremacy of law, of intelligence and property. "Choose ye whom ye will serve." Will you make justice, honor, fidelity, and truth the palladium of your liberties, or will you make injustice, perjury, and fraud the foundation of your policy? We have pled our cause. If you refuse to adjudicate our claims we will yield to the inevitable, but we shall appeal from Phillip drunk to Phillip sober. We submit our cause to the judgment of an enlightened public opinion, and to the advancement of a Christian civilization.[14]

Isaiah R. Reed's Speech

Attorney Isaiah R. Reed of Beaufort then spoke in favor of Smalls's proposal, beginning with an exposition on the "diametrically opposed" ideas of liberty and slavery that existed from the earliest years of American settlement. Americans' "love of liberty . . . budded and bloomed into unmistakable and impressive sentiment and words of the preamble to the Federal Constitution, namely, 'We, the people of the United State, in order to form a more perfect union, establish justice, insure domestic tranquility, provide for the common defense, promote the general welfare and secure the blessings of liberty to ourselves and our posterity do ordain and establish this Constitution for the United States of America.'" Pointing out that the South Carolina delegates signed this document, Reed asked:

Still the question may be asked, Liberty to do what? Well, among some things other than those stated above, it was liberty to have the accuser and accused face to face; liberty to be tried by a jury of their own countrymen;

liberty to be taxed and pay taxes to their own established government, and liberty to vote for and be ruled by their own ruler.

After the great confrontation of liberty and slavery in the Civil War, Reed added, the nation "did form a more perfect Union, it did establish justice, it did ensure domestic tranquility, it did provide for the common defense and secured the blessings of liberty to all of the citizens and their posterity when the 13th, 14th and 15th amendments were accepted and made the Negroes full-fledged citizens of the United States and of the States." He urged the delegates:

> You have charged that the Negroes are ignorant and that they are prone to elect ignorant and unscrupulous men to office. Does not the intelligence of the delegates here elected from Beaufort refute that charge?
>
> You have suffered the Negroes to harness in tandem and drive your costly steeds through the thoroughfares; you have suffered them to serve the delicacies of your festal boards; in short, you have suffered them to attend many other vocations of life; which come nearer to your person and nearer to your property than casting a ballot.
>
> In conclusion, I say that all such things produce bad and revolutionary citizens and stop the citizens from defending and honoring the peace and dignity of the State. That these citizens should be defended by a fair and impartial suffrage that would not commit them to the mercy of arrogant and unscrupulous registrars, and managers who could invert, subvert, convert, divert their political wishes. I, therefore, favor the substitute of my colleague from Beaufort.[15]

The other black Republican delegates also spoke, and Smalls closed out the debate with a very long speech in support of his suffrage resolution.

Tillman Speaks, and Smalls Responds

Then, on Friday, November 1, 1895, Senator Benjamin R. Tillman, chair of the Committee on the Right of Suffrage, spoke at length in support of his committee's report. During the course of his extraordinarily long address, he denounced the Constitution of 1868, Reconstruction, and the Republicans, especially black Republicans. He singled out several persons for criticism, giving particular attention to Robert Smalls. He recited in detail his version of the trial of November 1877, at which Smalls was convicted. In strident, sarcastic, and biting language he convicted Smalls all over again nearly twenty years later. In seconding Tillman's motion, another delegate, J. C. Sheppard, also attacked Smalls.[16]

At this time, as was fully expected, Robert Smalls asked for and was given the floor, whereupon he delivered what was perhaps the most eloquent speech of his entire career. (It is a particular note on civility that Senator Tillman requested that Smalls's address be printed in the official convention journal.) Smalls then addressed the convention on Saturday, November 2:

Mr. President, I had thought that I would not find it necessary to have a word to say in regard to this contest for the right of freemen, for the question had been ably presented by others; but to my surprise I find the distinguished gentlemen from Edgefield, Mr. Tillman and Mr. J. C. Sheppard, going away from the all important question, the right to let free Americans cast an honest ballot for honest men.

By those gentlemen I am arraigned here and placed on trial for an act said to have been committed in 1873 in South Carolina. It is true, sir, that I was arrested in the state in 1877, charged by the Democrats of the state with receiving a bribe in 1873. . . .

Now, let me say that after that trial and after I was arrested I appealed to the supreme court of the state. The supreme court held that opinion off over one year, as the record will show. After I had run for congress a second time the supreme court rendered a decision sustaining the action of the lower court. After that was done, under Section 641 of the Revised Statutes, I took an appeal to the Supreme Court of the United States. I went to Washington and appeared before that court. The record shows it, I went before Chief Justice Waite, and he granted the appeal and docketed the case.

No sooner was this done, and no sooner had I returned to South Carolina, than, without a single word from me, or friend of mine, directly or indirectly, Governor Simpson, of South Carolina, issued and sent to me in Beaufort a pardon, which I have here in this paper.

Why should this matter be dragged into this debate? Why, sir, it is to inflame the passions of delegates against Republicans and force them to vote for this most infamous Suffrage Bill, which seeks to take away the right to vote from two-thirds of the qualified voters of the state.

It has been claimed that there has been a compromise in my case, but this is not true. I refused all offers of compromise, but there were compromises made but I was not included; I received no advantage there from. I have here a copy of a compromise entered into by the state of South Carolina and the United States District Attorney for South Carolina, which I send to the desk and ask that it be read, which speaks for itself:

Mr. President, I am through with this matter. It should not have been brought in here. All the thieves are gone; they are scattered over this floor, and I shall serve them to the best of my ability.

My race needs no special defense, for the past history of them in this country proves them to be as good as any people anywhere. All they need is an equal chance in the battle of life. I am proud of them, and by their acts toward me I know that they are not ashamed of me, for they have at all times honored me with their votes.

I stand here the equal of any man. I started out in the war with the Confederates; they threatened to punish me and I left them. I went to the Union army. I fought in seventeen battles to make glorious and perpetuate the flag that some of you trampled under your feet.

Innocent of every charge attempted to be made here today against me, no act or word of yours can in any way blur the record that I have made at home and abroad.

Mr. President, I am through, and shall not hereafter notice any personal remark. You have the facts in the case; by them I ask to be judged.[17]

The day after his historic address to the convention, Smalls received word from home that his wife, Annie, was gravely ill. He took an indefinite leave of absence from the convention and rushed home. He was able to arrive before her death on Tuesday, November 5. She was buried in Tabernacle Baptist Church cemetery beside Smalls's first wife, Hannah.

After more than a week taking care of family affairs, Smalls returned to the convention in Columbia on November 14. He was on hand to support the resolution introduced by Beaufort delegate Isaiah J. Reed and surprisingly supported by Tillman, which established South Carolina State College.

On Wednesday, December 4, 1985, convention president John C. Evans announced that all convention business had been completed. He then asked all delegates to affix their signatures to the final document by county, beginning with those from Abbeville. When it was Beaufort's turn, Smalls, who was the only member of the Beaufort delegation present to represent the black delegates, asked to be excused from signing as he did not wish to endorse a constitution containing such an article on suffrage. He was unanimously excused.

One delegate offered a resolution that members not signing the constitution should not be paid their per diem and travel expense. Smalls rose and said that he would walk home from Columbia to Beaufort rather than sign the instrument. The resolution was not put before the convention.[18]

Accomplishments of the Black Republicans

What, it might be asked, did the six Republican delegates gain at this convention? Their loss was historic: theft of blacks' right to vote, in general, for some seventy years, until passage of the voting rights act of 1965. Their tangible gains were few, notably the very important and historic inauguration of a state-supported higher educational institution for African Americans.

Reflection on the participation of these six black delegates reveals that despite their devastating losses, they accomplished a number of important, though intangible, gains. First they stayed the course in a public forum overwhelmingly hostile to their interests. They also demonstrated a mastery of rhetorical and forensic skills as well as constitutional history, illustrating the important lesson that excellence in rhetoric, persuasion, and deportment knows no race, creed, or previous condition of servitude. It would be difficult to find a group of legislators today, black or white, state or national, who could best these men. Smalls's strong support for the constitutional ban on interracial marriage was widely heralded, but his amendment to extend the ban to include unions of unmarried couples—with children of such unions to bear the father's name and have the right to inherit from him—met with laughter and resounding defeat in South Carolina but acclaim nationwide.

A final intangible gain these men earned in this convention is reputation. They advanced the reputation of the African American people for seriousness of purpose, conviction on equality for both races, moderation, competence and comity. This gain was captured by Sarah Smalls and Mary J. Miller and recognized by the press and many constituents.

For himself, the fifty-six-year-old elder statesman regained a measure of the luster he lost two decades earlier with his trial and the collapse of Reconstruction. The impact of Smalls's performance at the 1895 Constitutional Convention is apparent in the media. Even a newspaper that had staunchly opposed Smalls over the past two decades modified its view. After giving generally fair coverage to the speeches of the black delegates at the convention, the Democratic-leaning *News and Courier* editorialized "we believe it safe to say that he could not be convicted before a jury of impartial white men anywhere on the same evidence today. Perhaps some of the lawyers or citizens of Columbia will take the trouble to correct or confirm what we have said in the interest of justice."[19] More than a century later, despite substantial progress and promising initiatives, the lawyers and citizens of Columbia had not yet restored the reputation of Robert Smalls as the *News and Courier* demanded of them.

PART V

Families Are Forever

At the 1992 Smalls family reunion Furman Williams, the oldest member of the family and the only one who knew Robert Smalls personally, handed out a statement he had written, "Our Forever Family." He challenged the descendants assembled to always keep the spirit of the family flourishing. It is in that spirit that the following three chapters examine the Smalls family down through the generations who have struggled, with a remarkable degree of success, to accomplish that task. Robert Smalls certainly would be proud of them all.

The family has been a source of enduring strength for African American people although it has not always had the traditional husband-and-wife family structure. This is why Robert Hill found "flexible family roles" to be among the six strengths of African American families down through the generations. This is also why Joyce Ladner discovered family relations to be among the "ties that bind" the African American community together.

Robert Smalls's legacy includes a variety of family structures. Some are nuclear families, some extended families, and some augmented families, which include members not related to the others by blood or marital ties. His very first family—which consisted of his mother, Lydia, himself, and for a time his grandmother—was at once a nuclear and an extended family. His second family consisted of his owner Henry McKee and McKee's wife and children, who bore no blood relation to Smalls, but because he lived in their home, they played a key role in helping his mother raise him. Some readers will dismiss the McKees as Robert Smalls's family because they were his owners and he their "property." However, sociologists and scholars in other scientific disciplines consider a group a family if it functions as a family.

Smalls's third family of record was the one he created by his marriage to Hannah, when they were both held in slavery. This family included Hannah, his stepchildren, and their own children. There is no doubt that this nuclear and extended family brought great comfort to Smalls and they to him.

The relationship that Smalls would have been the first to recognize as mutual and reciprocal was his fourth family, the group that accompanied him on the escape from Charleston harbor into freedom. Smalls, his wife, children, and stepchild were a nuclear family. John Smalls, his wife, and child constituted another nuclear family, which was related to Smalls by augmentation. The members of the crew, who were not related by blood or marriage, nevertheless functioned as an augmented family, with all being responsible to and for each other.

Smalls's fifth family, established after the escape, consisted of the seventeen people who lived together in the same house, including nuclear, extended, and augmented family members. According to the implicit ecological perspective, family members not only relied on themselves for the care of their children and other members but turned to and were assisted by institutions in the community, which they supported and which helped them meet their basic human needs. Among these community institutions were churches, schools, workplaces, and later hospitals and lodges, all of which played important roles in helping these families raise their children and meet their own needs as well. While these families helped to build and sustain these community-based institutions, the relationship was again reciprocal.

In the following chapters we shall see how Smalls's descendants sustained and benefited from strong families and strong institutions in the community. Beyond that, we shall see how they related to institutions in the wider society, which sometimes sustained them but often constrained them in their struggles for life, liberty, and the pursuit of well being.

The Bampfields of Beaufort

Samuel and Elizabeth Bampfield and Their Children

April 24, 1877, was a red-letter day in Beaufort, South Carolina. Nineteen-year-old Elizabeth Lydia Smalls was going to marry twenty-eight-year-old Samuel Jones Bampfield, an attorney.

Introduction: The Wedding

The ceremony took place in the First African Baptist Church of Beaufort, situated a few yards from the Robert Smalls home. The wedding reception was held at this house, where Elizabeth had spent most of her young and already eventful life.

The crowd spilled over into the yard, which was filled with trees, shrubs, and flowers. Elizabeth had played in this yard as a child, as had her father before her. In the years ahead Elizabeth's children found pleasure in this beautiful and well-kept yard.

Descriptions of the wedding, its principals, and their descendants reveal some of the complex features of African American family life, then as now. And despite the hard times in which this family existed, their structural and functional diversity is reflected in the extraordinary lengths to which individuals and families went in order to meet the basic needs of their members, especially the children. Children were central to the family, which shared the responsibility of child rearing. Social closeness and mutual support were (and are still) at the heart of the meaning of family, as is revealed in child-naming and child-rearing practices. Moreover, this wedding revealed the family's distinct patterns of socioeconomic diversity, the strong value they placed on family and work, and preeminently the roles of religion, faith, and institutional church.

The Wedding Party

The matriarch of this wedding party was the bride's eighty-one-year-old grandmother, Lydia Polite Smalls. Lydia was unwell, but she would not have missed this occasion. Within a year she was gone. Descendants believe she was buried on the Ashdale Plantation, where she was born into slavery in 1796. At the time of her birth, she and the plantation were both owned by the John McKee family. At the time of her burial, the plantation was owned by her son, congressman and general Robert Smalls.[1]

The bride's fifty-one-year-old mother, Hannah Jones Smalls, presided at this wedding and oversaw much of the detailed planning and execution. Because mothers think of their daughters' weddings from the time of their birth, this day was the culmination of a nineteen-year dream for Hannah, who was considered a model of virtuous approbation. On first meeting her, Admiral Samuel Du Pont described her in a letter to his wife as "very superior."

Thirteen-year-old sister Sarah Voorhees Smalls was the bridesmaid. Despite the six-year age difference between the two sisters, descendants say that they were always close, affectionate, and caring toward each other. While Sarah no doubt looked forward to her own marriage someday, she had no way of knowing that it would be substantially less fruitful than this one and extremely brief. Nor could she know that during the course of her too-short lifetime she would discover talents and opportunities unknown to her older sister. But this day belonged to Elizabeth and Samuel.

Also in attendance at this wedding in their best dresses and manners were the bride's two older half sisters, born to her mother, Hannah Jones, before she and Robert Smalls were married.[2] Charlotte Jones, the oldest, was thirty-five years old at the time of this wedding, and Clara was thirty-three.

Charlotte was married to a man named Larry Williams, with whom she had several children. A daughter named Rebecca Williams was born in 1870. Another daughter, Susan Williams, was born in 1872. A son named Willie Williams was born in 1877, the year of the wedding.

Clara Jones was living with an English sea captain named Ryder in a house on Craven Street that was probably owned by Smalls. They had two daughters at the time of the wedding. Sarah Ryder, born in 1872, was five years old, and Beula Ryder, born in 1876, was one. These children and grandchildren of Hannah Jones were part of this family and certainly members of the wedding party.

Father of the Bride

It is beyond question that this day, April 24, 1877, was Robert Smalls's day in a special sense. His many titles—including captain, general, congressman, and chairman—were all hard won and well deserved. But on that day none could rival "father of the bride." For the occasion he likely wore his Prince Albert formal cutaway coat, striped pants, top hat, and high-buttoned patent-leather shoes.

Special Guests

The wedding and reception were filled with special guests. Among them were Samuel J. Bampfield's siblings, nieces, and nephews, who had come from Charleston and Hampton.[3] Another prominent guest from Charleston was the scholarly Francis L. Cardozo, founder of the Avery Normal Institute and Bampfield's mentor. Cardozo had recently been reelected to his third term as state treasurer, a position that many proclaimed was the second most powerful position in state government. Also at the wedding was Richard T. Greener, the first black graduate of Harvard University, who, like Cardozo, had graduated from the University of South Carolina School of Law while serving as the first black person on the faculty at the university. Greener used all his impressive intellectual gifts to advance the cause of the Republican Party and its leaders, both black and white. Former ambassador to Haiti, Dr. Alonzo Crum, Smalls's physician and political ally, was there with his wife, Ellen Craft. Ellen was the daughter of William and Ellen Craft, whose daring escape from slavery in Georgia in 1848 and their educational and humanitarian service after the war rivaled Smalls's experience and joined the two families together.[4] Also in attendance were Smalls's political colleagues who had purchased homes in his neighborhood. Prominent among these neighbors were Judge William J. Whipper, Samuel Green, and George Holmes.

Bampfield Family History

Who, then, was Samuel J. Bampfield? At that time he was known as the son of free black parents in Charleston. A hundred years after his death, however, it was learned that his ancestry was somewhat more complex. On his father's side Samuel J. Bampfield descended from a prominent British family, whose ancestry, some descendants believe, reaches back to British royalty.[5] Samuel's paternal grandparents were Joseph Bampfield Sr. and Antoinette Turnbull Bampfield. During the nineteenth century three of their sons immigrated to the new world. James Bampfield (1815–1879) went to Nova Scotia, where on July

21, 1846, he married a Canadian woman named Margaret Sheehan. Another brother, John Bampfield, married a woman named Hannah in England, and they moved to Australia sometime in the early 1860s. Their first child, Harry, was born there on August 27, 1866. Earlier, during the 1820s, their eldest brother, Joseph Bampfield Jr., had immigrated to the United States. He settled in Charleston, South Carolina, where he married a free black mulatto woman named Judith Robinson in about 1827. The couple produced eleven children, all of whom, following their mother's line as well as American custom and law, became know as "free blacks," then Negroes, and eventually African Americans.

Born in Charleston on December 5, 1849, Samuel Jones Bampfield was the youngest son of this free biracial couple. In order of birth, these children were Annie (1829), Thomas (1830), Joseph (1832), Caroline (1834), Jane (1836, died in infancy), Judith (1837, died in infancy), Maria (1839), Jane (1842), James (1842), John G. (1847), and Samuel Jones (1849).

John G. Bampfield

The seventh of the eight children born to Joseph Bampfield Jr. and Judith Robinson Bampfield was John G. Bampfield. After the Civil War John purchased large tracts of land in Yemassee, South Carolina; some of this land has remained in the family until the present time. John created quite a legacy in Hampton County. He married Margaret Jackson, and they had six children.

The Bampfield brothers from England had no association through the years, but in 1993 James Robert "Jim" Bampfield, representing the white Bampfields of Nova Scotia, and Samuel J. Bampfield's granddaughter Janet "Dolly" Davidson Nash of Beaufort, representing the black Bampfields of South Carolina, began communication.

Jim Bampfield, initiator of the reconnection, wrote to Dolly Nash in 1993: "I have done a fairly complete study of the Ontario, Canada branch of the family back to my great-great-grandfather, James Bampfield (1815–1879). . . . I have tried to trace the origins of the brother, Joseph Bampfield, who found his way to South Carolina, and must have migrated from England as early as the 1820s. He was married to Judith Robinson a free black woman and their first child Annie Bampfield was born in 1829. Samuel J. Bampfield, the youngest, was born 5 Dec. 1849. . . . Although I have not yet achieved what I set out to find, I am delighted that I have connected with some previously unknown cousins and I have learned a great deal about the history of Beaufort. I would very much like to share with you the family 'tree' I have put together and would certainly like to see what you have done."[6] Dolly Nash supplied Jim Bampfield with information and some photographs of the Beaufort Bampfields, and he included the Beaufort branch of the family in his unpublished genealogy. John Bampfield is the only one of these siblings that Dolly Nash knew personally: "I knew him when I was a little girl in the 1930s. He was the postmaster at Yemassee and had lots of land. . . . They took lots of his land to make room for the super highway I-95 in South Carolina. Some of his descendants still own some of that land."

While the future of collaboration and celebration among the black and white Bampfields of three continents and four countries is uncertain, it is clear now that—as with Thomas Jefferson's and George Washington's descendants— black and white Bampfields have made steps toward mutual recognition. And as Edward Ball has shown through his book *Slaves in the Family* (1998) and as Robert Smalls so eloquently stated in an address to the 1895 Constitutional Convention, racial cohabitation in America seems to have no beginning, and the end is not yet in view.

While all the Bampfield-Robinson descendants were considered African Americans by law and custom, some of them, because of their European features, passed for white through the years. One of the many contradictions of race relations in South Carolina is that for a brief period after the Civil War it was much better to be black and educated than to be white and uneducated.

Growing Up Black

Descendants emphasize that Judith Robinson was distinctly mulatto and exhibited strong American Indian features. Photographs of Joseph Bampfield and Judith Robinson Bampfield show that they could have just as well passed for a white couple as for a biracial one. They chose to live as "free blacks" and raised their children as African Americans.

Samuel Bampfield's black cultural identity was expressed in his education. By the time he was six years old in 1855, his parents had enrolled him in one of the schools operated by free blacks for their children. At this time eighteen-year-old Francis Cardozo (1837–1903) was a teacher in one of these schools, having spent eight years studying in them. It is conceivable that Bampfield knew and studied under Cardozo before the war.

In June 1865 the American Missionary Association employed Cardozo to head their educational mission for black students in Charleston. Cardozo wrote that his primary mission in returning to the South was to establish a normal school for the preparation of Christian teachers who would be in the vanguard of elevating the race.[7] In October 1865, when Cardozo opened the Saxton School, named for General Rufus Saxton, 600 girls and 400 boys were enrolled. Among these eager learners were sixteen-year-old Samuel J. Bampfield, future son-in-law to Smalls, and ten-year-old Annie E. Wigg, who later became Smalls's second wife. Twenty teachers, ten whites from the North and ten blacks from the South, struggled to educate their pupils. Cardozo concluded that a great deal of instruction was required to prepare these students for high-school-level work so that they could become teachers. In the fall of 1867 he determined that enough of these students were now ready to make a transition into a normal school. He reduced the enrollment to 438, with eight of the northern whites serving as the teaching staff. Later, when financial support was obtained from the Avery Foundation, a school was constructed on the present site and named Avery Normal Institute in 1868.

Eager to pursue his mission of producing black teachers who could help to lift the black population out of bondage, Cardozo did not wait for Avery Normal School to train such talent. He obtained scholarships for his brightest students to attend colleges that included Oberlin College (Walter Raleigh Jones, 1867–1870), Lincoln University (Bampfield, 1866–1872), and Howard University (T. McCants Stewart, 1869–1873). All three returned to South Carolina to play leadership roles during Reconstruction.

The records of Lincoln University show that Bampfield was a 1872 graduate of Lincoln, where his classmates included the illustrious Archibald and Francis Grimké.[8] Two other Bampfield family members also studied at Lincoln, supporting the important role played by historically black colleges in the creation of the early black middle class. Samuel Jones Bampfield II, nephew to his namesake, graduated from Lincoln in the class of 1893. He then earned his M.D. degree at Howard University and became the most distinguished black physician in West Virginia, serving both blacks and whites. Still another nephew, Thomas R. Bampfield, graduated from Lincoln University in the class of 1896 and went on to a career as a prominent businessman in New York City.[9] Our Samuel J. Bampfield was enrolled in the preparatory department for the academic years 1865–1866 and 1866–1867. He then spent two years studying in the law department, from which he graduated in 1872. Bampfield returned to Charleston to read law with a Judge Cage and was admitted to the South Carolina Bar.[10]

Sometime around 1873 Bampfield moved to Beaufort and became active in the Republican Party. Robert Smalls took the bright young attorney under his political wing. By 1874, when Smalls began his first term in the U.S. Congress, Bampfield had succeeded him as a member of the General Assembly.[11]

When Smalls went to Congress in 1874, his daughter Elizabeth joined her father in Washington as his congressional secretary and hostess. On their returned to Beaufort on recess during 1875, Smalls introduced seventeen-year-old Elizabeth to his twenty-six-year-old political protégé, attorney and state representative Samuel J. Bampfield. Descendants say that it was love at first sight between these two eligible, attractive, and well-educated young people.

Bampfield's political career continued to advance. In 1876 he was elected to the first of ten consecutive terms as clerk of court for Beaufort County, a career that spanned a period of twenty years. By all accounts he did an outstanding job and was well regarded and highly respected by all who knew him.

New Street House

In June 1877, a few weeks after their wedding, Elizabeth and Samuel Bampfield moved into their new home at 414 New Street in Beaufort, less than two blocks from Smalls's home. This house was their home for twenty-two years, and all eleven of their children were born there. The house is still standing and in good condition.

Samuel continued to grow in his profession and as a community leader, while Elizabeth with all her education, worldliness, political savvy, and ambitions for her people took up a traditional role of full-time wife, mother, and home manager. With a constantly growing family, she had a great deal of help with child care from her nuclear and extended family. Smalls was exceedingly devoted to his grandchildren; he spent a great deal of time at their house and entertained them lavishly in his own house nearby.[12] They also had a full-time live-in maid.

Samuel J. Bampfield's Career

Samuel Bampfield was an active political ally of his father-in-law. During his twenty years as clerk of Beaufort County courts, Bampfield compiled an outstanding and unblemished record of service. In 1891 Bampfield joined with G. W. Anderson, a schoolteacher, and I. Randall Reid, an attorney and deputy sheriff, to become founding editors of the *New South,* "a weekly of four pages carrying national as well as local news."[13]

In his memoir, William Elliott Jr., son of the attorney who ran against Smalls for Congress, was quite complimentary to Smalls and Bampfield. Of Bampfield he wrote,

> He was a remarkable Negro. . . . He was well educated and I remember that during the time I was in Beaufort he took up the study of Spanish. Many circuit judges said he was one of the best clerks of court in the state. Furthermore he had the manners of a gentleman."[14]

Bampfield was almost as staunch a Republican as his father-in-law. In his single term in the General Assembly, Bampfield joined forces with the Republican, black majority, with whom Governor David H. Chamberlain was fighting as he attempted to appoint white Democrats to judicial positions. Chamberlain opposed the legislature's nomination of William J. Whipper after he was nominated by the legislature with its strong unified black leadership, including Bampfield. This caused a major confrontation. And when the black Republican speaker of the house recommended reappointment of one Democratic judge, Bampfield took the floor in opposition, saying: "I have nothing against the man you recommend except that he is a Democrat." He continued, "The Republican Party is on the verge of a terrible crisis. And an out-and-out Republican judiciary is all that can save it from utter annihilation."[15]

Bampfield was thoughtful and reflective, always trying to think his way, the Republicans' way, and black people's way out of the looming predicament in which they found themselves. A decade later he became a leader in the political "fusion" movement because, as he announced in his newspaper, the experience of Reconstruction had demonstrated that blacks could not go it alone in politics. Bampfield saw the handwriting on the wall for the demise of the Republican Party before Smalls did. Writing in the *New South,* he argued that "safety and success for the Negroes of South Carolina lie in conciliation and not in antagonism in their dealings with the whites on state issues. Fourteen years experience has clearly shown it."[16]

In the 1888 election season Bampfield helped to organize the Fusion Party of Republicans, Democrats, and nonaligned whites and blacks. The Fusion ticket was successful in county elections. Bampfield was so popular that he won reelection handily on both Republican and Fusion tickets. Other Fusionists who won election generally replaced black Republican officeholders in the county. Elliott reported that "there were put into office whites as follows: Joseph Reed, County Treasurer; Thomas Tailbird, Probate Judge; Joseph Glover, Supervisor and *colored* as follows: S. J. Bampfield, Clerk of Court; George A. Reed, Sheriff and James Wigg, School Commissioner."[17]

This represented the first time that white Democrats had been elected to office in Beaufort County in nearly two decades and, as we now know, was a harbinger of things to come. Even though Smalls steadfastly voted Republican, because his son-in-law was leader of the Fusionists, Smalls was criticized as a sort of closet Fusionist by some defeated Republicans, who accused him of helping Bampfield. Smalls had indeed voted for Bampfield, but he did so on the Republican ticket. He also admitted that he voted for Reed for sheriff and for Thomas Tailbird, another Democrat. Elliott wrote: "It will be noted that the whites took the money handling jobs and the colored the others."[18]

A certain amount of drama was added to these election results because three black Republicans, including the attorney William J. Whipper, lost in the election. Whipper, however, refused to concede. He had been serving as probate judge, but, when the election results were announced, Whipper had lost his seat to the white Democrat Thomas Tailbird. According to Elliott, "Whipper refused to give up his office as probate judge, or the books thereof, and Tailbird brought an action [in the court] to get possession. Even after the State Supreme Court . . . decided the election for Tailbird, Whipper refused to surrender the books, which he had hidden. So he was put in jail and kept there until the books were produced."[19] After thirteen days in jail, Whipper agreed to turn over the books and office to Tailbird and was released.

As captain of the Beaufort militia, Smalls was obliged to arrest Whipper and take him to jail. It was characteristic of Smalls to honor and enforce the law fairly and without fear or favor. While in jail Whipper wrote a blistering diatribe against Smalls.[20] Afterward Smalls and Whipper served together in numerous roles in the Republican Party, sometimes in concert and other times in opposition to each other.

Bampfield's Other Roles

His descendants believe that Bampfield's most important role was that of husband and father. When Carter G. Woodson wrote *Robert Smalls and His Descendants* in 1947, he noted that Smalls had produced many descendants who made important contributions to the nation.[21] Most of these descendants were the children and grandchildren of Samuel and Elizabeth Smalls Bampfield.

Bampfield was also an active member of the Masonic Lodge, as was Smalls. Today the Beaufort Lodge is Samuel J. Bampfield Masonic Lodge No. 584. This lodge takes the responsibility of keeping clean the Bampfield family plot in the Mercy Cemetery, where Bampfield, Elizabeth, and seven of their eleven children are buried.

Bampfield—like Cardozo and a small band of mulattoes in Charleston, free before the Civil War—was a staunch Presbyterian. He constantly studied the scriptures and was elevated to the position of elder in the Presbyterian Church. But there was no black Presbyterian church in Beaufort after the war. So, while Smalls was a founding member of the First African Baptist Church in Beaufort, Bampfield took the lead in establishing Berean Presbyterian Church on Carteret Street. The half-dozen incorporators, mostly family members and close friends, constituted the bulk of the tiny, predominantly black congregation. The building is still standing and has been taken over by a private art studio.

The Constitution of 1895 brought to an end the election of blacks and Republicans in the state. In 1896, when Bampfield lost his seat as clerk of court, President William McKinley, a Republican, acted on the recommendation of

Smalls and appointed Bampfield postmaster of Beaufort. Bampfield died in 1899 at the age of fifty. His widow, Elizabeth, succeeded him as postmaster and served until the political winds of 1908 caused her removal.

To support her children Elizabeth then took a position as secretary to Rossa B. Cooley, the new head of Penn School. In 1910 Elizabeth and her children moved to Charlotte, North Carolina. She never remarried, though she survived her husband by more than fifty years. She died in Charlotte at age 101 in 1959. She, her husband, and seven of their children are buried in a prominent Bampfield family plot in the Sisters of Mercy Cemetery.

Julia Bampfield Stinson

Samuel and Elizabeth's firstborn child was Julia Bampfield (b. 1877), born in Beaufort. Her parents and grandparents saw to it that she got a good education, which she received at the Institute for Colored Youth in Philadelphia. In 1910 she moved with her mother to Charlotte. Later she taught school in Beaufort and then married William Henry Stinson. Also an educator, Stinson became principal of Beaufort High School, which in 1925 was renamed Robert Smalls High School. The Stinsons later moved to Charlotte, where he became head of the boarding-school department at Johnson C. Smith University, a school founded with support of the Presbyterian Church.

Julia and her siblings constituted the second generation of Robert and Hannah Smalls's descendants and continued the line of upward mobility established by their parents. This generation depended heavily on the historically black colleges in the South; most of them entered the teaching profession, largely in those segregated black schools. Julia and William Stinson had a eight children: Thelma (b. 1902), Edna (b. 1903 or 1904) William (b. 1905), Camilla (b. 1907), Julian (b. 1910), Alberta, Mary Helen (b. 1914), and Bampfield (b. 1917).

Thelma Stinson was the oldest of William and Julia's children. According to Dolly Nash, Thelma was married and had several children. In 2000, her daughter Julia Boyd Picket, who lived in Union Springs, Alabama, took in her aunt Camilla Stinson Duff (Thelma's sister who died in 2003).

The second Stinson daughter was Edna Stinson Robinson, who graduated from Fisk University and married Audrey Robinson, a plasterer. She taught school in Charlotte, North Carolina. The Robinsons had no children.

William Bampfield Stinson (1905–1981) grew up in Charlotte, North Carolina. He attended Johnson C. Smith University, following a family tradition, and then went to Columbia University. He moved to Washington State in the 1930s and then to Washington, D.C., where he was principal of the Browne

Junior High School. From the time he was a child, he was a consummate school-teacher. When he was young he frequently conducted school for other children from the steps of his family's house. Often the children went home and proudly told their parents something they had learned. When asked where they learned that, each child replied, "I learned it in Willie's school." William never married or had children.

Camilla Stinson Duff (1907–2003) graduated from Western Reserve University in Cleveland and became a supervisor of home economics instruction in the Cleveland public schools.

Julian Leigh Stinson (1910–1992) was named for his mother. He attended college at Johnson C. Smith and married Catherine Elizabeth Hairston. For a long time he operated a filling station in Charlotte, North Carolina.

Alberta "Roxie" Stinson Cannady, named for her maternal uncle Albert, graduated from Johnson C. Smith University and taught school in Gastonia, North Carolina. After she married David Cannady from Oxford, North Carolina, they moved to Detroit, where he was a vice-squad policeman. Their daughter, Julia Ann Cannady, lives in Michigan, and their son, David Cannady Jr., lives in Florida.

As of September 2006, (Mary) Helen Stinson Greenlee is the oldest living member and matriarch of this family. Born August 2, 1914, in Charlotte, North Carolina, to William and Julia Stinson, she graduated from Johnson C. Smith University in 1936 with a B.S. degree, but her love was dressmaking. In 1940 she married Dr. Charles E. Greenlee, who was later a captain in the U.S. Army. Her husband died in 2001. She currently lives in Pittsburgh, Pennsylvania. On April 21, 2004, Helen represented the descendants of Robert Smalls when she christened the LSV8-*Major General Robert Smalls* at its Moss Point, Mississippi, launching.

Bampfield Stinson (1917–1979) was given his mother's maiden name. After attending Johnson C. Smith University, he served in World War II, where he was wounded on two occasions and received a Purple Heart. He studied business administration at Western Reserve University in Cleveland and married Dorothy Peoples. They had no children.

Family names were often repeated through the generations. Another Bampfield family tradition was attendance at Johnson C. Smith University.

Sarah Bampfield Meyer

After Julia, Sarah Bampfield (1879–1923) was the second child born to Elizabeth and Samuel J. Bampfield. Named for her Aunt Sarah, Sarah Bampfield was educated at the Institute for Colored Youth in Philadelphia. She married Edward

Face Meyer, an accountant in the navy at Bremerton, Washington. They had two children, a boy named Bampfield Wallace Meyer, named after his grandfather, and a girl named Edwina Meyer, named after her father. Bampfield Meyer, the elder child, attended Hampton Institute and became a master brick mason.

Maria "Yaddie" Bampfield Simpson

Named after a paternal aunt, Maria (1883–1949), or "Yaddie," Bampfield was Elizabeth and Samuel J. Bampfield's third child. She graduated from Barber-Scotia College and married Charles S. Simpson, a physician who had attended the Shaw University Medical School in North Carolina. He practiced medicine in Beaufort for more than thirty years. His office was on West Street in the heart of a once thriving black business district. The Simpsons purchased the Smalls house at 501 Prince Street from Elizabeth, who had inherited it from her father. They renovated and preserved the house and inhabited it until they passed away. Both Simpsons were members of Berean Presbyterian Church, founded by Samuel J. Bampfield. Charles Simpson died in 1947, and Maria died a year later in 1948. Both Simpsons arranged to have their funerals in the parlor of their Prince Street home. They are both interred in the Bampfield family plot.

The Simpsons had one daughter, Laura Elizabeth (1917–1983), named for her two grandmothers. She studied for two years at Barber-Scotia and then transferred to Johnson C. Smith, where she earned a bachelor's degree in 1939. In the early 1940s she became a teacher at the Shanklin School, which was out in the country in Beaufort County. During this time she lived at home with her parents in the Prince Street house.

Laura inherited the Prince Street house from her parents, becoming the last of the Robert Smalls descendants to live there. She rented the house out for a time to officers from the U.S. Marine Corps stationed in the area. Meanwhile Laura and her husband moved to Washington, D.C., where she held a professional position with the U.S. government.

After both her parents died, Laura Simpson Brown sold the Prince Street house to Allen C. Mustard in 1949.

The Browns had no children. When Laura died, she was buried in the Beaufort National Cemetery because her husband was a veteran of World War II. Her husband died shortly after and is buried beside her.

Like Mercy and Tabernacle, the Beaufort National Cemetery is associated with Robert Smalls, who sponsored the measure creating it in 1885. At first confined to Union veterans, the cemetery has long been open to veterans of all wars. Soldiers from the Fifty-fourth and Fifty-fifth Massachusetts regiments are buried. Three groups buried in this cemetery related in some way to the Smalls legacy: some of his descendants, members of the Fifty-fourth Massachusetts Colored Infantry, and members of the First South Carolina Colored Regiment, which Smalls helped to recruit and transport.

Robert Smalls Bampfield

The Bampfield's fourth child, Hannah, died in infancy. Their fifth child, Robert "Robbie" Smalls Bampfield (1886–1964), was named for his paternal grandfather. He was married twice. His second wife, Ella, born in 1905, celebrated her one hundredth birthday on July 7, 2005. Robert Smalls Bampfield was educated at Johnson C. Smith University. He was a lieutenant in the U.S. Army, was wounded in action during World War II, and received a Purple Heart. Subsequently he worked as a railway mail clerk. Robert Smalls Bampfield was buried in Arlington National Cemetery, the only one of Smalls's descendants buried there.

Elizabeth Bampfield Hall

Known as "Lise," the Bampfield's sixth child, Elizabeth (1889–1975), was given her mother's name.

In 1935, when Elizabeth Smalls Bampfield had been blind for several years, she received a letter from Woolsey Hall, a graduate of Howard University Law School, asking permission to marry her daughter Elizabeth Lydia. After having someone read the letter to her, she pondered the matter for a while and then wrote to him in her own handwriting on September 16:

> You have asked me a tremendously momentous question and I haven't been able to bring myself to the place where I could answer yes. . . .
>
> Marriage is ordained by God. I have never made a match and I have never broken one after I am informed of the intentions of any of my children to marry. I have never put one thing in their way of going through with it and I shall not do it with you. Therefore I pray that everything will turn out for the best and that the union will be a happy one.[22]

Lise married Hall, who held a professional position in the U.S. Treasury Department and served by political appointment as a member of the Washington, D.C., school board.

In an extensive interview (September 15–17, 2000), Dolly remembered that in Washington, some people referred to Elizabeth Lydia Bampfield Hall's husband Woolsey Hall as "Mr. Bampfield." He responded, "I don't mind if you call her Mrs. Bampfield, but please call me Mr. Hall." Dolly continued, "He was a big Democrat and very important person in Washington. My aunt, Lise, was always a Republican. Must have been an interesting household."

Albert Barnes Bampfield

The Bampfields' seventh child, Albert Barnes Bampfield (1890–1980), was one of Robert Smalls's favorite grandchildren. Because he was similar in age and size to Smalls's youngest child, William Robert Smalls, Albert spent a great deal of time at the Smalls home. William Robert wrote about their closeness, remembering once when his father came home from Washington with two new suits, one for him and the other for Albert. Albert attended public schools in Beaufort and then received a bachelor's degree from Johnson C. Smith University. Afterward he was appointed as a railway mail clerk, a position he held for forty-three years, traveling principally between Augusta, Georgia, and Port Royal, South Carolina. His career was aided, no doubt, by the fact that his older brother Robert Smalls Bampfield had held a similar position with the same company.

In 1914 Albert married Lillian Smoot of Augusta, Georgia, a cousin of the distinguished novelist Frank Yerby, also from Augusta. Living in Augusta, Albert and Lillian Bampfield were prominent members of St. Mary's Episcopal Church, where Albert served for several years as a member of the vestry. They had no children.

Dolly Nash attended Albert Barnes Bampfield's funeral in Augusta, Georgia, on Saturday, December 13, 1980. Despite the high-church Episcopal rites, the event included black Protestant elements. The scripture reading was from the Twenty-third Psalm, and the songs "Abide with Me," "My Faith Looks Up to Thee," and "Just As I Am" would have made any low-church Baptist feel at home.

Janet Bampfield Davidson

The eighth child of Elizabeth and Samuel Bampfield was Janet Bampfield (1893–1975), Dolly Nash's mother. Janet completed the two-year course at Barber-Scotia College and became an accomplished dressmaker.

Janet Bampfield married Edward Estes Davidson in the early 1920s. He attended North Carolina Agricultural and Technical College and became a plasterer. His brother was a brick mason. Janet and Edward had two children: Janet "Dolly" (1924–2004) and Edward Estes (1925–1990).

The Davidsons moved to Philadelphia sometime before 1924. According to Dolly, "Both my brother and I were born in Philadelphia. . . . I was born in the

Presbyterian hospital in Philadelphia, and I'm still Presbyterian and proud of it." Her father had his own business in Philadelphia as a contractor. He did all the plastering in Dolly's home in Cape May, New Jersey, after her husband, John Nash, had built the house.

In her mother's later years, Dolly moved Janet Davidson to Cape May so she could care for her. Janet died of a stroke in 1975 at the age of eighty-two and was interred in the Bampfield family plot. Dolly Nash died on March 17, 2004. She was buried in Cape May.

Interview with Dolly

On September 15–17, 2000, the author and his wife spent three days as Dolly and John Nash's houseguests, reviewing the entire Smalls-Bampfield genealogy. Dolly shared her family's history in great detail, further bringing to life the story and legacy of Robert Smalls.

I asked, "When you were growing up did you know about the *Planter* story?" Dolly answered, "Yes, I knew about the *Planter;* I knew about the Prince Street house; I knew where he was born in the backyard. We used to go to Beaufort every summer to see Yaddie [Maria 'Yaddie' Bampfield Simpson] who lived in that house. She remained in Beaufort and lived in grandpa's house." Smalls was Dolly's great grandfather, but she always referred to him as "Grandpa."

Dolly attended public school in Charlotte and earned her bachelor degree in dance and physical education from Hampton University in Virginia, where she performed as solo dancer with the Hampton Dancers for three of her years in college. After Hampton she taught physical education at Claflin College in Orangeburg, South Carolina, for one year. At Hampton, Dolly met John Nash, who was a recently returned veteran of World War II. They were married in 1948. Both became schoolteachers, and John also became a master upholsterer. Over the years the Nashes were steadfast Hampton supporters, returning to the campus for visits and reading the *Hampton Magazine.*

Dolly told the author, "We moved there, from Philadelphia to Charlotte, when I was 18 months old. It was the Depression and things were tight. So we went to live with my grandmother, Robert Smalls's oldest daughter Elizabeth, who had moved from Beaufort to Charlotte in 1910 after her husband, Samuel J. Bampfield, had been dead for ten years. That is where I first learned a little bit about Robert Smalls's history. We never talked about it very much but everybody knew the story. I learned about the *Planter;* I learned that my grandmother [Elizabeth] was on the boat. I learned what grandpa did." Author: "Why didn't they discuss it more?" Dolly: "I think it must have been unpleasant. It wasn't a pleasant story . . . to be discussing slavery all the time."

The embarrassment among African Americans about the slavery experience has persisted down through the years almost to the present time. Even among scholars, it was at first and for a long time primarily white scholars who studied the experience of slavery and tended to discuss it from the perspectives and experiences of the white plantation owners. This is because, in part, historians are so dependent on written records. Because slavery was their business, plantation owners kept the written records.

Since America's beginning, business, commerce, and the generation and management of wealth have always been supreme. Indeed, historian Herbert Gutman, author of *The Negro Family in Slavery and Freedom* (1976), once observed that most of the history of slavery is not about the blacks at all. It is about white slave owners and what they did to the slaves and, to some extent, for the slaves. Not nearly enough has been written, he said, about what the slaves did for themselves.[23] A major insight from the Robert Smalls story is what the enslaved Africans did for themselves and what they did for others.

After finishing school in Charlotte and obtaining her bachelor's degree from Hampton Institute in 1947, Dolly received a master's degree in physical education and administration from Columbia University in 1953. One of the quirks of history, racism, and economics is that Dolly's education at Columbia University was paid for by the state of Maryland, where she was teaching at the time. At that time state policy was not to allow blacks to attend the University of Maryland and instead to pay their expenses to study at the out-of-state graduate school of their choice. Of course it cost the state much more per pupil to do it this way. (It was not until the 1950s, when attorney Thurgood Marshall won the case admitting future congressman Parren J. Mitchell to the University of Maryland graduate school to study sociology, that this policy changed.) "That was fine by me," Dolly said, "I much preferred Columbia to the University of Maryland. It was a better school, so I got a much better education than I would have gotten at Maryland."

Dolly related the following story about her husband. "I had known Boot [what she and a few other close friends call John Nash] for three years at Hampton. In 1945 when the war was over, people who wanted to go to college could do so because there was the GI Bill of Rights, which paid their way to any college or vocational school of their choice that they could get into. Boot had graduated from Hampton in the trade of upholstery, but he wanted to learn cabinet making. So he came back to Hampton to look for a wife. He found me, and I found some very fine furniture. So 52 years later here we are.

"After we got married in 1948 we moved to Easton, Maryland, where I got a teaching job. I taught at the Robert Russell Moton High School there for eight years" [a school for black children, named for a former president of Tuskegee Institute in Alabama].

"The second year after we were married, we started building this house. We bought the shell from a wrecking company because it was surplus, army material. It had been part of a 'Day Room' in the service. Boot bought this lot immediately after he got out of the service because he knew exactly what he wanted and what he wanted to do.

"In 1963 we built a two-story, eleven-unit motel. We built it from scratch on Lafayette Street" [the busy tourist-frequented thoroughfare to the Cape May beaches]. "Boot suggested that we name it the Planter Motel, which we did.

"In the office I hung a picture of the ship, *Planter,* which now hangs in my family room [at their Cape May house]. I got it from a lady whose husband, Theodore Blythewood, had brought it with him when he moved up here from Beaufort, South Carolina. That began my collection of *Planter* things.

"Now my living room is full of Smalls memorabilia. I have a sofa, which was once owned by Robert Smalls. One of the dining room chairs was his. The marble-top tables belonged to him. My uncle Robbie [Robert Smalls Bampfield] had all this in his house in Washington. When he died, his wife Ellie wanted to give it to somebody in the family and gave it to us. The sofa stayed in my husband's shop for ten years before he got around to upholstering it. And now you see what a beauty it is."

The red velvet covers capture the handsomeness of the piece, and it is easy to imagine Smalls sitting on it in the living room of the Prince Street house in Beaufort around the turn of the twentieth century. Dolly continued, "My cousin in Massachusetts now has the chair and the arm chair that went with the dining room furniture. I have two like that. The marble tops are either Bampfield or Smalls's furniture.

"I have pictures when they dedicated the bust designed by the artist M. Talmidge Etheridge in 1976. I was not able to go to the dedication but my cousin Buster's children were there to represent the family. They are Smalls's great-great-grandchildren. Young Michael Boulware Moore, great-great-grandson of Robert Smalls, unveiled the statue at the ceremony. And I have pictures of the Robert Smalls Parkway, established by the Beaufort County Council [at the request of the Robert Smalls High School Alumni Association].

"I have a picture of Smalls's grave site in the Tabernacle Baptist Church yard. I have pictures of the dedication of the new Robert Smalls Middle School in Beaufort. I was once invited to give a talk on Grandpa at the middle school. . . . And I have that original oil painting [abstract in pastel colors] you see on the wall there. It was painted by my great-aunt Sarah, Smalls's second daughter.

She is the one who stayed with him and took care of him and his property after his second wife, Annie Wigg, died.

"My brother, Edward, was one year younger than I, born in 1925, in Philadelphia. He moved with us to Charlotte when he was about six months old.

"When my parents moved to Washington, D.C., where my mother got a job in the U.S. Adjutant General's Office, they took him with them. We called him "Sonny" at that time. Because they did not have a very large apartment, I stayed in Charlotte with an aunt named Helen for fourteen years. Sonny went to Garden Patterson High School in Washington, D.C., and then Dunbar High School, but he never finished high school. Before he went into the service he was a messenger in the government."

Edward Estes "Sonny" Davidson (1925–1990), named for his father, was the only one of the Smalls descendants to serve in the U.S. Navy, as his famous great-grandfather had done before him. There were two other experiences that honored this family connection. During World War II the U.S. Navy established a separate facility, located in Great Lakes, Illinois, for the training of black naval personnel. They named it Camp Robert Smalls. Among the thousands of black recruits trained there was Edward "Sonny" Davidson, Dolly's brother and Robert Smalls's great-grandson. Most blacks served in low-level positions in the navy at that time, and Edward was trained and served as naval storekeeper. While Edward was in training at Camp Robert Smalls, William Robert Smalls, Smalls's youngest son, who had served as an army officer in World War I, was an executive with the National Urban League in Dayton, Ohio. As a gesture of historic recognition and in the acquisition of an accomplished speaker, the navy invited William Robert Smalls to give the commencement address. The family connection and history must have been palpable on this occasion.

After the war, Edward returned to Washington and, according to Dolly "got a very good government job." He was married briefly to Idella Davidson and longer to his second wife, Mattie Davidson. He had no children.

Helen Bampfield Givens

The ninth child of the Bampfields, born in the New Street house, was Helen Bampfield (1897–2001). She married Howard W. Givens, a Presbyterian minister. Helen attended Barber-Scotia College and Johnson C. Smith University and became a public school teacher. Indeed, she taught first grade in the same school in Charlotte for more than forty years. Her husband predeceased her. She lived to the age of 104 and died in 2001, eclipsing her mother's longevity by three years. The Givenses adopted a child, Lois Ariana, who married and had two children. Helen and Howard are buried in Oaklawn Cemetery in Charlotte.

Ariana Bampfield Boulware

The tenth Bampfield child was Ariana Bampfield (1897–1994). According to Dolly, she was called "Arie" by the family and was very bright. When she was a senior at Barber-Scotia College and final exam time came, she found herself in a difficult situation. Students could not take final exams unless all fees had been paid, and the check for her fees, which was usually sent to her by an older brother, had not arrived. She took her dilemma to the dean, who checked her records and informed her that students with straight-A records did not have to take the finals. She had straight-A's, with a 99 average in math.

After graduation, Ariana stayed home to take care of her mother who was ill. Later she married Caldwell Elwood Boulware, who was the first male teacher at Barber-Scotia, a women's college. Boulware was also from an achieving family. His cousin, Harold Boulware Sr. (1913–1983), graduated from Johnson C. Smith and the Howard University Law School. He became a distinguished, pioneering attorney and judge in Columbia, South Carolina, where he collaborated on notable civil rights cases. He was the lead attorney for *Briggs v. Elliott.*

Ariana and Caldwell Boulware had one daughter, Helen Boulware, who married Robert Moore.

Helen Boulware Moore, Ph.D., is a native of Durham, North Carolina. She received the bachelor of arts and master of science degrees from the University of Pennsylvania and was awarded the doctorate of philosophy degree in psychology from Boston College.

Dr. Moore is a former member of the faculty of Simmons College in Boston and is currently the managing partner and senior consultant with the Interactions Group of Lakewood Ranch, Florida. She is married to her business partner, Robert E. Moore, Ph.D., and is the mother of Michael Boulware Moore and Robin Elizabeth Moore.

Robin Elizabeth Moore, the great-great-granddaughter of Robert Smalls, was born in Boston. She attended Saint Mark's School in Southborough, Massachusetts, and earned her bachelors degree in electrical engineering from Brown University. She did additional study in music production and engineering at Berklee College of Music in Boston. She currently is a sound engineer at WGBH, the NPR radio station in Boston. She is also the owner of Dangerzone, a sound engineering production company in Marlboro, Massachusetts.

Michael Boulware Moore was born in Philadelphia. He is married to Carla S. Moore and is the father of David Michael Bampfield Moore, Lucas Michael Greer Moore, Israel James Pendleton Moore, and Robert Caldwell Moore. They have been kept aware of this legacy and are inspired by it. At the christening of the Army transport ship *Major General Robert Smalls,* while their aunt

Robin, grandmother Helen, and great-grandaunt Helen Greenlee were performing their official duties, these two under-ten youngsters were the life of the party. The Moores currently live in Atlanta.

Michael received a B.A. from Syracuse University and a M.B.A. from Duke University. He has had a rewarding business career with leadership experience in Fortune 500 and entrepreneurial companies, working in marketing, finance, and general management. He is currently a director at World 5Ø, a Fortune 500 networking company based in Atlanta.

Samuel and Elizabeth Bampfield's eleventh child was Samueletta, who died in infancy. The Robert Smalls family tree found on page xxi is a seven-generation genealogy of the Robert Smalls family compiled by Helen Boulware Moore. It is also available at http://www.robertsmalls.org, where it will continue to be updated.

Bampfields Continue Smalls Legacy

Samuel J. Bampfield died at the age of fifty. Elizabeth outlived him by nearly sixty years, which was not only longer than they had been together but longer than he was on this earth. Nevertheless, during his few short years on earth, it would be difficult to find another man who bested him in the struggle for life, liberty, and fraternity.

In reviewing the Bampfield genealogy, some factors stand out, honoring the legacy of their parents and grandparents and highlighting the strengths of family in the African American experience. The first factor is all the Bampfields' striving for upward mobility. Many of the disabilities that afflict African American youth today—drugs, alcohol, domestic violence, street violence, unwed teen pregnancy—seem to have bypassed the Bampfield family, despite the comparatively low level of health and public-health facilities and the racial oppression rampant during their time. Clearly their upward mobility, striving, and attainments—and the values and habits associated with that lifestyle—shielded them from a great deal of destructive behavior. Moreover, the close-knit family relations they experienced, maintained, and perpetuated provided an additional shield of protection from self-destructive behavior. A conspicuous manifestation of this family feeling is represented in the naming of children. It would be difficult to identify any generation that did not have children named for someone in a prior generation.

A strong attachment and commitment to education for themselves and others was a consistent theme in the Bampfield household. Elementary education, technical education, college education, and professional-school education, especially in teaching, law, and medicine, are generously sprinkled through this family. Here the historically black colleges and trade schools and boarding schools played a vital role in the uplifting of this family, as with others. Johnson C. Smith University, Barber-Scotia College, Howard University, Claflin College, South Carolina State, North Carolina A&T, and Hampton University were lifelines into the black middle class during the early twentieth-century.

Religion played a role in the Bampfields' survival and achievement. From Robert and Hannah Smalls down through the generations, religion and the church have been sources of survival and achievement among them. In Beaufort, several churches were extensions of the family: Tabernacle Baptist Church, where Lydia and Hannah were active members and where the Smalls are buried; the First African Baptist Church, of which Robert was a founding member in 1864 and a major financial supporter and where Smalls's family members held their weddings and funeral ceremonies; and Berean Presbyterian Church, founded by Samuel Bampfield, where his sister-in-law, Sarah Williams, played the organ. Samuel Bampfield brought the Presbyterian faith to this family of Baptists. When Elizabeth and her children moved to Charlotte in 1910, the Presbyterian college Johnson C. Smith helped to keep the faith alive in this family.

The overarching factor, however, in the lives and achievements of the Bampfield family was their "yearning to breathe free." After slavery, they could go and come, live and love as they pleased. And though history is replete with the limitations on their freedom, they were free within themselves, and as the poet Robert Frost might say, "That made all the difference."

This Bampfield branch of the Robert Smalls family vividly illustrates a major theme of this book, namely that strong families make strong communities and strong communities make strong families. This family was able to assist in the building of strong churches and schools, and in turn they were able to take advantage of these churches and schools to help them build strong families.

14

Hannah's Children

Descendants of the two girls born to Hannah Jones before she was married to Robert Smalls in 1856 have not been recognized by most writers as part of the Smalls family. Hannah's children initiated the biannual family reunions that began in 1984. A study of this branch of the family reveals how South Carolina State University became a major springboard for the black middle class.

When seventeen-year-old Robert Smalls wed thirty-year-old Hannah Jones in 1856, Hannah was already the mother of fourteen-year-old Charlotte Jones and twelve-year-old Clara Jones. There is no indication who their father was. Even though they were close in age to their new stepfather, descendants affirm that Smalls treated these girls as though they were his natural children. According to Furman Williams, the oldest living member of this family and one who knew Smalls personally, Smalls "made no distinction whatever between Hannah's children and their children."[1]

The genesis of South Carolina State University is multifaceted. In 1862 the U.S. Congress passed the Morrill Act, providing for the establishment of land-grant colleges to offer scientific, agricultural, and mechanical arts with substantial support from the federal government. In 1890 Congress amended the Morrill Act, requiring states that did not admit blacks to their land-grant colleges to establish separate colleges for blacks as a condition for receiving federal support. As early as 1872, under a Republican government, South Carolina had already established the South Carolina Agricultural and Mechanical Institute as a branch of the University of South Carolina located in Orangeburg on the campus of Claflin College, a Methodist college founded in 1869. Under the leadership of Thomas E. Miller and Robert Smalls, black delegates at the 1895 Constitutional Convention lobbied for an independent state college for blacks.

The resolution passed by this convention was implemented by the state legislature on March 3, 1896, creating the "Normal, Industrial, Agricultural and Mechanical College for the colored race." Smalls served as a member of the board of regents for the school from 1873 to 1876, with a term as vice president of the board in 1874. Miller, well educated and aggressive, became the first president. An 1872 graduate of Lincoln University in Pennsylvania, he was elected commissioner of schools in Beaufort County, serving in 1873 and 1874. He studied law at the University of South Carolina and was admitted to the bar in 1875. He served several terms in the state legislature from Beaufort County, one term in the U.S. Congress, and was a delegate to the 1895 Constitutional Convention. An active member of the Beaufort County Republican Party, he was a protégé, collaborator and, sometimes, opponent of Robert Smalls.

Miller recruited a faculty of some fifteen members in 1896, including Robert Smalls's daughter Sarah. He served until 1911 under severe financial and political penalties exacted by the conservative Democratic regime. Historians say that it was the 1954 Supreme Court decision in the *Brown* case that encouraged the state to expand and support South Carolina State College as a bulwark against pressure to admit blacks to Clemson and the University of South Carolina. Meanwhile, the college became a launching pad for the entry of blacks into the middle class. Robert and Hannah Smalls's descendants became the beneficiaries of this institution as students and faculty during the long reign of state-supported racial segregation.[2]

In 1870, according to the U.S. Census, Robert Smalls's extended family included his stepdaughter Charlotte Jones and her thirteen-year-old daughter Emily Brown. Some time later in 1870 Charlotte married Larry Williams. They had several children together; Rebecca was born in 1870, and Susan was born in 1872. A son, Willie White Williams, was born in 1877. Willie became the leading contributor and patriarch of this wing of the Smalls family.

In 1870 Clara Jones and her husband, an English sea captain named Ryder, lived in a house on Craven Street, probably owned by Smalls. Clara and her husband had two daughters together—Sarah Ryder (named for her Aunt Sarah Smalls), born in 1872, and Beula Ryder, born in 1876.

In 1886 a tragedy overtook this family. Charlotte and her two daughters, Rebecca and Susan Williams, perished in a fire that destroyed their home. Her son, Willie Williams, who saw the tragedy on his way home from school, later told his descendants, "My one thought was to run and tell Grandfather [Robert Smalls], who I thought could do anything." Willie ran to the Prince Street house screaming for "Grandpa," but Smalls was in Washington at the time. It is said that nine-year-old Willie developed a hatred for his grandfather for not saving the lives of his mother and sisters. Charlotte's sister, Clara, took Willie into her home and raised him with her own children, Sarah and Beula Ryder, supporting them all with her employment as a laundress. When Willie finished elementary school, Clara apprenticed him to a blacksmith and metal worker in Beaufort, preparing him with a lifelong trade. At nineteen Willie moved to Orangeburg with his Aunt Sarah Smalls, who went there to teach at South Carolina State.

Willie White Williams was a skilled craftsman and was able to get a job as a master mechanic in a shop owned by a German native named Von Oshen. In 1898, at the age of twenty-one, Willie was married to a young woman whom descendants know as Miss King. They produced one child, a girl named Willie Mae Williams, named for her father. The child's mother died at an early age, and the infant Willie Mae was raised by her maternal grandmother. In 1904 Willie White Williams wed Daisy John Gaither, named for her father, but not before, on the advice of her father, Willie bought some land and built a three-room house for her.

In addition to Willie's daughter from his first marriage, their children were Emma Francis Williams, Furman Franklin Williams, Daisy Bell Williams, John Clay Williams, William Henry Williams, Luther Bostic Williams, Jacob Cornelius Williams, Starks Johnson Williams, and Beula Louise Williams. Their adopted son was John Avon Williams.

Daisy studied at the normal school in Orangeburg, earning a teaching certificate in 1902 and teaching in the public schools of Fairfield County. Her son Furman Williams wrote: "The fabric of our family, Willie and Daisy, set the tone. Education (all you could obtain), responsibility, respect, family cohesiveness. We were always reminded that we were living in a racist society and they expected us to find methods to conquer that scourge of ignorance . . . and not at any time to embarrass ourselves, our family, or our community."

After Willie and Daisy were married in 1904 at her parents' church in Winnsboro, they settled into their three-room home at 139 Treadwell Street in Orangeburg. During that first year Willie's daughter Willie Mae was brought from her maternal grandmother's house into the home as an integral part of the family.

Willie continued his job as a blacksmith and metal worker. Eventually he opened his own blacksmith and wheelwright shop on Middleton Street in Orangeburg. In 1918 he was employed as an instructor at South Carolina State. He retired in 1953 and died in 1955.

Many children eventually headed to South Carolina State. Meanwhile, while managing this home and family, Daisy Williams pursued her career as a public-school teacher.

This family had the same strong educational values as the Bampfields. Just as the Bampfield family home in Charlotte, North Carolina, served as a way station for family members into Barber-Scotia College and Johnson C. Smith University, the Williams family home in Orangeburg, South Carolina, served as a way station for members into South Carolina State. As a consequence, all the children of Willie and Daisy Williams (except for their adopted son, John Avon) attended and graduated from South Carolina State. The siblings graduated as follows: Willie Mae Williams (half sister), 1918; Emma Francis Williams, 1924; Furman Franklin Williams, 1928; Daisy Bell Williams, 1930; William Henry Williams, 1936; Jacob Cornelius Williams, 1941; Starks Johnson Williams, 1942; and Beula Louise Williams, 1943.

As Furman Williams, the family historian, has observed, it was not only his siblings who attended South Carolina State, but members of the extended family as well. These included Catherine Gaither, his mother's sister, in 1915; Morrie Hamilton, his father's niece, in 1916; Luther Gaither, his mother's brother, in 1922; George Cromer, friend of the family; Irene Fisher, his father's niece, in 1914; and Joanne Williams, a cousin, in 1939. After she graduated in 1918, Willie Mae started teaching at Wilson High School in Florence, South Carolina. According to Furman, she "sent one of her graduates to live in our home and attend S.C. State every four years until 1964." Furman told the author at the 1992 family reunion that, when he was growing up, there were so many people coming into his home that he did not know which ones were related to him or how. It did not matter, he said, because as long as his parents let them in, they were family. Moreover, Furman said, "Our cousin Etta Mae's husband died and left three children. Cousin Etta left for New York to earn money to support her family. My mother and father made it their business to take these children into our home and sent them to school. After some time they moved back into their home and Marian and Henry Simmons graduated from State College."

Little wonder that the Williams home at 139 Treadwell Street was expanded to six rooms. By 1927 a second story had been added, with three bedrooms and bath facilities. "Our house was strictly an educational house for the extended family and to my knowledge no one paid board or lodging. All who entered this house were welcomed by my mother and father," reported Furman.

To hold this remarkable family together, Willie White Williams worked as a blacksmith, and Daisy John Gaither Williams not only presided over the household as matriarch but also taught in the public schools of Orangeburg. All the family members had assigned chores and helped with the housework. The two parents set the example, according to Furman: "the priority of nurturing the minds of their young children was paramount in their home, developing the need for good study skills. In our house as the child's first teachers, our parents, laid the foundation for values: building of self esteem and teaching how wrong racism was!"

Carter G. Woodson's 1947 accolade to the Robert Smalls descendants applied equally to this branch of the family. They became teachers, skilled tradesmen, seamstresses, attorneys, doctors, and public servants. They supported their churches and schools, which in turn served them well. Although they suffered many downturns—including death, divorce, and career change—they strove to honor family, faith, work, and education as handed down from their forebears. They are examples of sociologist Robert Hill's findings that historically the strengths of African American families have been their strong religious and work orientations, flexibility of family roles, and education.[3] Another sociologist, Joyce Ladner, found that "the ties that bind" African American families together consist of a set of basic beliefs and values; she too saw this trend in the legacy of Hannah's children.[4]

Growing Up in Orangeburg

Furman Williams described growing up in Orangeburg:

> Treadwell Street extended from Russell (Main) Street on the east to Ellis Avenue on the west; this was comparable to four city blocks.
>
> Along Ellis Avenue lived the following white families with boys my age: the Dukes, the Sims, the Wolfes, and the Websters. They all played baseball with the blacks on a lot at the corner of Ellis and Treadwell Streets. We had no racial problems there. The black and white parents mingled and watched the games. These boys became lawyers, newspaper publishers, judges, and postmasters.
>
> Our black neighbors included Lawyer and Mrs. Moore, Dr. & Mrs. McTeer, and Dartus and Mrs. Judson, farmers who allowed the neighborhood children to gather crops and pick cotton.
>
> . . . All of our neighbors appeared to have stable family lives with two parents in most homes and the children seemed not to have any problems with the two authorities. Most of the children I knew are now leading productive lives, and their children are among the responsible citizens of our time.

There is no doubt that looking back on his childhood and youth growing up in Orangeburg, Furman Franklin Williams—eighty-six years old at the time he completed this memoir in 1992—had a strong case of nostalgia, and deservedly so. Yet it is clear, a century later, that a young lad growing up in

Orangeburg today would face more, not fewer, obstacles to his healthy growth and development—more distraction, less community solidarity and cohesion. Surely no black person would want to turn the clock back to those days, and yet a lesson in this particular family history is that progress is not always and uniformly better. As Frederick Douglass would say, "The struggle continues."

15

Annie Wigg's Family

Smalls's first wife, Hannah, died at the age of fifty-seven on July 28, 1883, after nearly thirty years of marriage. Almost seven years later, Robert Smalls, at forty-four, took a new wife on April 9, 1890. She was a thirty-four-year-old schoolteacher from Charleston, Annie Elizabeth Wigg. She was younger, more beautiful, and better educated than her predecessor and had grown up in an entirely different world. Smalls had married Hannah when she was nearly twice his age, and he married Annie when she was ten years his junior. Hannah had always wanted Smalls to withdraw from elective politics and settle down in a steady job with a daily routine, playing with the children and grandchildren and sleeping in his own bed. For years she had given to him all he demanded of her. Alas, by the time Smalls had done as she wished in 1890, it was left to a younger woman to enjoy the fruits of Hannah's labor. Following the pattern his daughter Elizabeth had set with her 1877 wedding, Smalls scheduled his second marriage ceremony at the First African Baptist Church with the reception in their Prince Street home.

William "Willie" Robert Smalls wrote that, while Smalls's marriage to Hannah had been a marriage of convenience, his dad's marriage to his mother was out of "pure love." Even the Democrat, anti-Smalls newspaper the *News and Courier* gave a positive notice to this wedding:

> The bride is an exceedingly handsome woman of respectable connection, and the interest felt in her was attested by the large assemblage of whites as well as colored people, who attended the church to witness the ceremony, which was performed at the First African Baptist Church. . . .
>
> The bride was elegantly attired in white silk, with lace overdress entrain and an elegant flowing veil. . . .

The residence of the groom, only one block from the church, was brilliantly illuminated, and thither the bridal party with their many friends repaired, and the celebration of the nuptials was concluded by an expensive and elegant supper. The entire community extended to the happy couple their warmest congratulations.[1]

This newspaper could have used the same words to describe Elizabeth and Samuel Bampfield's wedding thirteen years before. That the paper ignored the earlier wedding and recognized this one was due, no doubt, to the changed political climate. In 1877 Smalls was battling to hold back the tidal wave of Democratic takeover of the South Carolina government. By 1890 Smalls was no longer an active candidate, and the Democrats had long solidified their control over the state, except for Beaufort County. The Democratic *News and Courier* could afford to exhibit a measure of magnanimity toward Smalls's wedding.

The Reverend Pollard of the St. Mark's Episcopal Church, Charleston, performed the wedding ceremony. Also from Charleston came Ellen Craft, Annie's close friend, who later became godmother to their son. Willie reported proudly that his parents were given a silver tea set for a wedding present by one of their white friends.

Annie Wigg brought a breath of fresh air to the household where Robert and his twenty-seven-year-old daughter, Sarah, were struggling to bring comfort to each other. His older daughter, Elizabeth, and her husband, Samuel J. Bampfield, had already produced six grandchildren.

Born August 24, 1856, in Savannah, Georgia, Annie Wigg was the second of Archibald and Susan Morell Wigg's four children.[2] Her parents enrolled her in private schools in Charleston and the Avery Normal Institute under Francis Cardozo. Annie's father died on August 5, 1865, and her mother on November 24, 1887, in Beaufort.

Annie was a teacher in the public schools in Charleston at the time she met Smalls.

Robert and Annie's only child, William Robert Smalls (christened William Robert Wigg Smalls), was born on February 27, 1892, in the master bedroom of the Prince Street house. Annie died on November 5, 1895, after a brief illness. Their son believes that his mother was killed by political pressure and the violence accompanying the 1895 Constitutional Convention. Sarah sent word to her father that his wife was deathly ill. Smalls hurried home from the convention to be with her. Their son, who was three years old at the time, said years later that his mother died in his father's arms and that her last words to him were "take care of my son." After a funeral service in the First African Baptist

Church, where they were married just five years earlier, Smalls buried his second wife in the Tabernacle Baptist Cemetery just to the left of his first wife, Hannah.

When he learned of his mother's death, young Willie ran and hid in the clothes hamper in the hall closet. It took the firm hand of his father to coax him to come out.

Sarah took Annie's place in helping her father raise her young brother, giving up having a family of her own to do so. She was married briefly. On April 2, 1900, she married Dr. J. P. Williams of Aiken, South Carolina, and moved to Pueblo, Colorado, with her husband. After a very short time, however, she returned to her father's home in Beaufort.

When Sarah returned, she continued to teach and was principal in the school founded by her father. She also served as an organist at the Berean Presbyterian Church, founded by her brother-in-law, Samuel Bampfield. However, Sarah's primary role was to manage her father's health, properties, and other affairs.

William Robert "Willie" Smalls described his sister in his correspondence with Dorothy Sterling:

> Sarah was dignified and erect for all her tiny size. Once, when a white tenant's boy came to bring the rent, he asked at the door, "is Sarah in?" Sarah never raised her voice. She simply said, "Go back home and when you come back ask for Miss Smalls."
>
> Sarah didn't like spirituals. She was tiny, no more than five feet, tall and plump. She wore her dark hair, brushed back with a knot that stood up high, and she dressed plainly. She had classic features.
>
> She loved flowers, and music. She was a good pianist and had an above average soprano voice.

Sarah never married again or had children of her own. However, it might be said that she played the role of a mother in taking care of her father, siblings, extended family, and students. Although she suffered from severe asthma, she took care of her father until his death on February 23, 1915. She died August 22, 1920, at the age of fifty-seven and is buried in the Tabernacle Church Cemetery next to her father, mother, and stepmother.

Smalls suffered from the personal losses of his first son, his mother, his first wife, and his second wife. But he was not one to sit and cry. There was urgent work to do for his cause, his people, his party, and his state. After a week at home, Smalls returned to the convention in Columbia, where he made his most memorable speech, "my people need no special defense."

William Robert "Willie" Smalls often spoke and wrote of his childhood. His recollections, as documented in his letters to Dorothy Sterling, provide a personal view of Robert Smalls as a father and a man.

> My fondest memories are those many nights, when my father and I would be alone in our bedroom—as we shared the same bed until my teens. During the winter months, we would go to our room early, as nine o'clock was always his hour for retiring. We would build a big fire in the fireplace in the room, and with me on his knee, I would listen to stories of the war and adventures that marked many milestones in his life. . . .
>
> I visited personally with him at least two presidents of the United States (McKinley and Teddy Roosevelt). . . . I sat with him in two national conventions . . . , several fraternal conventions (Masonic) etc. Even though only a child, I still have vivid memories of some of them.

One of the national conventions Willie remembered attending with his father was probably the 1900 Republican National Convention, held in the Centennial Exposition Building in Philadelphia. Willie also went to an Odd Fellows convention with him.

Growing Up in Beaufort

Willie Smalls also wrote about going to work with his father:

> I used to go with my father to the Customs House, where he worked, and go swimming from the dock behind the Customs House. I used to take the Customs House skiff and row down to the bend in the [Beaufort] river and swim back to the dock. Once at high tide, I missed the dock, so I climbed back into the boat. Unknown to me, Pa had been watching from the Customs House porch. [Robert Smalls was such an expert swimmer that he could have rescued Willie if necessary, which is no doubt why he was keeping watch over him.] He said nothing to me. But the next day when I asked if I could go swimming, he said no, I could not go.

Smalls was a friend of Frederick Douglass. Willie recalled that Douglass came to visit his father and brought along his grandson Joseph Douglass, who was a violinist. Willie accompanied him on the piano as the two played for Smalls, who was ill. The Smalls family loved music. Sarah taught Willie to . dance, and she often played the piano while boys and girls danced and Robert watched.

In 1900–1903, from age eight to eleven, Willie played in the prestigious Allen's Brass Band, founded by his father primarily for his political campaigns.

He was the only youth to play with the otherwise all-adult male band. Willie wrote:

> I was the only boy among men. Allen, himself [a friend and beneficiary of his father], taught me to play the clarinet. We played on Memorial Day parades, funerals. We played slow tunes on the way to the cemetery, then on the way back we'd liven it up with "These Dry Bones Shall Rise Again."

With no electricity until 1913, the Smallses' home had a wood stove in the kitchen and six fireplaces, for which Willie carried in wood. The family used kerosene lamps and had elaborate kerosene chandeliers.

During the summer months, Sarah was too sick with asthma to come to the table, which was waited on by various housekeepers referred to as "Mrs." Two Bampfield boys, Allie and Robbie, often ate there too. According to Willie, there was not much talk at the table.

Stories of "Pappa"

His father told Willie this story:

> Two Negroes had killed a man looking for moonshiners. He was a constable looking for illicit sales; there was much bootlegging at that time. They were arrested and held in the Beaufort jail awaiting trial. While awaiting trial a lynch mob gathered outside Beaufort and began a march to the jail to lynch the accused. Papa devised a plan. At a given signal Garret, who was his boatman, was supposed to sound the fire alarm. When this town bell rang, everyone in on the plan was to throw a faggot and set fire to a white house nearby.
>
> Word got around about this, and the [lynch] mob was halted before they got into town. Whites turned out and stopped them. The two Negroes were later tried in court and convicted. They were hung and their bodies returned to Beaufort for burial.

According to Willie, the execution was all right with Smalls. For him, justice was done, and mob violence was prevented. "My father was fearless. Not afraid of anybody or anything. He was never intimidated until his dying day." The following story was a typical example.

> My father wore a signet ring on his finger. When he got mad, he turned the ring inside his hand. One time he slapped a white man in the face with his open hand with that ring in it. At the same time he struck the man with his cane. The incident occurred when the man was coming out of the liquor store, saw my father, and called him an insulting name. Pappa slapped him

and hit him with his cane. The *Charleston News and Courier* carried the story saying my father was armed with pistols and knives, etc. and something should be done about it.

Willie's Education

Willie's formal education began in 1896 at age four, when his sister Sarah took him with her to Orangeburg, where she was a member of the new state college faculty. She enrolled him in the kindergarten division of the college. When Sarah married in 1900 and moved to Pueblo, Colorado, with her husband, Willie, now age nine, was returned to his father's home in Beaufort. After a very short time with her husband, Sarah also returned to her father's home.

Between 1900 and 1903 William Robert Smalls attended the school two blocks from their home, of which his father had been a founder. "Sarah taught there; she was principal. Her nieces and nephews also studied there. She would not allow them to call her 'Aunt Sarah' in school. She insisted that they address her as Miss Smalls, like the other children."

After attending the school in his neighborhood, eleven-year-old Willie Smalls went to Boston in 1903:

> I attended the Dwight Grammar School while living with Mrs. Arianna Sparrow, the same family my sister Elizabeth lived with when she attended school in West Newton, MA, many years prior.
>
> Finishing grammar school I could no longer stay at the Sparrows' in Boston because of death in the family, so my father sent me to Washington, D.C., where I entered the Academy at Howard University, under the protective wing of Kelly Miller [a South Carolinian who founded and for years headed the sociology department at Howard]. Next I went to Armstrong Technical High School, and then to the University of Pittsburgh.

Even after Willie left home, his father actively followed and supported his son's education, maintaining frequent correspondence with Willie and those caring for him.

Harvard, Pittsburgh, or Military Academy

Smalls, of course, had the highest aspirations for his son, so his real preference would have been for Willie to study and graduate from West Point or Annapolis. On March 8, 1911, he wrote to President William Howard Taft, a Republican for whom he had campaigned, requesting an appointment for Willie:

> Seeing by the papers that there is a large number of vacancies in both the Army and Navy for want of students at West Point and Annapolis, and

having no member of Congress to whom I might recommend my son for appointment to either of these Academies as a student, and at the same time knowing that you have a certain number of these appointments to both of these Institutions, and that the practice has been, and I am informed still is, that the President generally appoints the sons of those who have or are serving in the Army or Navy, I respectfully recommend for your consideration, my son William R. Smalls.[3]

The letter went on to cite Willie's educational background and military training at the Manuel Training School. Smalls expressed a distinct preference for an appointment to West Point.

Small's second choice for his son was Harvard, but when Willie said he preferred the University of Pittsburgh Smalls did not argue. Willie did well there. After earning a bachelor's degree, he earned a master's degree in social work from the University of Chicago and taught school in Texas. At the age of twenty-two, William Robert Smalls married Martineau "Marty" Grey of Pittsburgh. Although Willie and Marty planned a grand wedding ceremony in the Prince Street house, his father was too ill. They got married in Texas, where Willie was teaching, and came to Beaufort for their honeymoon. Willie joined in the U.S. Army during World War I, serving as a first lieutenant. He then taught at several colleges, including Morehouse College in Atlanta. He gave forty-four years of service to the Urban League movement in four cities and was an official of the Urban League in Ohio. He was also a longtime member and officer of the NAACP.

Willie and Marty had two children, a boy whom they named Robert Smalls III and a girl whom they named Annie Elizabeth (called Anne), for her mother and paternal aunt. Robert III was married twice. His first wife was Beatrice Hollis; they had no children. He then married Lillian Prymus and had one child, Helen, who married Roy Dunn and had two children, Shenitta Ewing and DeJuan Prymus. Shenitta had two children: Quivon Ewing and Lakoble Ewing. DeJuan married Victoria Luna and had two children: Alexis Prymus and Christopher Prymus. Willie and Marty's daughter, Annie, was married to Wendell Pat Grigsby. They had two children, Linda Martineau Grigsby and Michael Wendell Grigsby. Linda has two children: Shyra and Leah. Michael has a daughter, Kathryn Elizabeth Small Grigsby.

Willie Smalls spent his last years in Toledo, Ohio. According to his granddaughter Linda Grigsby, who lived with him for several years, he was an accomplished and well respected leader among blacks and whites. Two events, however, marred his life. When he moved into an otherwise all-white neighborhood in the progressive 1960s, unknown people burned down and destroyed his home. Later, for reasons unknown to his descendants, he was dismissed from his post at the Urban League by National Urban League director Lester B. Granger. According to Linda, that made her grandfather very sad. She thinks he never got over the dismissal. William Robert Smalls died in Toledo, Ohio, in 1970 at the age of seventy-eight.

That William Robert Smalls was a credit to his family traditions is suggested by his obituary, which appeared in the *Toledo Blade* on July 31, 1970:

W. Robert Smalls, 78, of 210 Vistula Manor, executive secretary of the Frederick Douglass Community Association from 1944 to 1949, died Thursday in Riverside Hospital. Mr. Smalls was a native of Beaufort, SC. He was with the Urban League 44 years, serving in Cleveland, the Minneapolis St. Paul area, and Kansas City. When he was in Toledo, the Frederick Douglass Community Association was part of the Urban League. Mr. Smalls was a graduate of the University of Pittsburgh and did graduate work at the University of Chicago. Before joining the Urban League, he taught college for several years. In 1940, he became the secretary of the Urban League in Warren, retiring in 1967 when he moved back to Toledo. A World War I veteran, Mr. Smalls was a member of St. Andrews Episcopal Church, Alpha Phi Alpha Fraternity, National Association of Social Workers for which he was state chairman two terms. A Mason 40 years, he was a member of Compositive Lodge F&AM. He was committee chairman and the treasurer of the vocation guidance group of Kiwanis. He was member of the National Association for the Advancement of Colored People.

Surviving are his wife, Martineau, son, W. Robert, III of Kansas City, MO, daughter, Mrs. Ann Grigsby of Washington, DC, two grandchildren.[4]

16

A Summing Up

What Is He to Us?

After the turn of the century Robert Smalls's life was filled with disappointments, sadness, illness, and resignation. While he continued to enjoy visits from prominent people, including Booker T. Washington and Frederick Douglass, his disappointments were many; chief among them was his failure to gain a final appointment as collector of customs, marking the end of his political career. His illness from long-standing diabetes took a downward turn, resulting in the amputation of one of his feet. His daughter Sarah suffered from severe bouts of asthma. Throughout, however, he kept his spirits alive. In his last letter to Booker T. Washington, Smalls penned his own epitaph, writing in part: "During the twenty odd years I have held the positions of collector, I have succeeded to so manage affairs that when I leave it, I will do so with credit to myself, my family and the race."[1]

Smalls died on Tuesday, February 23, 1915, at his home on Prince Street in Beaufort. He was seventy-six years old. His funeral at the First African Baptist Church was attended by a record crowd of black and white mourners. Allen's Brass Band, Smalls's favorite, led the procession to the Tabernacle Baptist churchyard, where he was buried between his first wife, Hannah, and his second wife, Annie. His death was noted in the *New York Age,* which called him as "one of the race's most noted characters."[2]

The meaning of Smalls's life and legacy for our time has been expressed by two events, which occurred in 2004. One is an act by the state senate authorizing establishment of a commission to study the feasibility and cost of a monument honoring Smalls on the statehouse grounds. Introduced by Senators

Darryl Jackson, Maggie Glover, Robert Ford, and Clementa C. Pinckney. Joint Resolution S.987 reads in part:

> Whereas, it is fitting and proper to honor this outstanding son of The Palmetto State by placing a marker on the grounds of the Capitol Complex that chronicles his many achievements. Now, therefore, Be it enacted by the General Assembly of the State of South Carolina: SECTION 1. There is hereby established on the grounds of the State House a monument to recognize the life and many accomplishments of the late United States Congressman Robert Smalls. The design and location of the monument shall be determined by the commission appointed pursuant to Section 2 of this joint resolution. The monument shall be erected as soon as is reasonably possible after the design and location are approved by the General Assembly by concurrent resolution.[3]

A second honor to Smalls and his legacy was the naming of a new army transport vessel the *Major General Robert Smalls,* christened on April 21, 2004. The ship is a 313-foot army logistic vessel designed to carry two thousand tons of deck cargo. It has a beam of 60 feet and a depth of 19 feet. It was constructed by the V. T. Halter Marine Company of Gulfport, Mississippi, at a cost of $25 million. Although it suffered some damage from Hurricane Katrina in 2005, the *Major General Robert Smalls* was still scheduled for a ceremonial launching in Baltimore, Maryland, with crew assembled in spring 2007.

Responding on behalf of the family at the christening ceremony in 2004 was Robin Moore, great-great-granddaughter of Robert Smalls. Her statement included the following remarks:

> America loves a rag to riches, "Horatio Alger story." We love to celebrate someone "pulling himself up by his bootstraps," creating something from nothing, and actually making real, the promise of the American Dream!

In this context, the story of Robert Smalls is really the quintessential American success story. At a time when he had no reasonable expectation for anything better, Robert had the ability to envision a better life for himself, for his family, and for a better country.

> . . . Beyond that, he had the courage and skill against overwhelming odds to actually <u>do</u> something about it.
>
> . . .The story of his life provides our nation with a spectacular example of the best of the American spirit. The *Major General Robert Smalls* will be a shining testament of his life and work. We thank you again, for honoring the legacy of his achievement in this way.[4]

This statement reflects well on the entire career of Robert Smalls. Anita Baker sings a song titled "Sometimes You Win, Sometimes You Lose," in which she advises, "Bad luck will creep upon you and catch you by surprise." Still, she urges her listeners to persevere in the face of obstacles; "You can win, you can win," she sings, "and everything will be all right." A similar message is frequently delivered from the pulpits of African American churches. In a message delivered on Sunday, July 25, 2004, Reverend Charles B. Jackson Sr. of the Brookland Baptist Church in Columbia, South Carolina, taking his text from the book of Romans, exhorted his congregation to expect ups and downs in life but that with faithful service they would overcome evil with good and would be blessed. Likewise followers of Dr. Martin Luther King Jr. during the civil rights movement sang with faith and confidence, "We Shall Overcome," an anthem recited by President Lyndon B. Johnson on signing the Civil Rights Act of 1964.

Robert Smalls had more than his fair share of winning and of losing. Yet to the very end of his life, he held on to the faith taught him by his mother, Lydia Polite; to the confidence he learned at the hands of his owner, Henry McKee; and to the optimism learned from life experiences that taught "sometimes you win and sometimes you lose." Most of all, throughout his life, he was guided by a "yearning to breathe free," a quest at the heart of this authentic American hero.

We have seen that in each of the three branches of the Robert, Hannah, and Annie Smalls descendants, prime values were handed down through the generations. These are strong self-concept, strong achievement and work orientations, flexible family roles, strong kinship bonds, and strong religious orientation—the bedrock African American values.

Smalls's life and legacy also exemplify the ten lessons set forth by sociologist Joyce Ladner in *The Ties that Bind* (1998). The first lesson was "remember where you came from." The second, "trust in the Lord"; third, "respect is a two way street"; fourth, "don't make excuses"; fifth, "do an honest day's work"; sixth, "make a way out of no way"; seventh, "every child can learn"; eighth, "keep the can do spirit"; ninth, "stand tall"; and tenth, "your word is your bond."[5]

During his early-childhood socialization phase, Smalls acquired a strong self-concept, strong religious orientation, strong moral values, strong personal integrity, and a strong set of instrumental life skills. He was not born with these. He learned them from his childhood experiences, and he applied them appropriately in his battles for life and liberty. He never forgot that they had come primarily from his mother, Henry McKee, and his family.

Smalls's mother, Lydia, taught him that they were Africans, as were his grandmother and great-grandmother, who had been among those captured into slavery and brought to the New World against their wills. His mother also taught him to be forgiving, kind and obedient. More important, she taught him to love and trust in God, to love his mother and himself. While bringing him up in a house of bondage, she taught him that he was as good as anybody else, that slavery was wrong, and that surely he would be free some day. She never let him forget that, though he was a privileged bondsman, he was a bondsman nevertheless. It was his mother's teaching before he was twelve years old that enabled him to stand in front of overwhelmingly hostile faces at the 1895 Constitutional Convention and declare "I stand before you a man, as good as any other man."

And what about his instrumental life skills, those skills a father is supposed to teach his son? He had no father of record, but Henry McKee served as a substitute father, teaching Smalls how to swim and handle boats, how to hunt with firearms, how to ride and care for animals, and other skills necessary to be a man. While Henry McKee stands condemned before the world for the fact that he did not set Smalls free, he should be commended for giving Smalls the skills and the confidence to set himself free when the time came.

At any early age Smalls evinced his assimilation of his mother's values toward freedom and his owner's indulgence. His violation of the curfew, his sobbing at the whipping of a bondswoman, his characterization of the cruelties of other planters are all examples of this teaching. Thus Smalls was trained early in life for his career as a freedom fighter by his enslaved but strong mother and by his young, white, wealthy, owner.

It must also be remembered that, before his twelfth birthday, Smalls discovered Frederick Douglass's teachings, which had a lifelong effect on Smalls's disdain for slavery and his confidence in his race. How sweet it must have been in decades later for him to meet and entertain Douglass in his own home, to be mentored by this icon, and to become a close friend and colleague of a man he so admired.

The Beaufort Baptist Church was also integral to Smalls's early childhood socialization. The Reverend Richard Fuller taught the black congregants that God loved them and so did he. Fuller also taught them that they should love themselves, despite the fact that God had chiseled them out of ebony rather than ivory, both precious materials in God's sight. Important in this respect are the other planters whom Smalls was allowed to accompany on their inspection of their properties. He learned character differences between kindly owners and others. The Beaufort River was important in Smalls's development. The river taught him not to fear the water and to use it for his own ends. All these human and natural influences helped to make Smalls a young man of strong virtues.

Growing up in Charleston during his young-adult socialization, ages twelve to twenty-three, was pivotal to Smalls's growth. Coming into manhood on the waterfront was an important experience, which could not have been equaled in any other place. There he learned to load and unload ships and to meet and mingle among men from various parts of the globe. He learned to stand tall among his peers and his seniors as well. By the time he was fifteen, he was already head of his work crew. Life went upward from there. He later said that some of the best years of his young life were the seven years he spent learning and plying the trades of the waterfront. Wandering about the city of enormous diversity in relative freedom gave him confidence and self-determination. Experiences in black and white churches helped to deepen his religious convictions. Meetings of secret societies helped to sharpen his quest for freedom.

Among the most enduring experience of growing up in Charleston was the opportunity to build his own family. It was simultaneously a nuclear and an extended family, which over the years transformed into a strong augmented family. The experience of saving money and arranging to purchase his wife and daughter while still enslaved himself must stand out as one of the boldest ventures of his early manhood. The marriage lasted for nearly three decades.

Smalls's Confederate military service has not been widely examined but it, too, was in keeping with the teachings of his mother to do his best in whatever job he undertook or was assigned. The careful planning that led to the capture of the *Planter* has also not been recognized. Some treated it as a spontaneous act. The seizure of the *Planter* was a major turning point in Smalls's life. Were it not for that event, we would probably not know his name today. It was far from an individual act but rather a family affair, bring together nuclear, extended and augmented family members in a collaborative act of daring and purpose. Nothing can match the capture of the *Planter* in its historical significance, but it should not overshadow his piloting of the *Keokuk* in the assault on Fort Sumter, the *Planter* through the mission that made him its captain, or the crippled *Planter* to Philadelphia in terms of the sheer danger and the courage these events required of Smalls and his crew.

It was evident in Smalls's postwar life in Beaufort that he "never forgot where he came from." One setting he had come from was the John and Henry McKee family holdings. And despite the fact that for generations the McKees held him, his brother, and his mother in slavery, he never held any animosity toward them. Quite the opposite, he viewed them as family. The Civil War had made Smalls free and wealthy; while the same event left the McKees destitute. Smalls never failed to assist them. Nor was it a grudging or niggardly assistance. He had already named one of his children (Elizabeth Jane) after the McKees and would later name another (William Robert). When the McKees returned to Beaufort after the war, Smalls conveyed them to visit their friends and on at least one occasion entertained them in his home. He bought them a house and some tillable land and secured employment for their daughter Jane in Washington. He proffered a position at the U.S. Military or Naval Academy for a McKee lad. He introduced a bill in Congress to reimburse the McKees and others who had lost property during the war. An act that endeared him to descendants and Beaufort citizens alike was his taking Mrs. McKee into his home (once her home) and caring for her in her widowhood, old age, and infirmity.

Smalls knew, instinctively perhaps, and can certainly teach us today that the best way to build a strong family is through home ownership. His bold and imaginative action in purchasing the Prince Street house in which he and his mother had served as slaves, redounded through history. The house remained in the family for more than ninety years.

Without a doubt Smalls's greatest legacy is his "achievement orientation" in the field of education. His self-education, providing the best education available for his children, building a school for black children in Beaufort, and as his contributions to public and higher education in the state are enduring monuments to his legacy.

Smalls is most remembered in South Carolina for his achievements in politics and government—all remembered because of his successes and failures. His rise was spectacular—founder of the state Republican Party, congressman and state legislator, collector of customs, and delegate to the Constitutional Conventions of 1868 and 1895. His ego and ambition—and perhaps some misdeeds —caused him to fall short of his aspirations. Still it must be said that he was a brave, intelligent leader in the decade of biracial political democracy in South Carolina, which has not been equaled even to the present time. The struggle he led in the 1895 Constitutional Convention, is at least on a par with the struggle for voting rights in the civil rights era of the 1960s.

And finally, Robert Smalls's life and legacy speak to us today as the seventeenth-century English poet John Donne wrote in his "Meditation XVII": "No man is an island entire of itself; every man is a piece of the continent, a part of the main." He knew also that group action is no substitute for personal responsibility: "any man's death diminishes me, because I am involved in mankind; and therefore never send to know for whom the bell tolls; it tolls for thee." Near the Tabernacle Baptist churchyard, where Smalls is buried, stands a bronze bust of him with an inscription from his most famous speech: "My people need no special defense, for the whole history of them in this country proves them to be the equal of any people, any where. All they need is an equal chance in the battle of life." An even more striking statement occurred in his November 2, 1895, speech to the Constitutional Convention, defining his lifelong credo and his courage, confidence, and dignity: "I stand here today a man, as good as any other man."

NOTES

Prologue

1. Woodson, *Robert Smalls and His Descendants*, 29.

2. Billingsley, *Climbing Jacob's Ladder*; Raboteau, *Slave Religion*; Franklin and Schweninger. *Runway Slaves*; Franklin, *From Slavery to Freedom*; Du Bois, *The Souls of Black Folk*; Frazier, *The Negro Church in America*.

Chapter 1—Slavery, Religion, and Family in the Robert Smalls Legacy

1. Raboteau, *Slave Religion*; Lincoln and Lawrence, *The Black Church*; Billingsley, *Mighty like a River*.

2. Du Bois, *The Souls of Black Folk*.

3. Lincoln, Introduction to *Mighty like a River*, xx.

4. Raboteau, *Slave Religion*, 158.

5. Edgar, *South Carolina: A History*, 63.

6. Franklin and Schweninger, *Runway Slaves*.

7. Rushton, *Robert Smalls*.

8. St. Helena's Episcopal Church History Committee and Vestry, *The History of the Parish Church of St. Helena, Beaufort, South Carolina. Church of England 1712–1789. Protestant Episcopal 1789–1990*.

9. Rowland, Moore, and Rogers, *The History of Beaufort County, Volume 1: 1514–1861*.

10. Ibid., 287.

11. Ibid.

12. William Robert Smalls to Dorothy Sterling, August 31, 1955, Dorothy Sterling Papers.

13. Edgar, *South Carolina: A History*, 293.

14. Rowland, Moore, and Rogers, *The History of Beaufort County*, 1:355.

15. Much of this information on the Beaufort Baptist Church has been taken from sources generously provided to the author by the Reverend Hodges, including the undated "Tabernacle Baptist Church, Detailed History," by church clerk Charlotte Brown, and a brief account of the first fifteen pastors of the church from Solomon Peck (1864–1865) to the Reverend Dan R. Bodison (1963–1900), "Building a Super Aggressive Church: Tabernacle Baptist Church, 'Old Glory,'" edited by Bodison. We are also informed by Rowland, Moore, and Rogers's treatment of this church in *The History of Beaufort County*, 1:301, 409–11.

16. Cuthbert, *The Life of Richard Fuller*, 103.

17. Brown, "Tabernacle Baptist Church, Detailed History," and Bodison, ed., "Building a Super Aggressive Church: Tabernacle Baptist Church, 'Old Glory.'"

Chapter 2—In the House of Pharaoh

1. The 1870 census reported Lydia's age as seventy-four. That means she was born in approximately 1796, and, when Smalls was born in 1839, she would have been approximately forty-three. Other biographers, following Dorothy Sterling, have reported her birth as 1790, citing a reference Lydia made to having been born when George Washington was president. Washington was elected in 1789 and took office in April 1790. This earlier birth date means she would have been forty-nine years old at her son's birth, which seems unlikely. Moreover, in 1796 George Washington was still president, leaving office in 1797. He died on December 14, 1799. Washington's visit to the Beaufort District in May 1791 might have brought him to the attention of Lydia's mother. None of these facts supports 1790 as Lydia's birth year. Throughout this book we have calculated her age based on what she reported to the 1870 census.

2. Undated manuscript by Janet Bampfield Davidson, from the Collection of Dolly Nash; Mabel Runnette to Sterling, March 26, 1956, Dorothy Sterling Papers.

3. Davidson manuscript.

4. Testimony before American Freedmen's Inquiry Commission in 1863, a federal commission inquiring into the conditions of slavery, conducted at Smalls's home in Beaufort; republished in Blassingame, ed., *Slave Testimony*, 375.

5. Ibid.

6. Ibid., 378.

7. Ibid., 379.

8. U.S. Census of Beaufort County, for 1840, 1850, and 1860.

9. Runnette to Sterling, Dorothy Sterling Papers.

10. One source cites Jim Hayes, ed., *Antiquarian: Autographs and Documents*, list 230, p. 8: "Jacob Goldsmith, son of Moses Goldsmith and half brother of Robert Smalls" (www.haveautographs.com). Moses Goldsmith (1815–1884) was a wealthy Charleston merchant. He and other family members are buried in Shearith Israel Congregational Burial Ground in Charleston County.

11. Miller, "The Suffrage," 7.

12. Sterling, *Captain of the Planter*, 31.

13. Bailey, Morgan, and Taylor, eds., *Biographical Directory of the South Carolina State Senate 1776–1985*, 3:1482.

Chapter 3—On the Waterfront

1. Edgar, *South Carolina: A History*, 290.

2. Ibid., 280.

3. Ibid., 279–80.

4. Ibid., 286.

5. Ibid., 287.

6. Powers, *Black Charlestonians*, 48.

7. Ibid.

8. Ibid., 52.

9. Ibid., 9.

10. Ibid., 10.

11. Ibid., 31.

12. Ibid., 10.

13. Ibid.

14. Ibid., 20.

15. Ibid.

16. Blassingame, ed., *Slave Testimony*, 373–79.

17. Powers, *Black Charlestonians*, 21.

18. Ibid.

19. Robertson, *Denmark Vesey*, 4.

20. Powers, *Black Charlestonians*, 23.

21. Ibid.

22. Blassingame, ed., *Slave Testimony*, 373–79.

23. Brown, *A Guide to Gullah Charleston*, 28.

24. Ibid., 21.

25. Powers, *Black Charlestonians*, 49.

26. Ibid., 48.

27. Robertson, *Denmark Vesey*, 15.

28. Uya, *From Slavery to Public Service*, 10.

29. Ibid., 7–8.

30. Blassingame, ed., *Slave Testimony*, 373–79.

31. S.C. Department of Archives and History, Public Programs Document Packet no. 1: *Jehu Jones: Free Black Entrepreneur*, 2; Document Packet no. 2. *Jones: Time of Crisis Time of Change.*

32. Uya, *From Slavery to Public Service*, 7; Sterling, *Captain of the Planter*, 46–51.

Chapter 4—The Seizure of the *Planter*

1. Cowley, *The Romance of History in the Black County and the Romance of War in the Career of Gen. Robert Smalls.*

2. Thornbrough, ed., *Black Reconstructionists.*

3. Billingsley, *Black Families in White America.*

4. Edward D. Sloan, Jr., shared his extensive files on the *Planter* and its original owner John Ferguson with the author at Sloan's home in Greenville, S.C., on June 21, 1998. Sterling, *Captain of the Planter*, 45; Uya, *From Slavery to Public Service*, 7–8. For complete official records of this venture, see Rawson, ed., *Official Records of the Union and Confederate Navies in the War of the Rebellion*, 1:5.

5. Uya, *From Slavery to Public Service*, 7–8.

6. Miller, *Lincoln's Abolitionist General.*

7. Sterling, *Captain of the Planter*, 69.

8. Uya, *From Slavery to Public Service*, 15.

9. Delany, *The Condition Elevation, Emigration, and Destiny of the Colored People of the United States*, 177.

10. Harley, *The Timetables of African American History*, 142.

11. Lieutenant J. F. Nichols to Commander E. G. Parrott, May 13, 1862; quoted in Alexander, *Robert Smalls*, 3:6.

12. Miller, *Lincoln's Abolitionist General,* 1.

13. Du Pont to his wife, May 13, 1862.

14. Du Pont, Report to the Navy Department, May 14, 1862, quoted in Alexander, "Robert Smalls," 3:5.

15. Scott, *War of the Rebellion,* series 1, vol. 15.

16. Marsh, *Official Records of the Union and Confederate Navies in the War of the Rebellion,* series 2, vol. 1.

17. Scott, *War of the Rebellion,* series 1, vol. 15.

18. *New York Daily Tribune,* June 17, 1862.

19. Miller, *Lincoln's Abolitionist General,* 11–12; Uya, *From Slavery to Public Service,* 16.

20. Miller, *Lincoln's Abolitionist General,* 5.

21. Uya, *From Slavery to Public Service,* 16.

22. Westwood, "Mr. Smalls: A Personal Adventure," 3.

23. Miller, *Lincoln's Abolitionist General,* 6.

Chapter 5—Early Duty for the Union Forces, 1862

1. Alexander, "Robert Smalls," 3:24.

2. Ibid., 6:7.

3. Ibid., 6:20.

4. Rose, *Rehearsal for Reconstruction,* 40–48, 79, 237.

5. Foner, *Reconstruction,* 52.

6. Laura Towne, quoted in ibid.

7. Edgar, *South Carolina: A History,* 366.

8. Alexander, "Robert Smalls," 7:3.

9. Ibid., 7:2.

10. Quarles, *The Negro in The Civil War,* 40.

11. Du Pont to his wife, October 31, 1862.

12. *New York Daily Tribune,* September 10, 1862.

13. Du Pont to his wife, October 31, 1862.

14. *New York Times,* October 3, 1862.

15. Ibid.

16. Du Pont to his wife, October 31, 1862.

Chapter 6—Robert Smalls and the USS *Keokuk,* April 7, 1863

1. Other members of the 2000 study team that went to Fort Sumter were Dr. Bobby Donaldson, Dr. Dean Patrick, Judith Crocker Billingsley, LMSW, and the author. Wilcox and Ripley, "The Civil War at Charleston."

2. Ibid., 42.

3. Ibid.

4. "CSS *Virginia,*" *Wikipedia.*

5. Wilcox and Ripley, "The Civil War at Charleston," 42.

6. *New York Times,* April 17, 1863.

7. Ibid. See also abstract log of the USS *Keokuk* and additional notes by Rhind. Wilcox and Ripley, "The Civil War at Charleston," 42.

8. Ibid.

9. Ibid.

Chapter 7—Robert Smalls and the *Planter* at War, 1862–1866

1. Smalls to quartermaster general, December 16, 1882.
2. Rufus to Smalls, January 3, 1883.
3. Engagements supported by the Steamer *Planter* from May 31, 1862, through April 25, 1865, quoted in Alexander, "Robert Smalls," 8:1.
4. Brennan, *Secessionville,* 42.
5. Ibid., 32.
6. Captain E. G. Parrot to Admiral Du Pont, May 20, 1863, quoted in Alexander, "Robert Smalls," 6:15.
7. Emilio, *A Brave Black Regiment,* 11.
8. Uya, *From Slavery to Public Service,* 22.
9. Miller, *Lincoln's Abolitionist General,* 21.
10. Ibid.
11. Miller, *Lincoln's Abolitionist General;* Uya, *From Slavery to Public Service.*
12. Uya, *From Slavery to Public Service,* 26.
13. Ibid.
14. Ibid., 26–27.
15. Berlin, *Free at Last,* 310.
16. Quarles, *The Negro in the Civil War,* 322.
17. *New York Times,* February 13, 1865.
18. Quarles, *The Negro in the Civil War,* 328.
19. Miller, *Lincoln's Abolitionist General,* 24.
20. Sterling, *Captain of the Planter,* 156.
21. Ibid., 157.
22. French and Gary, *The Trip of the Steamer Oceanus,* 83–86.
23. Ibid., 43–44.
24. Ibid., 86.
25. Ibid.
26. Ibid.

Chapter 8—In Beaufort after the War

1. Billingsley, *Climbing Jacob's Ladder,* 36.
2. Bailey, Morgan, and Taylor, eds., *Biographical Directory of the South Carolina State Senate 1776–1985,* 3:1484.
3. Miller, *Lincoln's Abolitionist General,* 46–47; from a letter dated January 14, 1868, in Mrs. Samuel F. Du Pont's papers, document W-9-39920.
4. William Robert Smalls to Sterling, November 29, 1957, Dorothy Sterling Papers.
5. Elliott, "Memoir," 9.
6. The various houses Smalls owned in Beaufort were shown to the author by Helen Fields and Dolly Nash in 1994. Willie Smalls never lived in the house at 712 East Street. For information on the Enterprise Railroad, see Powers, *Black Charlestonians,* 169–70.
7. Woodson, "Robert Smalls and His Descendants," 47.
8. William Robert Smalls to Sterling, November 29, 1955, Dorothy Sterling Papers.
9. Ibid.
10. Ibid.
11. Family oral history.

12. Marscher and Marscher, *The Great Sea Island Storm of 1893*. See also http://www .mupress.org/webpages/books/marscher.html (accessed November 12, 2005).

13. Marscher, "After the Great Storm," 31.

14. Marscher and Marscher, *The Great Sea Island Storm of 1893*.

15. Bailey, Morgan, and Taylor, eds., *Biographical Directory of the South Carolina State Senate 1776–1985*, 3:1485.

16. *Beaufort Gazette*, July 7, 1991, A3.

Chapter 9—Mr. Republican

1. Miller, *Lincoln's Abolitionist General*, 39.

2. Ibid., 48.

3. Ibid.

4. Ibid., 49.

5. Ibid., 51.

6. Ibid., 148.

7. Foner, *Reconstruction*, 357.

8. Uya, *From Slavery to Public Service*, 72.

9. Ibid., 65. *Journal of the House of Representatives of the General Assembly of the State of South Carolina, Being the Regular Session of 1869–'70*, 413.

10. Uya, *From Slavery to Public Service*, 65.

11. Ibid., 63.

12. Ibid.

13. Ibid., 72.

14. Miller, *Lincoln's Abolitionist General*, 64.

15. Ibid.

16. *Republican*, January 4, 1871, reported in Uya, *From Slavery to Public Service*, 80.

17. Uya, *From Slavery to Public Service*, 82.

18. Miller, *Lincoln's Abolitionist General*, 65.

19. Ibid.

20. Uya, *From Slavery to Public Service*, 71.

21. Rowland, personal communication with the author, Beaufort, 2000.

22. Foner, *Reconstruction*, 544.

23. Ibid., 571.

24. Ibid.

25. Uya, *From Slavery to Public Service*, 71.

26. *Congressional Record*, 44th Congress, 1st Session, 3272–75, 4876; Uya, *From Slavery to Public Service*, 930.

27. *Congressional Record*, 4681.

28. Ibid., 4605–7.

29. Ibid.

30. *News and Courier*, September 20, 1890; *Palmetto Press*, September 25, 1890.

31. Miller, *Lincoln's Abolitionist General*, 105.

32. Underwood and Burke, eds., *At Freedom's Door*, 90.

33. http://www.Grinnell.edu/offices/ce/news/0726200611/, accessed February 11, 2007.

Chapter 10—They Tried to Cut Him Down

1. Edgar, *South Carolina: A History,* 408.

2. Ibid.

3. *Congressional Record,* 45th Congress, 2nd Session, cited in Miller, *Lincoln's Abolitionist General,* 120.

4. Miller, *Lincoln's Abolitionist General,* 97. Uya, *From Slavery to Public Service,* 101. See also "Select Committee on Recent Elections in South Carolina," Charleston, December 30, 1876. House of Representatives, 44th Congress, 2nd Session, miscellaneous document 31, part 3, 197–99. Smalls's testimony.

5. William Robert Smalls to Sterling, no date, Dorothy Sterling Papers. See also Gergel and Gergel, "To Vindicate the Cause of the Downtrodden"; J. Clay Smith, "The Reconstruction of Justice Jonathan Jasper Wright"; Uya, *From Slavery to Public Service,* 87.

6. Allen, *Governor Chamberlain's Administration in South Carolina.*

7. Miller, *Lincoln's Abolitionist General,* 103–4.

8. Ibid., 103.

9. Ibid., 104.

10. Ibid., 104–5.

11. Reynolds, *Reconstruction in South Carolina,* 457. See also Rowland, Moore, and Rogers, *The History of Beaufort County;* Foner, *Reconstruction;* Underwood and Burke, eds., *At Freedom's Door;* and Edgar, *South Carolina: A History.*

12. Underwood and Burke, eds., *At Freedom's Door,* 166.

13. Powers, *Black Charlestonians,* 139.

14. Underwood and Burke, eds., *At Freedom's Door,* 114.

15. *Charleston News and Courier,* October 6, 1877.

16. Transcript of trial, S.C. Department of Archives and History, 1–6. All quotations from statements and testimony at Smalls's trial, sentencing, and appeal are from this source.

17. *Charleston News and Courier,* November 27, 1877.

18. Transcript of trial.

19. W. B. McKee to Governor Wade Hampton, S.C. Department of Archives and History, box 14, folder 14, Robert Smalls.

20. White, *Charleston News and Courier,* July 15, 1878.

Chapter 11—Consummate Politician, 1877–1889

1. Thomas, *Black over White,* 95.

2. Miller, *Lincoln's Abolitionist General,* 124.

3. *Charleston News and Courier,* September 28, 1882.

4. *Congressional Record,* 49th Congress, 1st Session, 538, 2640, and appendix, 319–20. See also Miller, *Lincoln's Abolitionist General,* 155.

5. Elliott, "Memoir," 507.

6. Ibid.

7. Smalls to Whitfield McKinley, May 11, 1912, Robert Smalls file, Carter G. Woodson Papers.

8. Smalls to McKinley, May 22, 1912.

9. Senator Knute Nelson to Smalls, May 30, 1912, Robert Smalls file, Carter G. Woodson Papers.

10. Smalls to Booker T. Washington, April 22, 1913. Robert Smalls file, Carter G. Woodson Papers.

Chapter 12—Robert Smalls and the Constitutional Convention of 1895

1. The primary source document for this chapter is *Journal of the Constitutional Convention of South Carolina, Tuesday, September 10–Wednesday, December 4, 1895.* See also Sarah V. Smalls, *Speeches at the Constitutional Convention by General Robert Smalls,* and Mary Miller, "The Suffrage: Speeches by Negroes in the Constitutional Convention." All three of these sources may be found in the South Carolina Department of Archives and History and the South Caroliniana Library at the University of South Carolina. Smalls's and Miller's collections of speeches may also be found at the Library of Congress and the Schomburg Center for Research in Black Culture, New York Public Library.

2. *Journal of the Constitutional Convention of South Carolina,* 2.

3. Ibid., 8.

4. Ibid., 12.

5. Sarah V. Smalls, *Speeches at the Constitutional Convention.* See also *Journal of the Constitutional Convention,* 472–76.

6. Mary J. Miller, "The Suffrage," 122. See also *Journal of the Constitutional Convention,* 410, 415.

7. Miller, "The Suffrage," 2.

8. Ibid., 3.

9. Ibid., 4.

10. Ibid., 5.

11. *Journal of the Constitutional Convention,* 42–43.

12. Ibid., 111–12.

13. Miller, "The Suffrage." See also *Journal of the Constitutional Convention,* 122.

14. Ibid., 411–12.

15. Ibid., 415–16.

16. *Journal of the Constitutional Convention,* 443–71.

17. Ibid. 472–76.

18. Ibid., 727.

19. *Charleston News and Courier,* November 4, 1895.

Chapter 13—The Bampfields of Beaufort

1. William Robert Smalls to Sterling, March 27, 1955, Dorothy Sterling Papers. A major source of information for this chapter is the author's September 15–17, 2000, interview with Dolly Nash; all Dolly Nash quotations are from this interview. See also Helen Boulware Moore's Smalls genealogy on page xxi and online at http://www.robertsmalls.org.

2. Williams, "Family History"; also interviews with the author, Norfolk, Virginia, July 1992, and Beaufort, South Carolina, July 1994.

3. James Bampfield, "A History of the Bampfield Family."

4. Craft, *Running a Thousand Miles to Freedom.*

5. Bampfield, "A History of the Bampfield Family."

6. The oldest son of John G. and Margaret Bampfield was James H. Bampfield, who married Johnnie Elizabeth Watts. They had two children, Ethel Blanche Bampfield Denmark and Gwendolyn Bampfield Wright, both of whom graduated from Florida A & M University and the Hunter College School of Social Work. Ethel, a retired social worker, is married to the renowned artist James Denmark; they have two children. Gwen, who has a law degree from Rutgers University, is a municipal judge in Hampton County, South Carolina, and a leader in the HIV/AIDS Council. In 1993 Jim Bampfield of the Canadian Bampfields contacted Ethel and Gwen, who put him in contact with Dolly Nash. Jim Bampfield to Dolly Nash, March 13, 1993.

7. Drago, *Hurrah for Hampton!* 48.

8. Lincoln University archivist Susan Pevar found this information on Bampfield in the university records. Sherman Pyatt, archivist at the Avery Center, provided helpful assistance.

9. Pevar to author, December 4, 2002–February 19, 2003.

10. Underwood and Burke, eds., *At Freedom's Door,* 100–101.

11. The author is deeply indebted to Gerhard Spieler, long time columnist for the *Beaufort Gazette* and inveterate researcher and writer on the role and contributions of Samuel J. Bampfield.

12. William Robert Smalls to Sterling, November 29, 1955, Dorothy Sterling Papers.

13. Spieler, "Samuel J. Bampfield Remembered," *Beaufort Gazette,* September 2, 1980.

14. Elliott, "Memoir," 39.

15. Holt, *Black over White,* 186.

16. Spieler, "Samuel J. Bampfield Remembered."

17. Elliott, "Memoir," 9.

18. Ibid., 38.

19. Ibid.

20. Ibid.

21. Woodson, "Robert Smalls and His Descendants."

22. From the personal files of Dolly Nash.

23. Gutman to author, on visit to Morgan State University in 1978.

Chapter 14—Hannah's Children

1. For the history of this branch of Smalls's family, sources include the U.S. Censuses of 1870, 1880, and 1890; oral-history interviews at family reunions, including talks with Dolly Nash and Furman Franklin Williams; and Furman Williams's unpublished "Family History," the major source for this chapter.

2. In a program for the first commencement exercise at South Carolina State University, May 1–6, 1897, is listed a recitation titled "Our Banner" and delivered by William Wigg Smalls. This item confirms that five-year-old William Robert Wigg Smalls, son of Robert and Annie Wigg Smalls, who had been dead for two years, was enrolled in the kindergarten of the Colored Normal Industrial, Agricultural, and Mechanical College. This program also confirms that Sarah Voorhees Smalls was a member of the first faculty. She had taken her brother along when she went to teach there in 1896.

3. Hill, *The Strengths of African American Families.*

4. Ladner, *The Ties That Bind.*

Chapter 15—Annie Wigg's Family

1. The editor, *Charleston News and Courier,* April 10, 1890.

2. William Robert Smalls to Sterling,1955, Dorothy Sterling Papers. The quotations from William Robert Smalls in this chapter are from Smalls's letters to Sterling.

3. Robert Smalls to President William Howard Taft, March 8, 1911. Carter G. Woodson Papers.

4. Obituary for William Robert Smalls, *Toledo Blade,* July 31, 1970.

Chapter 16—A Summing Up

1. Smalls to Washington, April 22, 1913, Booker T. Washington Papers, Library of Congress.

2. Obituary for Robert Smalls, *New York Age,* March 4, 1915.

3. Joint Resolution S.987, South Carolina General Assembly, 115th Session, 2003–2004.

4. Robin Moore, unpublished speech, April 21, 2004.

5. Ladner, *The Ties That Bind.*

BIBLIOGRAPHY

Primary Sources

Manuscript Collections

Du Pont Papers, Hagley Museum and Library, Wilmington, Delaware

William Johnson Papers, Manuscript Department, University of North Carolina Library, Chapel Hill, North Carolina

Dorothy Sterling Papers, Amistad Library, Tulane University, New Orleans, Louisiana

Booker T. Washington Papers, Library of Congress, Washington, D.C.

Carter G. Woodson Papers, Library of Congress, Washington, D.C.

Unpublished Manuscripts

Bampfield, James R. "A History of the Bampfield Family." April 1993. In possession of the author.

———. Letter to Dolly Nash, March 13, 1993. In possession of the author.

Bodison, Dan R. "Building a Super Aggressive Church: Tabernacle Baptist Church, 'Old Glory.'" N.d. Collection of Tabernacle Baptist Church, Beaufort, S.C.

Brown, Charlotte. "Tabernacle Baptist Church, Detailed History." N.d. Collection of Tabernacle Baptist Church, Beaufort, S.C.

Davidson, Janet Bampfield. Unpublished manuscript, after 1910. Personal collection of Dolly Nash, in possession of Helen Boulware Moore.

Elliott, William, Jr. "Memoir." N.d. South Carolina Department of Archives and History, Columbia, S.C.

McKee, W. B. Letter to Governor Hampton. N.d. South Carolina Department of Archives and History (box 14, folder 14, Robert Smalls), Columbia, S.C.

Miller, Mary. "The Suffrage: Speeches by Negroes in the Constitutional Convention— The part taken by Colored Orators in their fight for a fair and impartial ballot being provided for in the fundamental law." Unpublished, 1895, South Caroliniana Library, University of South Carolina, Columbia, S.C.

Smalls, Robert. Letter to Quartermaster General, December 16, 1882. In possession of the author.

Williams, Furman Franklin. "Family History: The Descendants of an African American Family." N.d. In possession of the author and in Dolly Nash files in possession of Helen Boulware Moore.

Published Primary Sources

Colored Normal Industrial, Agricultural, and Mechanical College. Commencement Program, May 3, 1897.

Holland, Rupert Sargent, ed. *Letters and Diary of Laura M. Towne Written from the Sea Islands of South Carolina 1862–1884*. Cambridge, Mass.: Printed at the Riverside Press, 1912.

Marsh, C. C. *Official Records of the Union and Confederate Navies in the War of the Rebellion*. Series 1, vol. 12; series 2, vol. 1. Washington, D.C.: U.S. Government Printing Office, 1901, 1921.

Rawson, Edward K. *Official Records of the Union and Confederate Navies in the War of the Rebellion*. Vol. 1. Washington, D.C.: U.S. Government Printing Office, 1901.

Scott, Robert N. *War of the Rebellion: A Compilation of Records of the Union and Confederate Armies*. Series 1, vol. 15. Washington, D.C.: U.S. Government Printing Office, 1886.

South Carolina Department of Archives and History. Public Programs Document Packet no.1: *Jehu Jones: Free Black Entrepreneur.*

———. Public Programs Document Packet no. 2: *Jones: Time of Crisis Time of Change.*

———. *South Carolina Fraud Report*. 1878.

———. *The State of South Carolina in the Court of General Sessions County of Richland. The State v. Robert Smalls. Indictment: Accepting a Bribe*. South Carolina Department of Archives and History, Richland County General Session R.ll 905, box 4, Robert Smalls, November 17, 1877.

South Carolina General Assembly. *Joint Resolution S.987 of the South Carolina General Assembly*, 115th Session. Columbia: S.C.: General Assembly, 2004.

———. *Journal of the House of Representatives of the General Assembly of the State of South Carolina, Being the Regular Session of 1869–'70*. Columbia, S.C.: John W. Denny, 1870.

———. *Journal of the Constitutional Convention of South Carolina, Tuesday, September 10–Wednesday, December 4, 1895*. Columbia, S.C.: Charles A. Calvo Jr., State Printer, 1895.

Smalls, Sarah V. *Speeches at the Constitutional Convention by General Robert Smalls with the Right of Suffrage Passed by the Constitutional Convention*. Charleston, S.C.: Enquirer Printing, 1896.

Tillman, George Dionysius. *Smalls vs. Tillman: To Oust a Member of Congress Who Has Certificate of Election according to the Laws and under the Broad Seal of His State Is Tyranny*. Washington, D.C.: U.S. Congress, 1882.

U.S. Census Bureau. *U.S. Census of Beaufort County for 1840, 1850, and 1860*. Washington, DC: U.S. Government Printing Office, 1840, 1850, 1860.

U.S. Congress. *Congressional Record*, 44th Congress, 1st Session, 3272–75, 4876; 4641; 4605–07.

———. *Congressional Record*, 44th Congress, 2nd Session, Appendix "An Honest Ballot is the Safeguard of the Republic" Speech of Honorable Robert Smalls in the House of Representatives, February 24, 1877, 123–26.

———. *Congressional Record*, 49th Congress, 1st Session, January 24, 1883, 538, 319–20, 2640.

———. *In the House of Representatives, Forty-Seventh Congress: Robert Smalls, Contestant vs. George D. Tillman.* Washington, D.C.: U.S. Government Printing Office, 1882.

U.S. House of Representatives. Committee on Elections. *Robert Smalls vs. William Elliott.* Washington, D.C.: U.S. Government Printing Office, 1888.

———Committee on Naval Affairs. *Authorizing the president to place Robert Smalls on the Retired List of the Navy.* 47th Congress, 2nd Session, January 23, 1883. Rept. no.1887.

———. Committee on the Judiciary. *Arrest and Imprisonment of Hon. Robert Smalls.* Washington, D.C.: U.S. Government Printing Office, 1878.

———. *Select Committee on Recent Elections in South Carolina.* 44th Congress, 2nd session. December 30, 1876. Misc.. Doc. No. 31, part 3, pp. 197–99.

———. *Tillman vs. Smalls, Fifth Congressional District of South Carolina.* Washington, D.C.: U.S. Government Printing Office, 1878.

Newspapers

Charleston News and Courier, October 6, 1877; July 15, 1878 [article by Thomas G. White].

New York Age, March 4, 1915.

New York Daily Tribune, May 20–September 10, 1862.

New York Herald, May 20, 1862.

New York Times, October 3, 1862–April 17, 1863.

Secondary Sources

Reference Works

Bailey, N. Louise, Mary L. Morgan, and Carolyn R. Taylor, eds. *Biographical Directory of the South Carolina State Senate 1776–1985.* 3 vols. Columbia: University of South Carolina Press, 1986.

Biographical Directory of the United States Congress 1774–1989. Washington, D.C.: U.S. Government Printing Office, 1989.

Harley, Sharon. *The Timetables of African American History.* New York: Simon & Schuster, 1995.

Books

Alexander, Kitt. *Robert Smalls.* N.p: Published by the author, n.d.

Allen, Walter. *Governor Chamberlain's Administration in South Carolina.* New York: Putnam, 1888.

Ball, Edward, *Slaves in the Family.* New York: Farrar, Straus & Giroux, 1998.

Berlin, Ira, Barbara J. Fields, Steven Miller, Joseph P. Reidy, and Leslie Rowland, eds. *Free at Last: A Documentary History of Slavery, Freedom and the Civil War.* New York: Free Press, 1992.

Billingsley, Andrew. *Black Families in White America.* New York: Simon & Schuster, 1968; revised, 1988.

———. *Climbing Jacob's Ladder: The Enduring Legacy of African American Families.* New York: Simon & Schuster, 1992.

———. *Mighty like a River: The Black Church and Social Reform.* New York: Oxford University Press, 1999.

Blassingame, John, ed. *Slave Testimony: Two Centuries of Letters, Speeches, Interviews, and Autobiographies*. Baton Rouge: Louisiana State University Press, 1977.

Brennan, Patrick. *Secessionville: Assault on Charleston Harbor*. Camphill, Calif.: Savas, 1996.

Brown, Alphonso. *A Guide to Gullah Charleston*. Charleston: Gullah Tours, 1993.

Cooper, Michael L. *From Slave to Civil War Hero: The Life and Times of Robert Smalls*. New York: Lodestar Books, 1994.

Cowley, Charles. *The Romance of History in the Black County and the Romance of War in the Career of Gen. Robert Smalls, the Hero of the Planter*. Lowell, Mass., 1892.

Craft, William. *Running a Thousand Miles to Freedom; or the Escape of William and Ellen Craft from Slavery*. London: William Tweedie, 1860.

Cuthbert, J. H. *The Life of Richard Fuller*. New York: Sheldon, 1879.

Delany, Martin R. *The Condition, Elevation, Emigration, and Destiny of the Colored People of the United States*. New York: Arno Press, 1969.

Drago, Edmund Lee. *Hurrah for Hampton! Black Red Shirts in South Carolina during Reconstruction*. Fayetteville: University of Arkansas Press, 1998.

Du Bois, W. E. B. *The Souls of Black Folk*. Chicago: McClurg, 1903.

Edgar, Walter. *South Carolina: A History*. Columbia: University of South Carolina Press, 1998.

Emilio, Luis F. *A Brave Black Regiment: The History of the Fifty-fourth Regiment of Massachusetts Volunteer Infantry, 1863–1865*. New York: Da Capo, 1995.

Foner, Eric. *Reconstruction: America's Unfinished Revolution*. New York: Harper & Row, 1988.

Franklin, John Hope. *From Slavery to Freedom: A History of American Negroes*. New York, Knopf, 1947.

Franklin, John Hope, and Loren Schweninger. *Runway Slaves: Rebels on the Plantation*. New York: Oxford University Press, 1999.

Frazier, E. Franklin. *The Negro Church in America*. New York, Schocken, 1964.

French, Clement, and Edward Gary. *The Trip of the Steamer Oceanus to Fort Sumter and Charleston, S.C.* Brooklyn, N.Y.: Union Steam Printing House, 1865.

Garrison, Webb B. *Creative Minds in Desperate Times: The Civil War's Most Sensational Schemes and Plots*. Nashville, Tenn.: Rutledge Hill Press, 1997.

Gutman, Herbert. *The Black Family in Slavery and Freedom, 1750–1925*. New York: Pantheon, 1976.

Hill, Robert B. *The Strengths of African American Families, Twenty-Five Years Later*. Lanham, Md.: University Press of America, 1999.

Ladner, Joyce A. *The Ties That Bind: Timeless Values for African American Families*. New York: Wiley, 1998.

Lincoln, C. Eric, and Lawrence H. Mamiya. *The Black Church in the African-American Experience*. Durham: Duke University Press, 1990.

Littlefield, Daniel. *Rice and Slaves: Ethnicity and the Slave Trade in Colonial South Carolina*. Baton Rouge: Louisiana State University Press, 1981.

Marscher, Bill and Fran. *The Great Sea Island Storm of 1893*. Macon, Ga.: Mercer University Press, 2004.

Meriwether, Louise. *The Freedom Ship of Robert Smalls*. Englewood Cliffs, N.J.: Prentice-Hall, 1971.

Middleton, Stephen, ed. *Black Congressmen during Reconstruction*. Westport, Conn.: Greenwood Press, 2002.

Miller, Edward A. *Gullah Statesman: Robert Smalls from Slavery to Congress, 1839–1915*. Columbia: University of South Carolina Press, 1995.

———. *Lincoln's Abolitionist General: The Biography of David Hunter*. Columbia: University of South Carolina Press, 1997.

Powers, Bernard E., Jr. *Black Charlestonians: A Social History, 1822–1885*. Fayetteville: University of Arkansas Press, 1994.

Presgraves, James C., and S. Louise Presgraves, eds. *Old Churchyard Cemetery of St. Helena's Episcopal Church, Beaufort, South Carolina*. Beaufort: J. C. and S. L. Presgraves, 1987.

Quarles, Benjamin. *The Negro in the Civil War*. Boston: Little, Brown, 1953.

Raboteau, Albert J. *Slave Religion*. New York: Oxford University Press, 1978.

Reynolds, John S. *Reconstruction in South Carolina: 1865–1877*. Columbia, S.C.: The State, 1905.

Robertson, David. *Denmark Vesey: The Buried History of America's Largest Slave Revolt*. New York: Knopf, 1999.

Rose, Willie Lee. *Rehearsal for Reconstruction: The Port Royal Experiment*. New York: Oxford University Press, 1964.

Rowland, Lawrence, Alexander Moore, and George C. Rogers Jr. *The History of Beaufort County, Volume 1: 1514–1861*. Columbia: University of South Carolina Press, 1996.

Rushton, Margaret, and others. *Robert Smalls: Slave Hero, Statesman and His Environs 1839–1915*. Beaufort: Humanities School of Beaufort, 1999.

Sterling, Dorothy. *Captain of the Planter: The Story of Robert Smalls*. Garden City, N.Y.: Doubleday, 1958.

Sterling, Philip. *Four Took Freedom: The Lives of Harriet Tubman, Frederick Douglass, Robert Smalls, and Blanche K. Bruce*. Garden City, N.Y.: Doubleday, 1967.

St. Helena's Episcopal Church History Committee and Vestry. *The History of the Parish Church of St. Helena, Beaufort, South Carolina. Church of England 1712–1789. Protestant Episcopal 1789–1990*. Columbia, S.C.: R. L. Bryan, 1990.

Spieler, Gerard. *The History of Robert Smalls School*. Beaufort, S.C.: Robert Smalls Association, July 1991.

Thomas, Holt. *Black over White: Negro Political Leadership in South Carolina during Reconstruction*. Urbana: University of Illinois Press, 1977.

Thornbrough, Emma Lou, ed. *Black Reconstructionists*. Englewood Cliffs, N.J.: Prentice-Hall, 1972.

Underwood, James Lowell, and W. Lewis Burke, eds. *At Freedom's Door: African American Founding Fathers and Lawyers in Reconstruction South Carolina*. Columbia: University of South Carolina Press, 2000.

Uya, Okon Edet. *From Slavery to Public Service: Robert Smalls, 1839–1915*. New York: Oxford University Press, 1971.

Wilcox, Arthur, and Warren Ripley. *The Civil War at Charleston.* Charleston: News and Courier and Evening Post, 1986.

Articles and Chapters

A.M.E. Church Review. "Captain Robert Smalls Addresses the General Conference of 1864, Daniel A. Payne Presiding." *A.M.E. Church Review* 70 (January-March 1955): 22–23, 31.

Billingsley, Andrew. "Family Reunion: The Legacy of Robert Smalls—Civil War Hero." *Maryland Humanities* (Winter 1993): 14–17.

————. "Robert Smalls in Beaufort Today." *Carologue* 14 (Spring 1998): 8–15.

"Christening Ceremony: Major General Robert Smalls." *Jet* 105 (May 10, 2004): 6.

"CSS Virginia." *Wikipedia: The Free Encyclopedia.* http://en.wikipedia.org/wiki/CSS_Virginia (accessed November 8, 2005).

Gergel, Richard, and Belinda Gergel. "To Vindicate the Cause of the Downtrodden." In *At Freedom's Door: African American Founding Fathers and Lawyers During Reconstruction.* Edited by James Lowell Underwood and W. Lewis Burke, 36–71. Columbia: University of South Carolina Press, 2000.

Hine, William C. "Thomas E. Miller." *Carologue* (Spring 1996).

Lincoln, C. Eric. Introduction to *Mighty like a River: The Black Church and Social Reform,* by Andrew Billingsley. New York: Oxford University Press, 1999.

Marscher, Fran. "After the Great Storm: The Nation's First Hurricane Relief Effort." *Sandlapper* (Summer 2005): 31. http://www.knowitall.org/sandlapper/Summer 2005/PDF/Hurricane.pdf (accessed November 12, 2005).

Obituary for Robert Smalls. *New York Evening Post,* May 17, 1862.

Obituary for William Robert Smalls, 1892–1970. *Toledo Blade,* July 31, 1970.

Smith, J. Clay. "The Reconstruction of Justice Jonathan Jasper Wright." In *At Freedom's Door,* 72–89.

Spieler, Gerard. "Samuel J. Bampfield Remembered." *Beaufort Gazette,* September 2, 1980; "New Street House Has Story." *Beaufort Gazette,* September 17, 1980; and "Uncovered Grave Marker Does Injustice to Bampfield." *Beaufort Gazette,* January 28, 1997.

Washington, Wayne. "Forgotten Mission of Liberation." *Columbia State,* October 16, 2005.

Woodson, Carter G. "Robert Smalls and His Descendants." *Negro History Bulletin* 11 (November 1947): 27–33, 46.

Theses

Shirley, William Harrison. "A Black Republican Congressman during the Democratic Resurgence in South Carolina: Robert Smalls, 1839–1915." Master's thesis, University of South Carolina, 1970.

Uya, Okon Edet. "From Servitude to Service: Robert Smalls, 1839–1915." Ph.D. dissertation, University of Wisconsin, 1969.

INDEX